Mathew Brady

HISTORIAN WITH A CAMERA

Books by James D. Horan

FICTION

King's Rebel
Seek Out and Destroy
The Shadow Catcher
The Seat of Power
The Right Image
The Blue Messiah
The New Vigilantes

NONFICTION

Action Tonight
Desperate Men
The Pinkerton Story (with Howard Swiggett)
Desperate Women
Confederate Agent
Pictorial History of the Wild West (with Paul Sann)
Mathew Brady: Historian with a Camera
Across the Cimarron
The Wild Bunch
The D.A.'s Man
The Great American West
C.S.S. Shenandoah: The Memoirs of Lieutenant-Commanding James I. Waddell
The Desperate Years: From the Stock Market Crash to World War II
Timothy O'Sullivan: America's Forgotten Photographer
The Pinkertons: The Detective Dynasty That Made History
The Life and Art of Charles Schreyvogel:
   Painter-Historian of the Indian Fighting Army of the American West
The McKenney-Hall Portrait Gallery of American Indians
The Gunfighters: The Authentic Wild West

Mathew Brady

HISTORIAN WITH A CAMERA

By James D. Horan

PICTURE COLLATION BY

Gertrude Horan

BONANZA BOOKS · NEW YORK

© MCMLV JAMES D. HORAN

LIBRARY OF CONGRESS CATALOG CARD NUMBER: 55-10171

This edition published by Bonanza Books,
a division of Crown Publishers, Inc.

(O)

MANUFACTURED IN THE UNITED STATES OF AMERICA

TO MY BELOVED PARTNER

GERTRUDE

Table of Contents

LIST OF ILLUSTRATIONS IN THE TEXT

The photographs are contained in the Picture Album, following page 90,
and are indexed in the Picture Index

AN AUTHOR'S REPORT ON HIS SEARCH INTO THE LIFE OF MATHEW B. BRADY

NO great photographer has ever impressed his personality on the nation in which he lived more strongly than Mathew B. Brady. Perhaps this is partly because no other photographer has more completely absorbed the spirit of his times, so that mid-nineteenth century America and the American Civil War are linked with his name. Mathew B. Brady, who used his camera to record his country's history as Bancroft did his pen, produced the greatest pictorial essay of our times.

Until recently the bulk of Brady's photographs was to be found in three main collections; the Brady Collection in the National Archives, the Brady Collection in the Library of Congress, and the restricted Frederick Hill Meserve Collection, deposited in the New York Historical Society. The government-owned collections consist of thousands of wet plates, made by Brady and his staff on the battlefields of the Civil War. The Meserve Collection contains superb portraits of Lincoln and celebrities of his time. For years historians had been aware of the existence of a fourth collection, larger in scope than the others, which has been stored for more than half a century in a quaint red brick building at 494 Maryland Avenue, S.W., Washington, D.C., the home of the L. C. Handy Studios.

Levin Handy, Brady's nephew-by-marriage, had come to work for his famous uncle at the age of twelve. He started in the darkroom, coating negatives in the days when a photographer had to make his own "wet plates." Within a few years he was allowed to operate Brady's famous camera and for more than a quarter of a century he continued to make most of the portraits in Brady's famous Washington gallery at 627 Pennsylvania Avenue, N.W.

During that period, as Brady had done in his time, Handy photographed presidents, Cabinet members, Justices of the Supreme Court, foreign dignitaries, Edison with his first phonograph, Mark Twain, Robert Lincoln, Andrew Carnegie and thousands of others whose names were familiar to all Americans.

Upon Brady's death in 1896, Handy inherited all of Brady's wet plates and daguerreotypes. He combined Brady's work with his own and moved the historic collection to his own studio at 494 Maryland Avenue, S.W. For the rest of his life he used his camera to record history and became a one-man "photoduplication service" for the Library of Congress. Before his death in 1932 he was recognized as one of the country's outstanding photographers.

For years the famous collection, known as the Brady-Handy Collection, remained in its sturdy, old-fashioned wooden boxes while Handy's daughters, Mrs. Mary Handy Evans and Mrs. Alice Handy Cox, who inherited the collection, continued to carry on the work of the Handy Studios.

The collection took up virtually every available nook and cranny of the three-story building, and although both Mrs. Cox and Mrs. Evans were aware of the vast scope of history imprisoned on the fragile wet plates, they themselves did not know exactly how many plates were in the collection and what each contained.

For years Mrs. Cox and Mrs. Evans supplied, upon request, individual prints to biographers, publishers, government offices, museums, historical societies, etc. But at no time would they permit any historian, collector or photographer to examine the collection in its entirety.

In 1954, the Library of Congress, after protracted negotiations, purchased the Brady-Handy Collection for $5,000. The great number of wooden boxes, many unopened for more than half a century, were carefully deposited in the Library of Congress Annex, under the devoted care of Hirst Milhollen, himself a photographer and a friend. Mr. Milhollen is cataloguing the huge collection, a task which will require years of painstaking work and research.

One of the conditions of the purchase was that the collection be restricted for the next ten years. During this time Mrs. Cox and Mrs. Evans have control of the issuance of the prints. After September 14, 1964, all restrictions on the use of the collection will end.

Shortly after the collection was stored in the Library, Gertrude and I were given permission to examine the collection, to select any wet plates or daguerreotypes we wished, and to examine family documents, clippings and letters owned by Mrs. Evans and Mrs. Cox, that I might need to write a definitive biography of Matthew B. Brady, to be illustrated with his plates and those of Levin C. Handy.

"You will be the first, outside of the staff of the Library of Congress, to examine the collection," Mrs. Cox told us. "I think you will find it interesting."

To examine the plates, many still enclosed in brittle, yellowing jackets, was an unforgettable experience. Men and women who had made and changed history were no longer mere names in books. They became lifelike men and women, tall, short, bearded, crafty, gentle, brooding, bitter. There were the living dead of Andersonville, looking as if they had stepped out of Dachau, and the Lincoln conspirators, their ferocity clear in their faces. The Confederate generals who returned to Washington after the war as Senators and Congressmen could not hide their arrogance from the eye of the camera; the young Prince of Wales, later Edward VII, reminded one of a youthful Beau Brummel.

These portraits and thousands of others were examined, selected or rejected.

Each plate we selected was carefully indexed and locked in a separate vault, where it will remain for a period of time with exclusive reproduction rights.

In selecting the plates for this biography I found an abundance of riches, but in searching out the facts of Brady's life I discovered a vast drought of evidence. His family records helped but I had to spend many weary months examining old books, diaries, periodicals and newspapers from the eighteen-forties to the early nineties.

I thought it was unusual that Brady had not kept a diary, but I was amazed to discover that there did not exist among his family records a single letter, a note or a receipted bill in his own handwriting.

Mrs. Cox and Mrs. Evans told me that to the best of their recollection they had never seen a letter written by Brady, nor had they ever seen him write a letter in the years when he lived in their home at 494 Maryland Avenue.

One day in the quiet of the library of the New York Historical Society, the thought came to me with the suddenness of a blow: Perhaps Brady, the greatest photographer of them all, could not write, though there seemed to be no doubt that he could and did read.

Fig. 1. Signature found under Brady's portrait in the *Photographic Art Journal*, January, 1851.

At first it seemed almost unbelievable that this man who was the intimate of many of America's greatest men could not write a simple note, make out a photographic bill, or keep the more important records of his galleries and extensive photographic coverage—as vast during the Civil War as the modern newsphoto services are today.

The question would not rest, so I set out to prove that Mathew B. Brady could write. It was the most frustrating task of research I have yet encountered. The trail led from London to Washington and back to New York.

I began my search for evidence to prove that Brady could write in the Handy Studios with the help of Mrs. Cox and Mrs. Evans. The contents of desks, cupboards, forgotten boxes and family Bibles were carefully sifted and examined. After some weeks, a tiny calling card with the Maryland Avenue address scrawled on the bottom in pencil was found. Mrs. Cox and Mrs. Evans insisted that Brady had written the address a few years before his death when he was living with them. However, they both agreed, they had not actually seen him write it "but had assumed down through the years" that he must have. Their search had also produced three letters written to Levin Handy about Brady by his friend Riley, during his last illness in New York City.

The Treasury Department files in the National Archives produced a letter of recommendation which Brady had sent to the Treasury Department in 1880, for his onetime assistant, Tim O'Sullivan.

The body of the letter was written by someone else and Brady had signed it. The signature appears to be in the handwriting of a very old man, or a man who is ill or a man whose eyesight was so bad he could not guide his own hand.

At the time he signed the letter Brady was in his late fifties. His health, while not robust, was not so delicate that he could not lift a pen. We know his eyesight was so poor twenty-nine years before the date of the letter that he had stopped taking pictures—that is, personally handling the camera. Had it deteriorated so much in 1880 that he could barely sign his name?

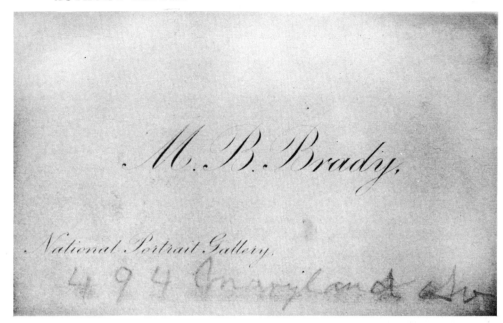

Fig. 2. According to Mrs. Cox and Mrs. Evans, this is a specimen of Brady's handwriting.

A wartime "Register" from his New York gallery, now in the Manuscript Division of the New York Public Library, produced a signature—again in pencil—which appears similar to the signature on O'Sullivan's recommendation. There are none in the Brady's Washington "Register" of 1870-1873, now a part of the Brady-Handy Collection, and I could not find any on the wet plate jackets, many of which crumbled at my touch.

Fig. 3. The signature at the bottom of Brady's letter recommending Tim O'Sullivan. See Fig. 37.

I found a notary public's record of the sale of Julia Handy Brady's New York City property in 1869. The notary stated that Brady signed the deed in his presence, but I could not find the deed, which of course was turned over to the purchaser, Mr. Nathan.

Mrs. Cox, Mrs. Evans, Mr. Milhollen, a number of autograph collectors and several historical societies and numerous historical writers all told me the same thing— they had never seen a Brady letter.

I was about to give up the hunt when a search of the manuscripts in the New York Historical Society produced one "Brady letter."

The body of the letter and the signature were in the same hand but it could not be Brady who had written it. The letter, an invitation to view his portrait of Washington Irving, was written in 1860. By this time Brady's eyesight, from the accounts of eyewitnesses and from reports in trade journals, was exceedingly poor. His signa-

ture should have been a scrawl but it was in a fine copperplate-type hand.

The letter obviously had been written by one of his assistants or a clerk.

Further research turned up a few other "Brady letters," reproduced in the book, but it is not certain that they were written or signed by him.

Several years ago in a book about Brady, Brady's so-called "Lecture-Book" was included. While the author did not say it was in Brady's handwriting, the reader was led to assume that it was.

All of the writing in the notebook was done by Mrs. Cox. As she explained, her father was preparing a series of Civil War scenes, small transparencies, for an exhibition Brady was planning in New York. Brady died before the work was completed. Handy did not abandon the project but completed the set of 124 transparencies, which are at present in the Brady-Handy Collection. He identified each picture, all copied from original wet plates, by writing in pencil on the strip of white tape which protected the edges of the transparencies. Sometime later Mrs. Cox wrote out a description of each transparency, basing her information on her own research and her father's reminiscences of what Brady had told him. This is the so-called Brady "Lecture Book."

The evidence I finally gathered to prove that Brady could write was far from impressive. He could read, and while nowadays the ability to read almost definitely affirms the ability to write, in the less literate days of the last century, that guarantee was not so definite. I had his signature on the bottom of a letter of recommendation someone else had written for him; a badly scrawled address in pencil which his grandnieces had always assumed was written by him; a signature in pencil in his New York "Register"; a signature under his portrait published in 1851; a signature on his bankruptcy papers; a notary's statement that he had signed a deed;

a statement submitted to the Joint Committee on the Library in 1881 (the volume in which the original correspondence was filed is missing from the bound volumes of original documents on file among the records of the Senate); and several letters bearing his name but probably written by someone else.

However, Beaumont Newhall, the well-known historian of photography, did find an authentic Brady letter. On June 17, 1843, Brady wrote a letter to Albert Sands Southworth, the Boston pioneer photographer, in which he tried to sell Southworth "a new style miniature case." It is evident that Brady's eyesight deteriorated so rapidly within the next few years that he could only scrawl his name by the 1850's.

To write a complete Brady biography, to present his life "in the round," so to speak, it is necessary to deal with the lives and times of the men with whom he was associated in the pioneer days of photography and the men who served under him during the war. Some of Brady's genius rubbed off on a few of them so we find that although Brady did not record the opening of the American West or the impassable jungles of the Isthmus of Darien, the skills and techniques he had initiated were carried on in these frontier outposts by men he had befriended and trained. Unfortunately some of these men are only names. We know nothing of their backgrounds, their hopes, dreams, their desires.

To write of Brady's life was a frustrating experience because of the lack of evidence but to examine the lives of Alexander Gardner and that indomitable man, Tim O'Sullivan, both an important part of Brady's life, was an almost helpless task. There was virtually nothing about them, although O'Sullivan, at least, clearly deserves his own biography. At one time I thought I had scored a major discovery when a friend directed me to the family with whom O'Sullivan had spent his last years on Staten Island. But the lead accomplished little; a few legends and that was all. In fact what happened was not unusual; the biographer, a total stranger, knew more than the "friends" of his subject.

To round out the picture of Brady and his men I examined newspapers, magazines, trade journals, unpublished collections of letters and unpublished journals of other men of the times. The result was disappointing; Brady and his men remain shadowy figures obscured by the mists of time.

I decided that, to tell with pictures the entire Brady story, it would be best to include in the photographic section of this book some of the work of his contemporaries, other war views, and the accomplishments of the most notable Brady alumni, Alexander Gardner and Timothy O'Sullivan.

When it came to the matter of the physical organization of this book, I thought it best to present the pictures as an album in a section of their own, following in general the same chronological pattern as the text. For easy reference the pictures are numbered and cross-indexed. In the course of preparation new Brady pictures turned up and a few were found to be less desirable and therefore here and there a number will be skipped or followed by an *a, b* or *c.*

This is also true of my Source Notes, which are in numerical order. In the final version a few items were deleted and the reader will find that some Note numbers are also skipped. These omissions are simply deletions. Because footnotes are distracting to many readers I have placed the actual Notes in the back of the book, leaving only the small superior numbers in the text.

There is a complete list of Picture Sources, a bibliography and also a list of Brady pictures from which engravings were made for *Leslie's Illustrated Newspaper* and *Harper's Weekly* during the years 1860-65.

ACKNOWLEDGMENTS

The efforts and courtesy of many people helped make this book possible and it is a pleasure to acknowledge their kindnesses and contributions.

Heading the long list must be Mrs. Alice H. Cox and Mrs. Mary H. Evans, daughters of the late Levin C. Handy, Mathew B. Brady's grandnieces. They are the owners of the famous L. C. Handy Studios in Washington, known to many historians, authors and publishers. Both ladies kindly gave me permission to be the first to go through the massive Brady-Handy Collection and were more than generous with their family material and their own memories of the grand picture-maker in his last years when he sat in the parlor of their quaint Maryland Avenue home and recalled the lost days.

Mr. Frederick Cox and Mr. Edgar C. Cox were unstinting with their time and efforts in locating lost documents and in searching through church records and newspaper files to answer many of my questions.

A major contribution to this book was made by Mr. Hirst Milhollen, to whose care the Brady-Handy Collection has been entrusted. Mr. Milhollen's advice, encouragement and enthusiasm were most helpful to an author surrounded by a mountain of wet plates and daguerreotypes.

I would be derelict in my duty if I did not mention the editorial skill, the sharp blue pencil and the tenacity for facts of Miss Helen Staeuble.

And I cannot forget the hospitality of our Colonel and his lady, Herbert and Ann Michau. As always, there is Anne O'Shea.

When the press of a deadline threatens, there is Ray Flynn, of the War Records, National Archives, to help us out.

The entire staff of the Photographic Division, Library of Congress, was exceedingly cooperative, courteous and helpful. I welcome this opportunity to thank Miss Alice Lee Parker, Miss Virginia Daiker, Milton

Kaplan and Carl Stange, and Miss Ramona Javitz, Print Division, New York Public Library, Robert Hill, Chief of the Manuscript Room, New York Public Library, and his valuable assistant, Edward Morrison.

I owe a special vote of thanks to Mr. James Heslin, formerly of the American History Room, New York Public Library, who spent much time gathering for me numerous technical books, early photographic volumes, pamphlets, etc.

It was Mr. Ivor Avellino of the New York Public Library's staff, who gathered together a Brady bibliography. Mr. Sylvester Vigilante of the New York Historical Society helped me enormously in gathering newspaper files of the Civil War and postwar years, along with a storehouse of books, pamphlets, excellent advice and suggestions. And it was Mr. Wayne Andrews, himself a fine author, of the Manuscript Room of the New York Historical Society, who found a "Brady letter" for me.

I owe a great deal of thanks to Arthur B. Carlson, Curator of the Maps and Prints Division, New York Historical Society, for his assistance in finding early New York street maps and building plans of Brady's studios.

As always, my bookseller friends, Messrs. William Kelleher, Peter Decker, Lou Klepper, Sam Stagler and Lockrow's in Albany, N.Y., made extensive searches.

Historians, fellow authors, editors, museums and collectors volunteered their suggestions and gradually the photographic section of Brady's life and times began to round out. Gardner's excellent frontier scenes were found in the Kansas State Historical Society; Vincent Mercaldo combed through his Archives and produced prints taken by Brady or one of his men of downtown New York; The George Eastman House sent on a print of Tim O'Sullivan taken in the jungles of Darien; Ansco carefully made prints of the forty-four Brady wet plates found some years ago in an upstate New York barn; the Museum of the City of New York archives yielded a superb Brady print, and the Brady Collections in the National Archives and the Library of Congress were examined for exceptional war scenes.

This brings us to the time-battered question of "exclusive" or "unpublished" Brady pictures. To find the exact answer one must take each print and consult hundreds of biographies, newspapers, magazines, historical quarterlies, etc. Brady was the forerunner of today's gigantic newsphoto services. He made duplicates of his subjects, other photographers copied them, and, of course, the subjects of his photographs undoubtedly had prints made for themselves.

As Brady himself said sadly, "In those days a photographer ran his career upon the celebrities who came to him and many, I might say most, of the pictures I see floating about this country are from my ill-protected portraits."

Thus one cannot say positively that any particular print was never published. However, Brady was more or less eclipsed at the time of the invention, in 1880, of the halftone process and his pictures were neglected. When I use the term "unpublished" in describing a photograph I mean that I have not encountered it in any other book about Brady or his time.

The Brady prints best known and used most frequently are his war views. I have included many of these, though I thought it best, in the compass of this biography, not to give overemphasis to his superb, but more familiar, war pictures. It is just about impossible to label any of these "unpublished." Most of the books about the Civil War issued during the last half century have been illustrated by pictures taken by Brady or his assistants.

Of all the collections of Brady pictures the Brady-Handy Collection has retained its exclusivity simply because it has remained so long in private hands. The bulk of this fine collection has probably not seen the light of day for three-quarters of a century, particularly the portraits of Civil War and postwar figures. In a sense, the acquisition by the Library of Congress of the Brady-Handy Collection ultimately realized the desire expressed as early as 1871 by the Joint Committee on the Library to preserve in the Library these same portraits. In that year the Committee voted unanimously to recommend that Congress purchase two thousand of Brady's portraits for $5,000. The proposal was shelved. Besides the portraits of national figures and views of historic events, many of his early daguerreotypes were brought to light for the first time when the wooden boxes containing them were opened last fall.

To return to our long list of acknowledgments, Mr. Vincent Mercaldo of the Mercaldo Archives went through his large collection for early Brady stereos.

Mr. Emerson C. Ives, Quaker Hill, Pawling, N.Y., grandson of Francis B. Carpenter, the artist, graciously loaned me his Lincoln Brady print and excerpts from his grandfather's unpublished diary, which helped to establish the name of the operator who took some of the famous Lincoln pictures, and also the circumstances in which they were taken.

Miss Eleanor I. Ney, of Ansco, Binghamton, N.Y., was diligent in her search for Brady and Anthony material and was never too busy to answer my many queries.

The George Eastman House, Rochester, N.Y., supplied me with a picture of Tim O'Sullivan taken in the jungles of Darien, while Mark E. Nevils, Captain Theodore W. Goodman, USAF, PIO, George Carroll, aviation editor of the New York Journal-American, and the Public Relations Department of General Dynamics Corporation combined operations to obtain pictures of the Mathew B. Brady plane.

Miss Helen M. McFarland, Librarian of the Kansas State Historical Society was most helpful in obtaining for this book the Gardner negatives taken during the

Union Pacific track-laying after the Civil War.

Miss Grace M. Mayer of the Museum of the City of New York supplied an excellent Brady wet plate print of New York City during the Civil War along with some good advice, and Miss Elizabeth Baughman, Reference Librarian of the Chicago Historical Society, was eager to assist as always; as was Marjory Douglas, Curator of the Missouri Historical Society.

Major Alfred S. Byrne of the 69th Regiment Armory lent me a rare Brady picture of an army field mass.

Mr. George Feinstein, clerk in charge of the Division of Records, County Clerk's office, New York County, searched for many days to find for me the record of the sale of Mrs. Brady's real estate.

Mr. Claude G. Bowers interrupted a busy schedule to discuss the unpublished George W. Julian diary and other sources which mentioned Brady in the postwar years. Mr. H. Armour Smith, Yonkers, N.Y. spent the best part of a day going through his collection to locate his Mexican War daguerreotypes for me, which Mr. Michael Ciprioni so skillfully copied. Captain John D. Murphy, Assistant Public Information Officer, United States Military Academy, West Point, N.Y., searched diligently until he found the volume containing Stonewall Jackson's signature.

I owe a special note of gratitude to Miss H. M. Baumhofer, Chief, Film Depository Division, Wright-Patterson Air Force Base, Ohio, who shared with me her research material on Tim O'Sullivan, and to Karl Pretshold of the New York City Department of Health and his staff who helped me to locate Brady's death certificate.

I owe a large note of thanks to Florence and Maureen, that charming and irreplaceable pair, who again guarded the heirs and the hearth. It would have been impossible to do without them.

As always, my friend Mr. Howard Swiggett was ready to interrupt his own busy writing schedule to offer excellent advice.

Horan's Boondocks.
September, 1955.

PICTURE SOURCES

Numbers refer to picture numbers

Ansco, 85, 100, 104, 175, 193, 258-260, 351, 355, 363, 369

Author's Collection, 224-246

Brady-Handy Collection, Library of Congress, 1, 3, 4, 10, 11, 13, 15, 16, 18, 18a, 19, 36, 41, 43, 50, 53, 56-58, 60, 61, 64, 66-68, 71-73, 75-79, 83, 84, 93-96, 101-103, 105-107, 109-134, 136-138, 141, 145, 147-151, 153, 155, 157-170, 172, 173, 176-181, 185-191, 194-196, 198-217, 227-233, 235-243, 247-257, 261-263, 268, 269, 272-274, 276, 280, 283, 285-290, 292, 302-305, 307, 308, 310-314, 320, 323-325, 335-338, 340-350, 352-354, 356-362, 364-368, 370-378, 380-394, 396-404, 406-417, 420, 421, 423-426

Frederick Cox, 42

Mrs. Cox and Mrs. Evans, 419, 422

George Eastman House, 427, 428

Howard Theatre Collection, 315

Emerson C. Ives, 152

Kansas State Historical Society, 432-451

Library of Congress, 8, 9, 12, 14, 17, 20-22, 23, 24-26, 27-35, 37-40, 42, 44, 46-48, 51, 52, 54, 55, 59, 62, 65, 69, 80, 87-92, 99, 139, 140, 142-144, 146, 154, 156, 174, 218, 234, 265, 270, 277-79, 281, 284, 293-301, 306, 316-319, 321, 322, 326-334, 339, 395, 404

Mercaldo Archives, 192, 219-222, 245

Metropolitan Museum of Art, 2a

Museum of the City of New York, 7, 82, 223

National Archives, 63, 70, 74, 97, 135, 171, 182, 184, 264, 269, 271, 275, 282, 291, 329

National Park Service, 309

New York Historical Society, 244, 246

New York Public Library, 5, 429-431

Photographic Art Journal, 2, 27

Photo Miniature Magazine, 81

Sixth-Ninth Regiment, New York, 266

H. Armour Smith, 49, 86a, 86b, 86c

U. S. Army Air Force, 453

U. S. National Museum, 6

PART ONE

Brady of Broadway

⋯→──▶►●◄◀──┄⋯

Well, yes—if you saw us out driving
Each day in the park, four-in-hand-
If you saw poor dear mamma contriving
To look supernaturally grand,
If you saw papa's picture, as taken
By Brady, and tinted at that,
You'd never suspect he sold bacon
And flour at Poverty Flat.

From "Her Letter" by Bret Harte.

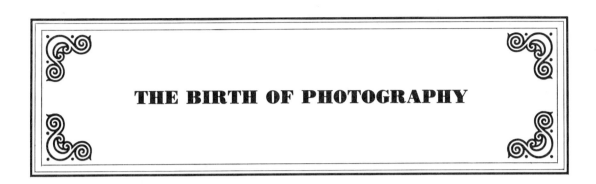

THE BIRTH OF PHOTOGRAPHY

UNTIL 1839 the world was blind. Vision was limited to the immediate spectator or the art of the artist, but the rest of the world and history could not see.

On a hot and sticky August day in the French Academy of Sciences where that year the heat was unbearable, every seat was occupied. Outside, more than two hundred persons jammed the courtyard. Since January, when Louis Jacques Mandé Daguerre, citizen of France, had exhibited pictures etched by some special magic on shiny copper plates, all France—the world—had been waiting for this day.

It was well known that the pictures had dumbfounded Francois Arago, the great French scientist and student of light, who had placed a bill before the government asking that an annuity be given to Daguerre and that his process be revealed and made available to the world. The French government had granted Daguerre an annual income of six thousand francs. In return, the father of the "daguerreotype" had agreed to release his process to the public.

Now the day of revelation had arrived. At the stroke of three Arago arose and began reading. He explained that Daguerre himself, because of a "little too much modesty," could not be prevailed upon to speak, or even to appear.

Arago spoke slowly. The scientists gathered from all over the world listened carefully—"copper plate . . . well cleaned and polished . . . iodine vapor . . . camera obscura . . ." The last words hung in the air, then Arago sat down to thunderous applause. In the courtyard the spectators cheered.

The veil had been torn from history's eyes. She could see. Photography had been born.

February 14, 1849, Washington city. A slim young

THE DAGUERREOTYPE.

We give below a description of this most interesting discovery, and take great pleasure in stating that several gentlemen of this city, among whom, we may name Dr. Chilton, President Morse, and Professor Draper, have fully succeeded in procuring fine specimens of photogenic drawing, by *means of this instrument*.

Translated from the original paper of L. J. M. Daguerre, (the inventor,) by J. S. MEMES, L L. D.

Practical Description of the Daguerréotype. Material to be employed in the photogenic process. Five steps of the process explained. Polishing the white coating with Iodine. The Camera. Mercurial process. Fixing the impression, with descriptions of the Apparatus.

THE designs are executed upon thin plates of silver, plated on copper. Although the copper serves principally to support the silver foil, the combination of the two metals tends to the perfection of the effect. The silver must be the purest that can be procured. As to the copper, its thickness ought to be sufficient to maintain the perfect smoothness and flatness of the plate, so that the images may not be distorted by the warping of the tablet; but unnecessary thickness beyond this is to be avoided on account of the weight. The thickness of the two metals united, ought not to exceed that of a stout card.

The process is divided into five operations:

1. The first consists in polishing and cleaning the plate, in order to prepare it for receiving the sensitive coating, upon which the light traces the design.

2. The second is to apply this coating.

3. The third is the placing the prepared plate properly in the camera obscura to the action of light, for the purpose of receiving the image of nature.

4. The fourth brings out this image, which at first is not visible on the plate being withdrawn from the camera obscura.

5. The fifth and last operation has for its object to remove the sensitive coating on which the design is first impressed, because this coating would continue to be affected by the rays of light, a property which would necessarily and quickly destroy the picture.

FIRST OPERATION.

Preparing the Plate.

The requisites for this operation are of:
A small phial containing olive oil.
Some very finely carded cotton.

Fig. 4. An early announcement of the birth of photography in *The American Repertory of Arts, Sciences, and Manufacturers*, March, 1840, with a translation of Daguerre's paper, which had been read before the French Academy of Science in 1839.

3

man walked up the path to the White House and knocked on the front door.

He was about twenty-six years old. His dark hair was thick and curly and his near-sighted brown eyes peered weakly through the thick lenses of his spectacles. He was wearing his best black broadcloth suit and he was carrying an oblong wooden box.

His name was Mathew B. Brady—"Brady of Broadway," as he was known in the newspapers—and he had come to the White House to take the first picture of a President of the United States in office.

In response to his knock an usher opened the door. When he gave his name he was invited inside and the servant went into the study where President Polk was working. Anyone who had known Polk before he had been elected to office and who had not seen him in four years would have been shocked at his appearance this day. An agonizing disease had etched deep lines in his face. His long hair, once black as a raven's wing, was now gray and straggly. His hands shook and his movements were feeble. Only his eyes were alive, black and searching.[1]

When his servant told him that Brady was calling he went out to greet him. When Brady asked which was the lightest room, Polk said the dining room, and Brady suggested that they take the "likeness" in that room.

President Polk led the way down the hall to the dining room and Brady followed respectfully at his elbow. In the dining room Brady drew aside the drapes, placed a chair near the window with the "immobilizer" (head clamp) behind it, then set up his daguerreotype camera.

Polk sat in the chair. The weak, lemonish winter sunshine fell on the sad and bitter face. The black eyes stared unblinkingly at the lens. Brady told the President it would take but a few seconds, then slipped the cover from the lens, counted thirty seconds under his breath, and put the cover back over the lens. That was all. He unscrewed the headclamp, thanked the President, gathered up his equipment with his precious copper plates and was ushered out of the White House.

Polk returned to his study and to his diary. With a firm hand he wrote the date, "February 14, 1849," and then went on to denounce the hordes of office seekers "who are willing to profess to belong to either party to obtain or hold office, all anxious to get in before I retire in the hope that they will not be turned out after I retire. I have great contempt for such persons and dispose of their applications very summarily. They take up much of my time every day. I yielded to the request of an artist named Brady of New York by sitting for my daguerreotype likeness today. I sat in the large dining room."

Back in New York, in his gallery at Fulton Street and Broadway, Brady placed Polk's daguerreotype among the collection of portraits of distinguished individuals with the intention of "making in the end a more complete collection than had ever before been made of the distinguished men of the nation."[2]

If, on his return to New York, Brady had walked about his spacious gallery, studying the portraits of the great men and women he had taken, and also noting, perhaps, the rich carpeting, the chandeliers, and the case after case of mounted daguerreotypes in rich rosewood frames, he would have been justly proud. This studio where he was on such intimate terms with presidents, diplomats, statesmen, actors and actresses, poets and pioneers, seemed a thousand years away from the small farmhouse where he was born in Warren County, N.Y., in 1823, when James Monroe was President of a farmer republic sprawled along the Atlantic and westward into the Mississippi Valley.[3]

If he had asked himself, while musing, what moment, what meeting had started him on his journey to fame in the new science of photography, he might have said it was the day he left for Saratoga . . . or perhaps his meeting with William Page, now becoming one of the great portrait artists of the nation . . . or when he walked into Professor Samuel F. B. Morse's bohemian "rookery" on Spring Street in New York City.

Francis Trevelyan Miller put Brady's birthplace as Cork, Ireland, but Brady, in a newspaper interview, claimed Warren County, New York, and put the year as "about 1823-24." We know nothing of his parents, who were believed to have been Irish immigrants. On Brady's death certificate their names are listed as Andrew and Julia and their birthplaces as the United States.

Mathew Brady's boyhood years are shadowy, but we know that Warren County—the terrible Border Wars of the American Revolution were only forty-two years past—was still the frontier where the curly horns of Butler's Rangers coming down from Fort Niagara to "bust the Valley" still echoed in the memories of many of its settlers.[4] At about sixteen he left home and traveled to Saratoga, the mecca of the farm lads who sought jobs and a look at the outside world.

Somehow—the circumstances are not known—Brady met young William Page, then a struggling young portrait artist, in his studio, and they became friends. There was a great deal of the artist in Brady and perhaps the shy farmboy came into the studio to watch a young man his own age bring life and color to a dead canvas. We do know from C. Edwards Lester, the art critic, and editor of *The Gallery of Illustrious Americans,* that Page took an interest in Brady and encouraged him to sketch, "giving him a bundle of his crayons to copy." They became close friends, traveling together to Albany where Brady laboriously copied the sketches, while Page sought out commissions.[5]

A letter about the Daguerre process published in

the New York *Observer* would bring about great changes in the life of Mathew B. Brady. It was from Samuel F. B. Morse, then in Paris, giving an account of his visit with Daguerre who, three months earlier, had placed on public exhibition specimens of his daguerreotypes, pictures taken on copper plates. Daguerre had been working on this process for ten years with Joseph Nicephore Niepce, and when Niepce died in 1833, Daguerre continued the experiments alone.[6]

Morse, who had been in Europe to secure a French patent for his electro-magnetic telegraph, had requested and was granted a private interview with Daguerre, who showed him his copper-plate pictures. In his letter to the *Observer* he described the plates as "one of the most beautiful discoveries of the age" and disclosed that he himself had been experimenting along the same lines in New Haven, Conn. It has been claimed, particularly by Morse's son, that Daguerre gave Morse "the secret" of the process at that time, but this is unlikely.[7]

From January to June of 1839, Daguerre and representatives of the French government worked out a contract in which the process was made free for all, Daguerre relinquished all rights to the patent and a government pension was established for him. The contract was signed in June and on August 19 the secret of the process was announced to the world by Arago.

Arago's description of Daguerre's process was not too complicated. A sheet of copper was coated with silver, well polished and cleaned. The surface, in a small box, was exposed to iodine vapors at ordinary temperature until the silverized surface turned a golden yellow color. The time required was anywhere from five to thirty seconds. The sensitized surface was then placed in a camera "five to ten minutes in the summer and from ten to twelve minutes in the winter. In the climate of the tropics two or three minutes should certainly be sufficient."

The daguerreotype plate on "which even an experienced eye could detect no trace of drawing" was developed by being exposed in a closed box to mercury vapors heated to 167° Fahrenheit.

The plate was then washed with the solution known to every photographer, amateur and professional alike, as "hypo," or, as Daguerre termed it, "hyposulphite of soda."[8]

Three days after Arago's speech at the Academy, stories of the announcement appeared in the leading newspapers of England and France. They were as quickly rewritten by correspondents of New York's major dailies and sent off.

The fever generated by the "new art" spread rapidly. In Paris Morse ordered a daguerreotype camera made according to the specifications laid down by Daguerre. Artists and amateurs in London followed his example.

The *British Queen,* the fastest ship of its time, left Portsmouth, England, on September 3, and arrived in New York on the 20th, returning Morse to America with his camera and also bringing to the United States the announcement of the birth of photography. Within a few days news stories describing the process were published in New York, Washington, Boston and Philadelphia.[9]

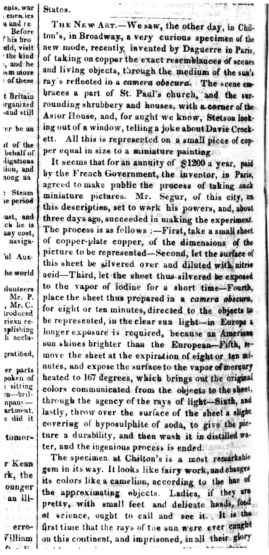

Fig. 5. One of the first news stories about photography ever published. From the New York *Morning Herald*, September 30, 1839.

Here was a new art—free! All one had to do was build a camera, coat and polish a copper plate and take a picture. The financial gains were obvious from New York to the farthest frontier. Americans, too, began to experiment with Daguerre's wooden camera and the process of daguerreotypy. One of them was Mathew B. Brady, whose camera would link the founders of the Republic with virtually the opening of the twentieth century.

Brady and Page left Albany sometime in 1839-40 for New York. Page opened a studio on Chambers Street and presumably Brady became his roommate. The New

York City in which Brady and Page found themselves was a feverish, filthy, mushrooming metropolis in the grip of the last years of a financial panic. The flood of immigrants from all over the world had quickened since the mid-thirties and the city's borders were constantly inching northward. There was little sanitation and the condition of the streets was disgraceful.[10]

After a few days of rain or an extended spring thaw it took a brave man to cross some of the streets, but the New Yorker of more than a century ago accepted his city's shortcomings with a philosophical indifference, ready to chuckle over the legend of the child who let go of his mother's hand and was lost in a pothole while crossing a downtown street or the elderly lady who glanced out of her window during the epidemic of 1832 when the city fathers had the streets scraped and cried, "Cobblestones at the bottom of the streets! How droll!"[11]

The Croton reservoir had been completed and it was no longer necessary to get water at the street corner pumps, but Knapp's safe drinking water was still selling for a penny a gallon. Down in the Five Points district epidemics of typhus, typhoid and dysentery still raged through whole sections of miserable rabbit-warrens. But despite its muddy streets, poor dwellings and the miserable existence of thousands of its citizens, New York was strident, bustling and alive and for two young men bursting with dreams and hopes it was the only place to live.

Brady soon found a position as a clerk in A. T. Stewart's large store, then located at Chambers Street and Broadway, and Page continued to paint portraits.[12]

One of Page's first moves was to visit his friend, Samuel F. B. Morse, then President of the National Academy of Design.[13] Brady went along and was introduced to Morse—and photography. This meeting was to be the great turning point in his life.

As Morse recalled sixteen years later, he took his first daguerreotype in September, 1839, with the camera he had had made for him in Paris. It was a view of the Unitarian Church taken from the window on the staircase of the third story of the New York University.[14]

There can be little doubt that he showed the copper plate with its image to the two young men. It was the first specimen of the photographic art they had seen and one can imagine their intense excitement. More than half a century later Brady recalled that after this meeting his life was inextricably enmeshed with the infant art of photography.

"I was introduced to Morse," he remembered, "who was then painting portraits at starvation prices in the University rookery on Washington Square. He had just come home from Paris and had invented upon the ship his telegraphic alphabet of which his mind was so full that he could give but little attention to a remarkable discovery one Daguerre, a friend of his had made in France.

"Daguerre had traveled in this country exhibiting dissolving views and Morse had known him. While Morse was abroad Daguerre and Niepce had after many experiments fixed the pictures in sensitive chemicals, but they applied it chiefly or only to copying scenes. Morse, as a portrait painter, thought of it as something to reduce the labor of his portraits. He had a loft in his brother's storeroom at Nassau and Beekman Streets with a telegraph stretched and an embryo camera also at work.

"Professor John W. Draper and Professor Doremus counseled me, both eminent chemists. It was Draper who invented the enameling of a daguerreotype and entered at last into the business, say about 1842-43. . . ."

At the time of this first meeting with Morse the inventor was going through one of the bitterest periods in his life. His attempts to finance his precious electromagnetic invention had left him almost penniless. The salary he earned at the University was small, and from his letters written during these years, it is evident that the daily struggle to survive was very hard indeed.[15] Photography and his invention shared his dreams; his telegraph was to give him glory and enduring fame, but photography paid his rent and bought his food.

Sometime about 1840 he opened what was perhaps the first school of photography in America, charging twenty-five to fifty dollars for a course in taking and developing daguerreotypes. Morse had only a few pupils, but their names stand out in the history of photography —Edward Anthony, Samuel Broadbent of Philadelphia, Albert S. Southworth of Boston—and the farmboy, Mathew B. Brady.

Money was tight in those days following the panic and fifty dollars must have seemed like a fortune to young Brady. We find a brief reference in an early New York directory to his early job as a jeweler's helper and it is possible Brady worked days at Stewart's and nights in some small shop, in that winter of 1840-41, to get together the fee necessary to enter Morse's school.[16]

The art of photography, meanwhile, was ever on the advance. New names began to appear in connection with the "new art." Among them was that of D. W. Seager, an Englishman residing in New York City, who probably inserted the first commercial photographic advertisement in this country; Dr. John W. Draper, a professor of chemistry at New York University; John Plumbe, who shared a love of photography with a dream of a transcontinental railroad.[17] Alexander Wolcott, who obtained the first photographic patent in this country, and Dr. James R. Chilton, a patron of the early photographers.

Morse, Draper, Plumbe, Seager, Wolcott, Doctor Chilton—they are America's photographic pioneers. They were Brady's friends, instructors, advisors and his competitors. Some, like himself, were poor, others were well-to-do. Two—Morse and Draper—were brilliant. To evaluate properly Brady's importance in the early years of photography it is important also to know them and their contributions.

Towering over them all, including Morse, is Draper. Son of a Wesleyan clergyman, he was writing articles on the solar system and contributing scientific essays to the *Ress Encyclopedia* while he was still in his teens.[18] In 1832 he came to the United States from England and lived in Virginia. Five years later he was appointed head of the Chemistry Department of the University of the City of New York. He was then only twenty-six.

It is little known that Draper had been keenly interested in solar light and that, when Daguerre's announcement stirred the world, he was conducting experiments to ascertain the effects of different kinds of light upon chemical changes.

Draper made the first photographic portrait of a human face of which copies are known to exist, probably late in 1839. As Draper explained, he first coated the face of the sitter with white powder, but after a few experiments he decided this was not necessary. On March 23, 1840, he displayed his portrait of his sister at the Lyceum of Natural History in New York. It had been taken on a brilliant day with a twenty-minute exposure. The picture was one inch in diameter. There is no doubt that Brady saw that picture.[19]

Another Brady associate was John Plumbe, who looked like a Corsican bandit with a thick black mustache, but was actually a man of tremendous vision and courage. In 1836 Plumbe was the Dubuque, Iowa, correspondent for every large paper in America. Already he was dreaming of a transcontinental railroad, and in January of that year drew up the first recognized plans for a railroad westward from Lake Michigan. He also organized the meeting (in a small store on Main Street in Dubuque), at which a petition for the railroad was drawn up and presented to the government in Washington.[20]

In 1839 his restlessness took him to New York, and when photography was born that summer, Plumbe immediately appointed himself one of its godfathers. His extensive experiments gave his name to the "Plumbetype," a form of early photography not generally known except to the professional historians. He established the first chain of Daguerreotype Parlors throughout the East, founded the Plumbe National Daguerrian Gallery and Photograph Depot in Washington, D.C., in 1840 ("Portraits taken in any weather, in exquisite style"). At one time his chain of studios included branches in New York, Boston, Philadelphia, Baltimore, New Orleans, Louisville, Saratoga, St. Louis, Albuquerque, Newport—even Paris and Liverpool. But his financial resources were stretched too thin and his business collapsed. His star loomed bright for a time, then faded out. A few years later he returned to the pages of history

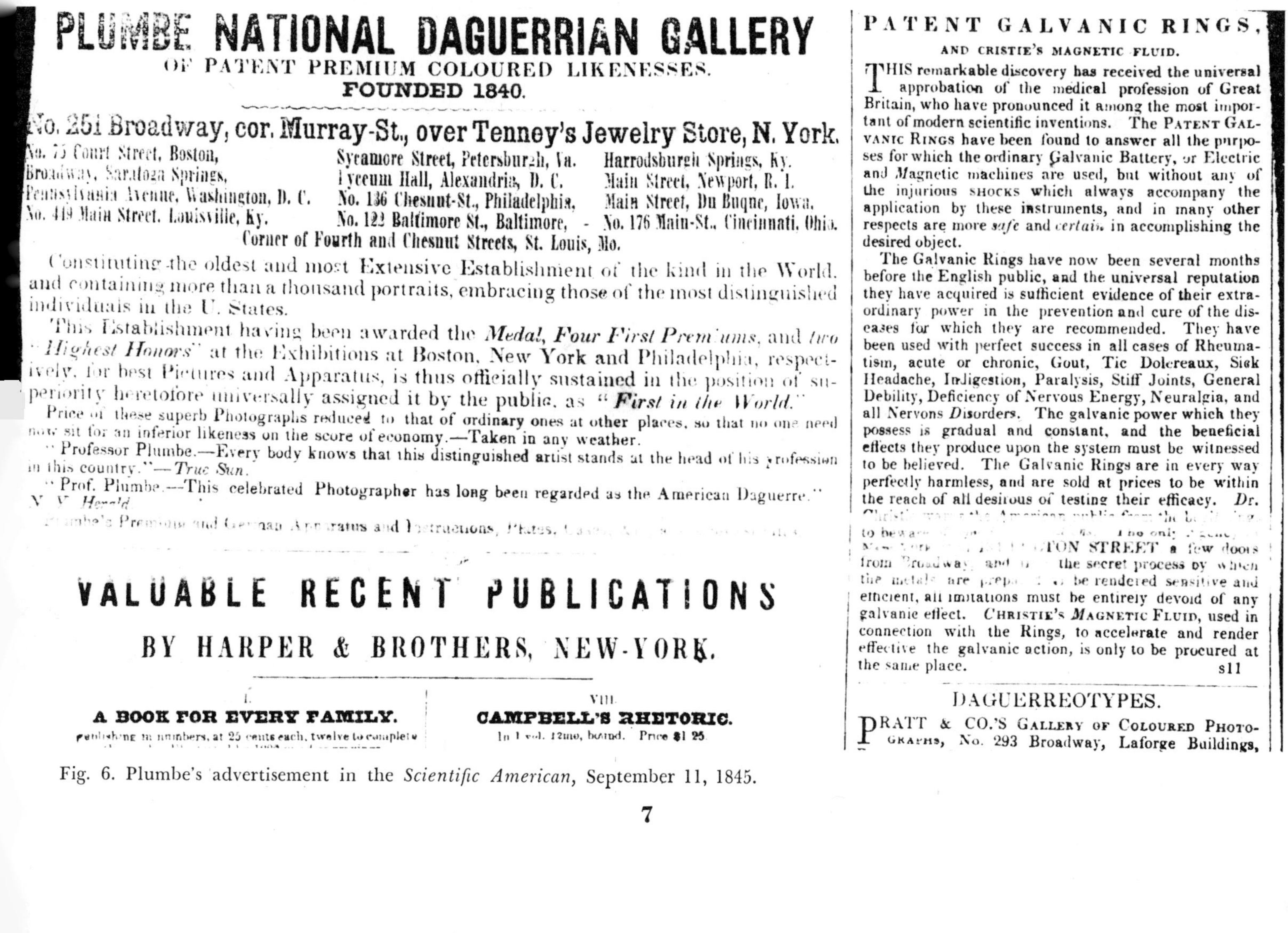

PLUMBE NATIONAL DAGUERRIAN GALLERY
OF PATENT PREMIUM COLOURED LIKENESSES.
FOUNDED 1840.

No. 251 Broadway, cor. Murray-St., over Tenney's Jewelry Store, N. York.

No. 75 Court Street, Boston, — Sycamore Street, Petersburgh, Va. — Harrodsburgh Springs, Ky.
Broadway, Saratoga Springs, — Lyceum Hall, Alexandria, D. C. — Main Street, Newport, R. I.
Pennsylvania Avenue, Washington, D. C. — No. 136 Chesnut-St., Philadelphia, — Main Street, Du Buque, Iowa,
No. 419 Main Street, Louisville, Ky. — No. 122 Baltimore St., Baltimore, — No. 176 Main-St., Cincinnati, Ohio.
Corner of Fourth and Chesnut Streets, St. Louis, Mo.

Constituting the oldest and most Extensive Establishment of the kind in the World, and containing more than a thousand portraits, embracing those of the most distinguished individuals in the U. States.

This Establishment having been awarded the *Medal, Four First Premiums*, and *two "Highest Honors"* at the Exhibitions at Boston, New York and Philadelphia, respectively, for best Pictures and Apparatus, is thus officially sustained in the position of superiority heretofore universally assigned it by the public, as "*First in the World.*"

Price of these superb Photographs reduced to that of ordinary ones at other places, so that no one need now sit for an inferior likeness on the score of economy.—Taken in any weather.

"Professor Plumbe.—Every body knows that this distinguished artist stands at the head of his profession in this country."—*True Sun.*

"Prof. Plumbe.—This celebrated Photographer has long been regarded as the American Daguerre." *N. Y. Herald.*

[illegible] Apparatus and Instructions, Plates, [illegible]

VALUABLE RECENT PUBLICATIONS
BY HARPER & BROTHERS, NEW-YORK.

I.
A BOOK FOR EVERY FAMILY.
publishing in numbers, at 25 cents each, twelve to complete

VIII.
CAMPBELL'S RHETORIC.
In 1 vol. 12mo, bound. Price $1 25

PATENT GALVANIC RINGS,
AND CRISTIE'S MAGNETIC FLUID.

THIS remarkable discovery has received the universal approbation of the medical profession of Great Britain, who have pronounced it among the most important of modern scientific inventions. The PATENT GALVANIC RINGS have been found to answer all the purposes for which the ordinary Galvanic Battery, or Electric and *Magnetic* machines are used, but without any of the injurious SHOCKS which always accompany the application by these instruments, and in many other respects are more *safe* and *certain* in accomplishing the desired object.

The Galvanic Rings have now been several months before the English public, and the universal reputation they have acquired is sufficient evidence of their extraordinary power in the prevention and cure of the diseases for which they are recommended. They have been used with perfect success in all cases of Rheumatism, acute or chronic, Gout, Tic Dolereaux, Sick Headache, Indigestion, Paralysis, Stiff Joints, General Debility, Deficiency of Nervous Energy, Neuralgia, and all Nervous *Disorders*. The galvanic power which they possess is gradual and constant, and the beneficial effects they produce upon the system must be witnessed to be believed. The Galvanic Rings are in every way perfectly harmless, and are sold at prices to be within the reach of all desirous of testing their efficacy. *Dr.* [illegible] TON STREET a few doors from Broadway, [illegible] the secret process by which the metals are [illegible] be rendered sensitive and efficient, all imitations must be entirely devoid of any galvanic effect. CHRISTIE'S *MAGNETIC* FLUID, used in connection with the Rings, to accelerate and render effective the galvanic action, is only to be procured at the same place. s11

DAGUERREOTYPES.

PRATT & CO.'S GALLERY OF COLOURED PHOTOGRAPHS, No. 293 Broadway, Laforge Buildings,

Fig. 6. Plumbe's advertisement in the *Scientific American*, September 11, 1845.

as a dust-covered man stepping down from an ox-cart. He had just completed a lonely six-month crossing of the western plains to make a "survey" for his transcontinental railroad.[21]

Another of Brady's contemporaries was Alexander S. Wolcott, a manufacturer of dental equipment and the first photographer to use a concave reflector to reduce the required exposure. On May 8, 1840, he obtained the first photographic patent, for the reflector, in this country.

Brady was still struggling to learn the art in Morse's school of daguerreotypy when Wolcott opened his first studio at the corner of Broadway and Chambers Street. In a few years his biggest competitor was Mathew B. Brady.

It was Seager (sometimes called Segur) who had made photography news. Over their coffeepots or squeezed in

the "cars" on their way to work, readers of the New York *Morning Herald* learned, on the morning of September 30, 1839, that they could see one of those daguerreotypes the whole world was talking about displayed in the window of Chilton's on Broadway. The man who had successfully made this remarkable specimen—a picture of St. Paul's Church and a corner of the Astor House—was one Mr. Seager.[22]

We can only imagine the amazed murmurs of the crowds which packed the front of the Broadway store as they gazed at the tiny little copper miracle . . . can one imagine one's own feeling at seeing for the first time a familiar scene magically etched on a copper plate . . . a picture!

The exhibition must have been a success because a few days later Seager inserted in the *Herald* an announcement of a lecture, probably the first photo-

Fig. 7. The first photographic commercial announcement in America. From the New York *Morning Herald*, October 3, 1839.

graphic commercial advertisement in America. Morse and Draper are listed as his sponsors. The group of photographic pioneers was still small in that winter of 1839 and the members were constantly exchanging information, praise and encouragement, and experimenting with new techniques. Seager had demonstrated his competence and experienced men like Draper and Morse were ready to endorse him.

The years 1841-43 of Brady's life are shadowy. He is listed in Doggett's *New York City Directory* 1843-44 (and 1844-45) as a jewel-case man. It is believed he shared quarters with Page on Chambers Street near Washington Street, but this is not certain. He recalled many years later that he was working at Stewart's store during this time, studying photography and experimenting in taking daguerreotypes.

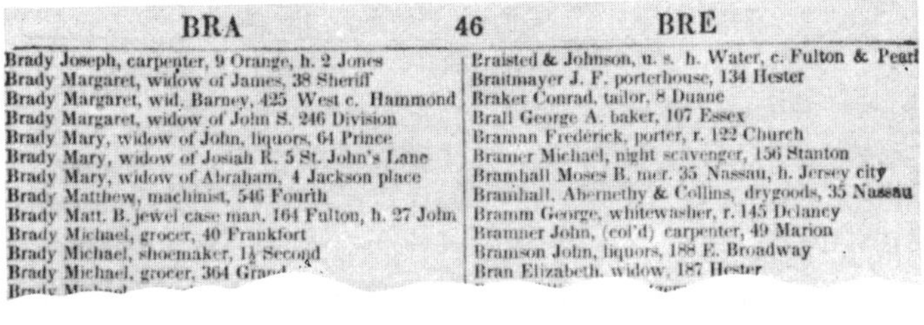

BRA 46 BRE

Brady Joseph, carpenter, 9 Orange, h. 2 Jones
Brady Margaret, widow of James, 38 Sheriff
Brady Margaret, wid. Barney, 425 West c. Hammond
Brady Margaret, widow of John S. 246 Division
Brady Mary, widow of John, liquors, 64 Prince
Brady Mary, widow of Josiah R. 5 St. John's Lane
Brady Mary, widow of Abraham, 4 Jackson place
Brady Matthew, machinist, 546 Fourth
Brady Matt. B. jewel case man. 164 Fulton, h. 27 John
Brady Michael, grocer, 40 Frankfort
Brady Michael, shoemaker, 1½ Second
Brady Michael, grocer, 364 Grand

Braisted & Johnson, u. s. h. Water, c. Fulton & Pearl
Braitmayer J. F. porterhouse, 134 Hester
Braker Conrad, tailor, 8 Duane
Brall George A. baker, 107 Essex
Braman Frederick, porter, r. 122 Church
Bramer Michael, night scavenger, 156 Stanton
Bramhall Moses B. mer. 35 Nassau, h. Jersey city
Bramhall, Abernethy & Collins, drygoods, 35 Nassau
Bramm George, whitewasher, r. 145 Delancy
Bramner John, (col'd) carpenter, 49 Marion
Bramson John, liquors, 188 E. Broadway
Bran Elizabeth, widow, 187 Hester

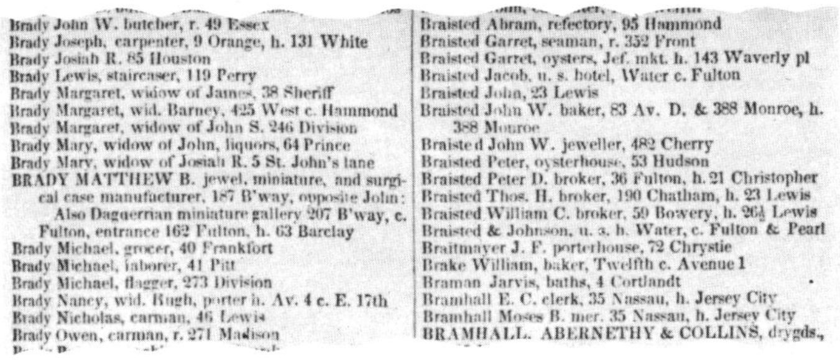

Brady John W. butcher, r. 49 Essex
Brady Joseph, carpenter, 9 Orange, h. 131 White
Brady Josiah R. 85 Houston
Brady Lewis, staircaser, 119 Perry
Brady Margaret, widow of James, 38 Sheriff
Brady Margaret, wid. Barney, 425 West c. Hammond
Brady Margaret, widow of John S. 246 Division
Brady Mary, widow of John, liquors, 64 Prince
Brady Mary, widow of Josiah R. 5 St. John's lane
BRADY MATTHEW B. jewel, miniature, and surgical case manufacturer, 187 B'way, opposite John: Also Daguerrian miniature gallery 207 B'way, c. Fulton, entrance 162 Fulton, h. 63 Barclay
Brady Michael, grocer, 40 Frankfort
Brady Michael, laborer, 41 Pitt
Brady Michael, flagger, 273 Division
Brady Nancy, wid. Hugh, porter h. Av. 4 c. E. 17th
Brady Nicholas, carman, 46 Lewis
Brady Owen, carman, r. 271 Madison

Braisted Abram, refectory, 95 Hammond
Braisted Garret, seaman, r. 352 Front
Braisted Garret, oysters, Jef. mkt. h. 143 Waverly pl
Braisted Jacob, u. s. hotel, Water c. Fulton
Braisted John, 23 Lewis
Braisted John W. baker, 83 Av. D. & 388 Monroe, h. 388 Monroe
Braisted John W. jeweller, 482 Cherry
Braisted Peter, oysterhouse, 53 Hudson
Braisted Peter D. broker, 36 Fulton, h. 21 Christopher
Braisted Thos. H. broker, 190 Chatham, h. 23 Lewis
Braisted William C. broker, 59 Bowery, h. 26½ Lewis
Braisted & Johnson, u. s. h. Water, c. Fulton & Pearl
Braitmayer J. F. porterhouse, 72 Chrystie
Brake William, baker, Twelfth c. Avenue 1
Braman Jarvis, baths, 4 Cortlandt
Bramhall E. C. clerk, 35 Nassau, h. Jersey City
Bramhall Moses B. mer. 35 Nassau, h. Jersey City
BRAMHALL. ABERNETHY & COLLINS, drygds.,

Figs. 8 and 9. Excerpts from *Doggett's New York City Directory*, 1843-44 and 1844-45, showing Brady listings. *Courtesy New York Historical Society.*

But whether he was still working at Stewart's, or at the jeweler's or both, attending Morse's school or experimenting with photography, we do know that young Brady had become an accepted member of the group of artists and early daguerreotypists who had made New York City the center of the world of photography.

He was a welcome visitor at Morse's studio, "the rookery,"[23] which he recalled years later. Here is the inside of Morse's "rookery" as Brady would have seen it in his day: telegraph wires stretched across the untidy room; at his table, oblivious to the hubbub, Morse tinkered with his precious electro-magnetic machine; nearby, on another table was Morse's wooden daguerreotype camera—the one he had ordered made for him in Paris. Strewn about on the floor were boxes and bottles filled with chemicals, canvases, paints, stiffened brushes, bits of clothing, finished daguerreotypes, smudged ones, shiny copper plates and newspapers.

A "glass palace"[24], which Morse hoped would help produce a better type of daguerreotype, was constructed sometime in 1840 on the roof of the University of the City of New York (now New York University), by Morse and Draper, who apparently went into partnership. But they soon parted and what results the glass house produced we do not know.

Brady, together with Page, also visited Morse at the inventor's second glass house, or "palace for the sun," built for him by Morse's brothers, Sidney and Richard, on the roof of the building they owned at the northeast corner of Nassau and Beekman Streets.

Morse was now "tied hand and foot," as he put it in a letter, to the taking of daguerreotypes. He was in debt for the equipment and furnishings for his studio and was "reaping little profit from it."

Sometime in 1844 young Brady, then about twenty-one, felt he had learned all that Morse could teach him and with the small cash capital he had saved from his long hours at Stewart's and the jeweler's, he decided to open his own gallery.

It was typical of him to choose the Times Square of his time, Fulton Street and Broadway. His first studio on the second floor of a loft building was crude and unfurnished but all his own. Brady, who had seen what the "sun palace" of Morse had produced in better pictures, hired a carpenter to construct skylights in the roof. He was the first photographer, as far as we know, to use these, which became standard equipment in most studios in later years.[25]

Brady must have opened his gallery early in the year 1844 because in the spring, when the American Institute held its first competitive photographic exhibition, Brady walked off with the silver medal for first honors. Plumbe also took honors, as did a newcomer to Broadway, Jeremiah Gurney, who was destined to become Brady's toughest competitor and one of the nation's finest photographers.[26] In the next four years Brady took the same top prize. In fact, in 1849 it had become so monotonous that *Humphrey's Journal* (one of the early daguerrean trade periodicals) announced with a casual air, "Mr. B. has won again."

But prizes and awards soon seemed minor matters. Brady had found himself. He was fast becoming the well-known "Brady of Broadway" and his fame as a photographer was beginning to spread beyond the boundaries of the city.

In an article written about him by C. Edwards Lester in a photographic journal his zeal and energy were described: "Availing himself of everything that was published and known on the subject at the time and catching hold of every new discovery and improvement, he multiplied his facilities to such an extent that he was soon able to produce pictures that were regarded as quite equal if not superior to all that had been made before. While he offered inducements to the best operators and chemists to enter his studios he superintended every process himself and made himself master of every department of the art, sparing no pains or expense, by which new avenues could be introduced to increase the embellishments of the art."

He once remarked that he never, "after upwards of 20,000 experiments, had grown so familiar with the process of daguerrotyping as not to feel a new and tremendous interest in every repeated result when after preparing his plate he stepped aside to wait in silence for Nature to do her work."

Brady was tireless. He worked from dawn until the light failed and then most of the night developing his daguerreotypes. In later years he estimated he had taken "thousands" of pictures in those first years.

Brady was a perfectionist by nature and his health suffered because of this trait. His eyes, never too strong, grew weaker and the lenses in his glasses grew thicker and thicker. But he prospered. According to one of his contemporaries, his fellow photographers knew him as a shy, greatly reserved man, but the people who suffered the discomfort of the head clamp while he trained his camera on them, discovered he had the traditional Irishman's sense of storytelling and a seemingly endless fund of anecdotes.[27]

In 1845 Brady, the commercial photographer, became Brady the historian, who used a camera as Bancroft did his pen. It was in that year that Brady began work on the tremendous project of preserving for posterity the pictures of all distinguished Americans, which he planned to publish in a massive volume with the glow-

ing title of *The Gallery of Illustrious Americans*.

With typical energy and tenacity, Brady began to seek out the great men of his time, pleading, begging, promising and cajoling them to pose for him. Brady's persuasiveness worked wonders. The "men and mothers of America," as Brady called them, followed the huge black finger pointing up the creaky stairs to his second floor studio.

It is hard to find any great American statesman, politician, writer, scientist or thinker of the time who did not visit him; nor any actor or actress of any note who was not attracted by his offer to lead him or her by the hand before his camera and into history.[28]

Once Edgar Allan Poe paid Brady a visit. He was brought by Willis Ross Wallace and as Brady remembered, the melancholy poet shrank from coming, "as if he thought it was going to cost him something." Brady added that he had copied the portrait of Poe for "many a poet."[29]

Brady's first major contribution to his historic gallery was a daguerreotype of Andrew Jackson, seventh President of the United States. "Old Hickory" was dying in the simple bedroom of his beautiful Nashville Hermitage in the spring of 1845 when Brady obtained his precious picture. He "sent to the Hermitage," he said in later years, and "had Andrew Jackson taken barely in time to save his sacred lineaments to posterity."

Whether Brady took the daguerreotype or hired a local photographer is not certain. Writing in *McClure's Magazine* Charles Henry Hart, an art expert, claimed that the original daguerreotype, which he described as "the most important one of Jackson in existence," was taken by a young photographer named Dan Adams of Nashville, Tenn.[30]

Hart made his claim under an engraving of Jackson "from the original daguerreotype by Dan Adams of Nashville, Tennessee, owned by Cole Andrew of Cincinnati, size 1½ inch by ¾ inch width but ¼ inch in diameter, enlarged by Truscott of Philadelphia."

Hart claimed the daguerreotype was taken in Jackson's bedroom at the Hermitage on the morning of April 15, 1845, when the "general" was very weak and his body dreadfully swollen with dropsy. His granddaughter, Mrs. Rachel Jackson Lawrence, told Hart, "I have a vivid recollection of the arrangement of taking his likeness in which I was greatly interested. He [Jackson] was greatly opposed to having it taken, was very feeble at the time. I still have an old plate taken earlier but they were (sic) nearly faded out."

In any case, the daguerreotype of Andrew Jackson remained on display in Brady's New York gallery for some time.

But Brady, as History's cameraman, was sometimes unsuccessful in persuading "the men of achievement" he admired to pose for him.

Once he made a trip to Boston to "catch the Athenian

TABLE OF GENERAL RULES FOR EXPOSURE OF THE PLATE IN THE CAMERA, IN TAKING EXTERIOR VIEW

The following table is compiled partly from observation, and partly from analogy, and applies only to the period from the month of October to February. The observations were made upon ordinary city views.

STATE OF THE WEATHER.	HOURS OF THE DAY.						
	8	9	10	11 to 1	1 to 2	2 to 3	3 and after
	MINUTES.	MINUTES.	MINUTES.	MINUTES.	MINUTES.	MINUTES.	MINUTES.
Very brilliant and clear, wind steady from W. or N. W., very deep blue sky, and absence of red rays at sunrise or sunset. Time employed......	15	8	6	5	6	7	12 to 30
Clear, wind from S. W., moderately cold, but a slight perceptible vapor in comparison with above. Time employed......	16	12	7	6	7	8	15 to 40
Sunshine, but rather hazy, shadows not hard, nor clearly defined. Time employed......	25	18	14	12	14	16	25 to 40
Sun always obscured by light clouds, but lower atmosphere, clear from haze and vapor. Time employed.	30	20	18	16	15	20	35 to 50
Quite cloudy, but lower atmosphere, free from vapors. Time employed......	50	30	25	20	20	30	50 to 70

It is impossible, at present, to state precisely the time required

Fig. 10. The first photographic exposure table published in America. From *The American Repertory of Arts Sciences, and Manufactures*, March, 1840.

dignitaries such as Longfellow"[31] whom he missed. When Longfellow did not appear for his appointment Brady took it philosophically and in his gentle way excused the poet for his rudeness because of "his great press of business."

Brady's business was expanding and it was inevitable that in his search for men and women of History, Brady should open a Washington gallery. According to the art critic C. Edwards Lester, Brady visited the "seat of government" and opened a branch gallery about 1847 in Washington city, the "only daguerreotypist in America honored by a visit at his studio from the President and his Cabinet. Mr. Polk and all the heads of departments, General Taylor and his Cabinet, with the new President and most of his Cabinet" gave him sittings at his gallery and at the President's mansion.

In 1849 Brady made a photograph of President Zachary Taylor and his Cabinet, the first set of photographic engravings of a President and his Cabinet ever published. He sent them to the office of his old friend, James Gordon Bennett. The New York *Herald* editor peered at the engraving.

"Why, man," he exclaimed after a moment. "Do Washington and his Cabinet look like that? Alas, they were dead before my time."[32]

Brady chuckled many times over this anecdote and used it more than once to put a great man at ease as he tightened his immobilizer. Brady tried many times to get Bennett before the camera but the camera-shy editor steadfastly refused, giving many reasons, but the chief one, that he "didn't have the time." Brady settled for Horace Greeley, Dana, Kipley, Stone and Fry and the other great members of the *Herald*'s staff. But Brady did get him before his camera. "He did, however, come in at last and I took him with all his staff once—son, Dr. Wallace, Fred Hudson, Ned Hudson, Ned Williams, Captain Lyons."

James Fenimore Cooper, author of the popular *Leatherstocking Tales,* was another great American Brady yearned to include into his album of illustrious Americans.

"I recall," said Brady, "being much perplexed to know how to get Fenimore Cooper. I never had an excess of confidence and perhaps my diffidence helped me out with genuine men. Mr. Cooper had quarreled with his publishers and a celebrated daguerreotypist, Chilton, I think, one of my contemporaries, made the mistake of speaking about the subject of irritation. It was reported that Cooper had jumped from the chair and refused to sit. After that, daguerreotypers were afraid of him.

"I ventured in at Biggsby's, his hotel, corner of Park Place. He came out in his morning gown and asked me to excuse him until he had dismissed a caller. I told him what I had come for. Said he, 'How far from here is your gallery?' 'Only two blocks.' He went right along, stayed two hours, had half a dozen sittings and Charles

Elliott painted from it the portrait of Cooper for the publishers, Stinger and Townsend."[33]

Washington Irving also found his way to the Broadway and Fulton Street studio, apparently without any advance pressure or influence by his friends, who were also Brady's friends. As Brady remembered his visit, Irving was "a delicate person to handle for his picture." The first sitting was satisfactory to Irving and he returned several times, not only to the Fulton Street gallery but also to the Washington studio.

It makes a wonderful picture to visualize Brady unfolding his wealth of tales about the great men whose daguerreotypes stared down at them from the walls, as he placed the sacred head ever so gently into the grasp of the rigid immobilizer . . .

In the winter of 1849-50 Brady took portraits of three great Americans—Clay, Calhoun and Webster. There has been much romantic embroidery woven about these three famous portraits, so it is only just that Brady himself tell when and how they were taken.

As he informed the Joint Committee on the Library many years later: "Clay's picture was taken in the City of New York during the winter of 1849. He was accompanied by William V. Brady, ex-mayor of New York, on this occasion and by Simeon Draper, Collector of the Port of New York. I made five different sittings on this occasion. In Washington in 1850 I made another sitting and Darby made his study at the same time for the oil painting. Calhoun visited my gallery in Washington in 1849 in company with his daughter, Mrs. Clemson, and the same artist, Darby, made his study for the painting. Webster visited my gallery in June, 1849, accompanied by Mr. Charles Stetson of the Astor House. Five different sittings were made on this occasion. Neagle, the New York artist, made his study for the painting at the same time. The material no longer exists to produce these portraits with such lifelike fidelity and accuracy as to facts . . ."[34]

The man who frustrated him most was the Swiss naturalist Jean Louis Rodolphe Agassiz. Brady yearned to get the great biologist, "with the noble head, the broad handsome face, usually illuminated with a charming smile" as one admirer recalled him, before his camera. But Agassiz failed him several times through a series of misunderstandings, inclement weather and the caprices of fate.

He came to America in 1846 for a series of lectures at Cambridge. He was a professor of natural history, Lawrence Scientific Institute, Harvard, from 1848-73. He spoke, as the *Herald* said, "with a vivid and picturesque English," and was soon a delight in the lecture halls. "He was as much at home before an audience of farmers and laborers as with the most erudite leaders of research," according to a biographer.

The following year Agassiz began lecturing several times a year in New York City and became a popular figure about the city. Crowds jammed his lectures and the New York City papers never failed to quote him at length.

Agassiz's habit was to come over from Boston in the day, lecture the same night and return to Boston by night. One day Brady said sadly to him, "I suppose you never mean to come?" "Ah," Agassiz replied, "I went to your gallery and spent two hours studying public men's physiognomies, but you were in Washington city."

There is evidence, however, that Brady finally secured the coveted picture, for Agassiz is listed in Brady's catalogue of views, published in 1870.[35]

It was inevitable that Jenny Lind would find her way

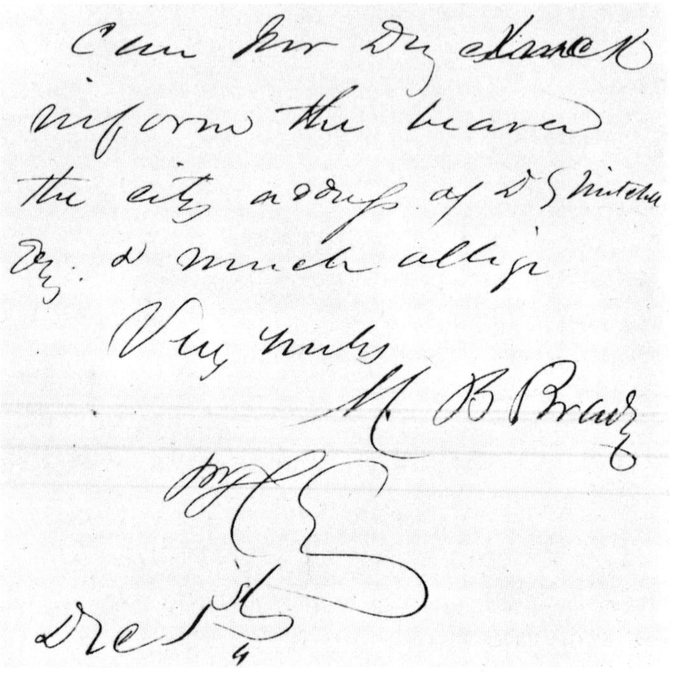

Fig. 11. A "Brady" letter requesting the address of Ik Marvel (Donald Grant Mitchell). Not written by Brady himself. *Manuscript Division, New York Public Library.*

to Brady's gallery. This is the way it happened:

P. T. Barnum, the master showman, had brought Jenny, "The Swedish Nightingale," to New York, and she had opened at Castle Garden at the then fabulous fee of $1,000 a night. Barnum had contracted to pay her that much though he had never heard her sing. Her voice, her smile, her beauty—and Barnum's masterpiece of showmanship—captured the country.

Brady and the other photographers tried in vain to get Barnum to bring Jenny in for a picture. But the shrewd showman just smiled and shook his head. Brady, as he recalled, luckily found an old schoolmate of hers in Sweden who lived in Chicago. He arranged for Jenny's sitting for Brady.

Jenny, like other celebrities, was charmed by the striking pictures of the great Americans on the walls of Brady's reception room and instead of a few minutes she stayed a few hours. Brady got his pictures, but

when Jenny was ready to leave there was heard the low murmur of the crowd waiting outside. Brady looked out and saw a solid mass of humanity pressed about the building. To protect Jenny, he and his operators escorted her out a rear door.

Brady was not the only American photographer to capture Jenny's charm on a daguerreotype plate. The *Daguerrean Journal* of November 1, 1850, states that Brady and "Mr. Root of this city have succeeded in getting a very fine daguerreotype likeness of Jenny Lind . . ."

Root was undoubtedly Marcus A. Root of Philadelphia, who was not only a fine photographer but the author of *The Camera and the Pencil*, published in 1864. He was photography's first historian.

However, it was not Root's but Brady's portrait of Jenny Lind which captured the country's fancy. It gained a large circulation both in daguerreotypes and the *cartes de visite*.

Brady was also successful in getting the great Fanny Elssler to his gallery with the aid of the ubiquitous adventurer Chevalier Henry Wikoff.

Wikoff came into the gallery one day to have his own portrait taken and, as always, casually mentioned the beautiful women with whom he associated. Fanny Elssler was his current "companion" and at the mention of her name Brady grew attentive. Fanny was the most popular idol in America at the time and the other daguerreotypers along Broadway had tried unsuccessfully to get her to pose.

When Brady cautiously asked Wikoff if he could persuade the great lady to visit his gallery, Wikoff assured him he could and made an appointment for the following afternoon.

The next day the triumphant Wikoff walked into Brady's gallery with Fanny on his arm. She was one of the most beautiful of all the women who smiled into the lens of Brady's camera. At the time she had captured the hearts of the gallants in Europe in whom she "inspired a remarkable passion."

Brady took several daguerreotypes of Fanny and after the sitting was over she walked about the gallery ordering copies of several portraits of noted Americans. Then with a last smile she took Wikoff's arm and they walked downstairs to Fulton Street.[36]

It seems strange, considering the intensity of Brady's love for photography, to find love for a woman sharing his heart. But here again we find ourselves groping, vainly trying to peer through the mists of history to know the woman who is hardly more than a name, a legend and a picture.

Her name is Julia, and there is a legend that as a child of four she was so beautiful that President Jackson wanted to adopt her; the pictures—by Brady of course—

show a young woman with a calm face framed by the long curls of the period.

Their courtship, as Brady remembered it, took place against the backdrop of a beautiful Maryland plantation—gay parties, hoopskirts, and young men who talked of nothing else but horses, duels and manners of the time. It was all in the days that were swept away by the Civil War.

Brady had been invited to the plantation by a wealthy Maryland planter who was brought to his Washington studio for some sittings. There was to be a picnic and a dance in the evening, the planter said, and would Brady like to come . . . ?

There was little time for picnics and dances in the life of this dedicated and shy young man but something made Brady accept the invitation. And under the trees with the gay young people, Brady fell in love with the 'young miss' of the plantation, Julia Handy. One newspaper clipping vaguely describes her "as a daughter of a prominent Maryland family, whose ancestry dates back before the American Revolution. There are the usual references to ancestors who fought with Greene or Knox, ending with a legend of Jackson wanting to adopt her.

Brady said in his last years, as he sat in the front parlor of his nephew's house, that the happiest moment of his life was on that evening when he took Julia into his arms and glided across the floor to the strains of a beautiful waltz. It may all be the dream of an embittered and defeated old man, but it is possible that this was the way Mathew and Julia fell in love.[37]

Though her given name was Juliet Elizabeth, she was called Julia all her life. The daughter of a Maryland lawyer, Colonel Samuel Handy, she was born in Somerset County. On her father's side she was kin to such Eastern Shore families as the Windsors, Goldboroughs and Tilghmans and on her mother's, "to the most famous families of northern Virginia. Her father did take her to Washington when she was a child of four—perhaps the root of the "Jackson legend."

They were married by Reverend George Whitefield Samson of the old E Street Baptist Church in Washington. Brady, of course, took his picture. But a search of the church records and the newspapers of the time fails to disclose the exact date.[38]

Even the year of the marriage is in doubt. Levin Handy, Julia's nephew, who supplied information for an account of Brady's life, said he thought they were married in 1860, but the only two newspaper accounts of her life indicate that the marriage took place in the late eighteen-forties or early eighteen-fifties.

The National Hotel in Washington was to be their permanent residence until Julia's death. They lived quietly, with Julia apparently devoting her whole life to her husband and his work. They had no children, but lavished their affection on Julia's brother's child, young Levin Handy.

ALBERT'S FAIR

IT was 1850 and Mathew B. Brady, the farm boy from upstate New York, was now one of the best-known photographers in the world, and owned one of the finest galleries in America.

He was sought out by the leaders of the nation who wanted their likeness preserved among Brady's famous daguerreotypes of the great men of the ages. The legend "By Brady" at the bottom of a portrait was *de rigueur* for fashionable society in the United States and Europe and it was a rare issue of *Harper's Weekly* that did not have a large engraving with a Brady credit line.

Brady knew the value of publicity and he called at Harper & Brothers when he had a rare print. In the fifties he was running what could be compared to the present picture syndicates. Brady once called his gallery "the magazine to illustrate all the publications in the land." "The illustrated papers," he said, "got nearly all their portraits and war scenes from my camera." A check of the issues of *Harper's* or *Frank Leslie's Illustrated Newspaper* in those years will show that ninety out of a hundred illustrations used are Brady's.[39]

The year 1850 was also a milestone in Brady's life; his dream of having his *Gallery of Illustrious Americans* published became a reality. One hundred and five years later his "gallery" is still an impressive volume.[40]

It is a huge book, weighs five pounds and is bound in thick brown covers, the title etched in gold, "containing portraits of twelve of the most eminent citizens of the American Republic since the days of Washington, all from the original daguerreotypes taken by Brady." *The Gallery of Illustrious Americans,* an impressive parlor piece, sold for $30.

The handsome engravings were made by F. D. D'Avignon and the text written by C. Edwards Lester, the foremost art critic of his day, although as Brady later remarked John Howard Payne "was to have written the letter-press."

Lester said in his foreword, "In the preparation of this book no department has been neglected. Mr. Brady has been many years collecting portraits for a National Gallery and in the accomplishment of his object he has experienced the utmost courtesy and encouragement from eminent men. His reputation in his art has been too long established to need commendation."

On the first day of the new year the book was issued by D'Avignon's Press at 323 Broadway.[41] It received fine notices from the *Herald* and other New York newspapers, but the public was apathetic and sales were disappointing.

Brady had paid D'Avignon a hundred dollars apiece for each one of the lithographic stones and Brady soon recognized the book as a critical success but a financial failure.[42] The price was cut to half within a year or two.

But he was not discouraged. He confidently predicted that his original plan of producing the whole of the twenty-four portraits would soon be completed, but as the months went by and the books gathered dust in the D'Avignon Press warehouse he reluctantly abandoned the project. (According to the lithographer and rare book dealer, Joseph Sabin, the work was finished in 1856, but there is no volume extant.)

While Mathew B. Brady was establishing his reputation as an historian with a camera, a young engineer who had abandoned the stolid career of a civil engineer for the unpredictable but attractive life of a pioneer photographer was also making a place for himself.[43] Edward Anthony had a good figure of average size, curly black hair, dark eyebrows, calm brown eyes, and a trim black beard.

One of his fellow engineers on the Croton Reservoir

and saloons. A large number of copies have been ordered from different portions of Europe. Among its patrons are numbered the most distinguished men of this country, with its institutions of learning science and art.

———— • ————

—We have been requested to publish the following fine stanzas, and do so with pleasure. We shall never refuse anything of real value connected with the Daguerrean art :

STANZAS,
Suggested by a visit to Brady's Portrait Gallery.

Soul-lit shadows now around me ;
   They who armies nobly led ;
They who make a nation's glory
   While they're living—when they're dead,
Land-marks for our country's future,
   Have their genius left behind ;
Victors from the field of battle ;
   Victors from the field of mind—

Doniphan, who trod the desert ;
   Scott, who conquered on the plain ;
Taylor, who would not surrender ;
   Butler, sleeping with the slain ;
Houston, San Jacinto's hero ;
   Fremont, from the Golden shore ;
Jackson, as a lion, fearless ;
   Worth, whose gallant deeds are o'er—

Webster, with a brow Titanic ;
   Calhoun's eagle look of old ;
Benton, freedom's valiant Nestor ;
   Kent, the jurist, calm and cold ;
Clay, " ultimus Romanorum ;"
   Cass, with deep and earnest gaze ;
Wright, of yore the Senate's Cato ;
   Adams, last of early days—

Pere de Schmidt, the Jesuit preacher,
   From the Rocky Mountains wild ;
Tyng, Melancthon of the pulpit ;
   Channing, guileless as a child ;
Barnes, who pondrous themes has written ;
   Bascom's eye, a gleaming bright ;
Anthon, whose unceasing labor
   Fills the student's path with light—

Audubon, from out the forest ;
   Prescott, from historic page ;
Bryant, pilgrim of our poets ;
   Forrest, vet'ran of the stage ;
Inman, looking palely thoughtful ;
   Huntington, with dreams of art ;
Father Mathew, mild, benignant ;
   Jenny Lind, who wins the heart.

Lawrence, type of merchant princes ;
   Colt, of our mechanic peers ;
Emerson, of Yankee notions ;
   Miller, of our Scripture seers ;
Mott, the hero of the scalpel ;
   Cooper, wizzard of the pen ;
Flagg, the glorious painter poet ;
   Powers, of arts own nobleman—

From the hills and from the valleys,
   They are gathered far and near,—
From the Rio Grande's waters,
   To Aroostook's mountain drear,—
From the rough Atlantic's billows,
   To the calm Pacific's tide,
Soldier, statesman, poet, painter,
   Priest and Rabbi, side by side.

Like a spirit land of shadows
   They in silence on me gaze,
And I feel my heart is beating
   With the pulse of other days ;
And I ask what great magician
   Conjured forms like these afar ?
Echo answers, 'tis the sunshine,
   By its alchymist Daguerre—

       CALEB LYON, OF LYONDALE.
Broadway, Dec. 12, 1850.

———— • ————

—WE would call the attention of our readers to our cover, the first, or title-page of which we are, we think justly, proud. It is plain, simple and beautiful. There is no profusion in its design ; nor is there anything wanting to indicate the idea of the artist—Daguerre, crowned by the Genius of American Art and Science—and we have had the satisfaction of hearing it pronounced by several literary men of taste and talent, the most beautiful engraving for a magazine ever yet produced. The other pages of the cover, it will be perceived, contain information of importance to every Daguerrean artist.

———— • ————

— We intend to devote portions of our future numbers to the Romance and Poetry of Daguerreotyping. There are a large number of artists through the Union whose peregrinations through the land give rise to numerous incidents, either of an instructive or amusing nature, which we should be pleased to weave into narrative for the benefit of our readers. Will not our friends, therefore, assist us, and send whatever may come under their observation ? We have already many anecdotes, which we shall relate as occasions may offer to give them point. These, and any others with which we may be favored, will serve to relieve the more scientific portion of our Journal of some of its monotony, and still be interesting for their connection with the art. We wish, also, by this means, to bring out the talent of the profession, which we believe now lies dormant for want of some such stimulant.

Fig. 12. A poem suggested by a visit to Brady's New York gallery. From the *Photographic Art Journal,* 1851.

project was James Renwick, son of Professor James Renwick of Columbia University, one of the commissioners engaged in determining the Maine-New Brunswick boundary. Probably aware of Anthony's interest in photography young Renwick told his father and Professor Renwick "hired" Anthony to take a series of daguerreotypes showing the territory which was the subject of dispute between Canada and the United States. The daguerreotypes were later submitted to Daniel Webster and Lord Ashburton, who composed the Boundary Commission and it is said, though there is no documentary evidence to support it, that Anthony's daguerreotypes helped determine the present border between the two countries and led to the signing of the Webster-Ashburton Treaty.

Upon his return from the northern expedition Anthony opened his daguerreotype gallery at 308 Broadway. Like Brady, Anthony had a passion for perfection in the making of fine daguerreotypes. In his first week of operation he wrote an advertisement setting forth the principles on which his business was to be based: "**My prices for the various styles (of daguerreotypes) will be found to be very low, but I look for a reputation more from their quality than from their low price, being convinced from former experience as a practical operator that nothing in the daguerrean business is truly cheap but what is good. . . .**"

After a few years he took in his brother Henry as a partner. He became the actual photographer in the studio, while Edward Anthony conducted a photographic supply business. Soon E. Anthony (later Ansco) was the largest photographic supply house in America. But Henry, who was constantly experimenting, was the first man in the world to take the so-called instantaneous photograph, thus becoming the father of the modern snapshot.[44]

About 1848 the Anthonys opened a Washington studio. Adopting a leaf from Brady's imaginative projects, they began collecting pictures of every Congressman and foreign notable and sending them to New York where they were placed on display at Anthony's Broadway studio as a "National Daguerrean Gallery" for many years.

Daguerreotype parlors could now be found all along Broadway. In 1840, among the total population, the census report listed no photographers officially, but a decade later, among the population of 23,191,876, there were 938. Ten years later the number had leaped to 3,154 and by 1870, with the total population at 39,000,000, there were 7,558 . . .[45]

When, in 1847, Brady opened his Washington gallery "to expedite the taking of pictures for his Gallery of Illustrious Americans" he was not the first capital photographer. Plumbe had arrived in September, 1839. His

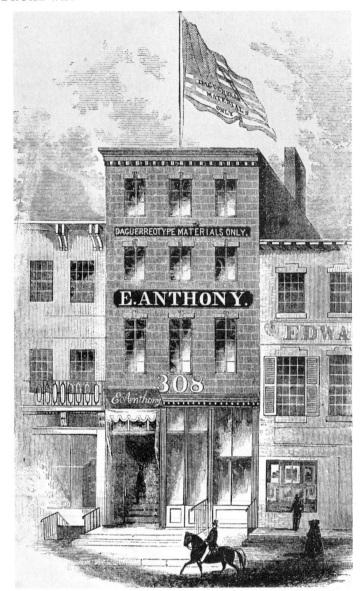

Fig. 13. Anthony's photographic supply house, the first of its kind in the world, at 308 Broadway, New York. *Humphrey's Journal,* 1860.

studio was in a loft over Todd's store, in what was then known as "Concert Hall," on the north side of Pennsylvania Avenue between 6th and 7th Streets, N.W. This building later became a part of the Metropolitan Hotel.

In New York, "galleries" sprang up everywhere. One could find an "artist"—as a daguerreotypist liked to call himself—in a jeweler's shop, a barber shop and even in a shoemaker's shop. Most of these "artists" were amateurs with a glib tongue. It is amusing to read in *Humphrey's Journal* of 1853 an indignant letter from a subscriber who had been "taken in" by one of the incompetents.

As the "patron" wrote to the editor, he was strolling down Market Street when he saw a large advertisement outside a "parlor where I could have my phiz taken for seventy-five cents."

Attracted by the advertisement, he walked into the building and found himself in a room ten by twenty feet, crowded with perspiring customers—men, women and crying children—and was immediately taken in tow by the receptionist, a "rowdy-looking fellow dressed in a baggy suit."

After an hour of wrangling the customer had his picture taken, "a miserable thing which he called my likeness." When he protested, the receptionist, with a great show of disappointment, showed him a larger portrait and said that for a few cents more he could produce a better one.

The customer reported he had stalked out after berating the "thief" in no uncertain language. "He is only trying to stick customers for higher-priced pictures, the grand secret of gulling the people."

The editor solemnly agreed that such practices were outrageous and promised to look into the matter.[46]

Presidents also were victims of the incompetents. John Quincy Adams, in his diary, tells of a visit to a photographer's studio during his tour of the Mohawk Valley in the hot summer of 1843. Walking down the main street of Utica "after shaking hundreds of hands," he stepped into a daguerreotype parlor with a friend.

"Four likenesses were made, two of them jointly with the head of Mr. Bacon—all hideous," Adams wrote.[47]

The new art also produced a flock of new trade journals which give a fascinating insight into the life, times and difficulties of the early photographers.

The *Daguerrean Journal*, probably the first photographic publication in the world, was first issued November 1, 1850, under the editorship of S. D. Humphrey. This same publication was known, at various times, also as *Humphrey's Journal*. The following year a second trade magazine appeared, *The Photographic Art Journal*, edited by H. H. Snelling of New York City.[48]

Both journals were wonderfully aggressive in obtaining and printing the news of the latest scientific developments in the fast-expanding art. Both were delightfully gossipy—"Sol Skylight" was the name of the popular columnist whose views appeared in *Humphrey's*—and the news that "Mr. B." as Brady was called, was moving uptown to a new gallery was just as important as the startling announcement that the Reverend Levi G. Hill had developed a new technique for taking daguerreotypes in color. And when Hill, whom Morse piously described as "a man of genius" was found to be the author of a hoax, that news was given the same amount of space.

The big photographic news in the winter of 1850-51 was the announcement by Queen Victoria that a great industrial exhibition (actually the first World's Fair) was to be held in London in the spring of 1851. The idea was Prince Albert's. The Crystal Palace, where the exhibition was to be held, was being built in Hyde Park at the enormous cost of almost a million dollars. Prizes were to be awarded for the best in art, science and literature, and photography was to be one of the

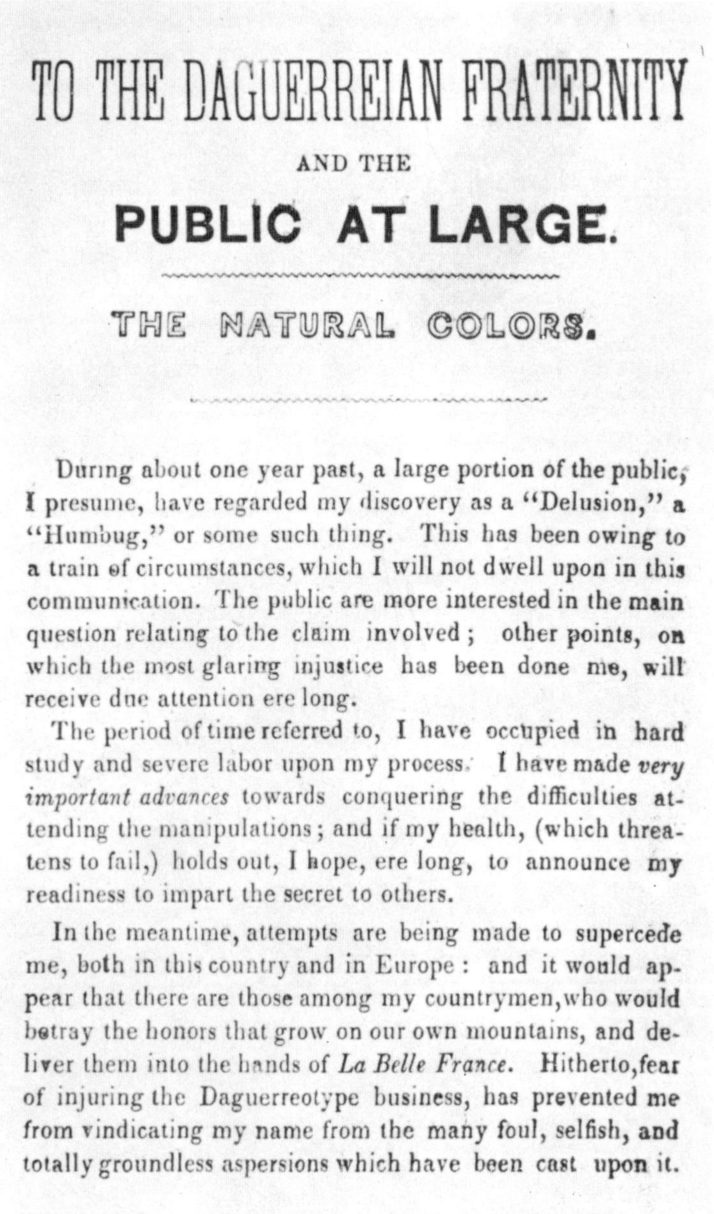

TO THE DAGUERREIAN FRATERNITY

AND THE

PUBLIC AT LARGE.

THE NATURAL COLORS.

During about one year past, a large portion of the public, I presume, have regarded my discovery as a "Delusion," a "Humbug," or some such thing. This has been owing to a train of circumstances, which I will not dwell upon in this communication. The public are more interested in the main question relating to the claim involved; other points, on which the most glaring injustice has been done me, will receive due attention ere long.

The period of time referred to, I have occupied in hard study and severe labor upon my process. I have made *very important advances* towards conquering the difficulties attending the manipulations; and if my health, (which threatens to fail,) holds out, I hope, ere long, to announce my readiness to impart the secret to others.

In the meantime, attempts are being made to supercede me, both in this country and in Europe: and it would appear that there are those among my countrymen, who would betray the honors that grow on our own mountains, and deliver them into the hands of *La Belle France*. Hitherto, fear of injuring the Daguerreotype business, has prevented me from vindicating my name from the many foul, selfish, and totally groundless aspersions which have been cast upon it.

Fig. 14. The Reverend Levi Hill's answer to the charge of fraud in announcing his color photography invention. *Courtesy New York Historical Society.*

major categories.[49]

Photographers the world over, particularly in New York, began to appraise their best pictures and to make preparations to send or take their most unusual, their most vivid and their most beautiful daguerreotypes.

Competition was intense. Daguerreotypists tried to hire interesting subjects ("any man or woman over one hundred years old") in advertisements in the trade journals in the months preceding the exhibition. One advertisement read, "Wanted, a Revolutionary veteran to come forward to have his likeness taken FREE"; one operator had the original idea of offering "FREE pictures to a dozen brothers or sisters or a group of five who represent as many generations," while another simply called for "twins or triplets, all over eighty."[50]

Brady did no advertising for freakish or unusual subjects. He already had his subjects in his files—great Americans, living and dead. He gathered forty-eight and shipped them to the Photographic Committee in London, where they were joined by the best works submitted by photographers from all the world.

Brady continued to work incessantly and it was apparent, even by 1851, that his eyes were weaker and the lenses in his spectacles thicker. He was never a robust man and the strain of his intense drive, which made him work often from dawn to late at night to perfect the taking of daguerreotypes, left him in a weakened state during the winter of 1850-51, which the newspapers of that time described as a rather severe season of sub-normal temperatures and much snow and ice.

His failing eyesight, which had become so acute that he was no longer a practicing operator, must have been a topic of conjecture in the world of photography at that time. What could be a more juicy morsel of gossip among photographers than the knowledge that the most famous photographer in America could no longer operate a camera because of his eyes. . . ?

The condition of Brady's eyesight finally broke into print in 1851—eleven years before the Civil War—in an article in the *Photographic Art Journal*, which declared: "Mr. Brady is not operating himself, a failing eyesight precluding the possibility of his using the camera with any certainty. But he is an excellent artist, nevertheless, understands his business perfectly and gathers about him the finest talent to be found. His daguerreotypes on ivory have attracted considerable attention; it may be said without flattery to be the most magnificent production of the art . . . Brady's proverbial enterprise is not to be questioned and his gallery is the most fashionable in the city . . ."51

About this time, Julia and Mathew were living quietly and evidently were not inclined to participate in New York's social life, for there is no mention of either Brady or his wife attending any of the functions given by members of the photographic fraternity, nor is there any listing of Brady's name on any committee, nor do we find him contributing a "paper" describing a discovery he might have made while experimenting.

Whether it was Brady's frail health and Julia's insistence that he take a vacation, or his natural interest as a photographer that made Brady decide to travel to Europe, we do not know, but we do know he and Julia sailed for London in July of 1851.52 They traveled with James Gordon Bennett, his wife and son. "Mr. B. has left the city and will be gone for some months." The July, 1851, issue of the *Daguerrean Journal* also disclosed that Brady intended to see Daguerre himself in Paris and was taking with him "some exquisite specimens of daguerreotypes for Daguerre and Niepce. These will establish his reputation for exquisite pictures in Europe as generally as it is here . . ."

But Brady did not get to meet the "father of the new art," as Daguerre was reverently called by many of the photographic journals. He died, while Brady was en route, on July 12. It is curious to note that the editors of the journal were not aware that Niepce, with whom Daguerre had made photographic experiments, had died in 1833.

Brady left his Broadway studio in charge of a young Southerner who had demonstrated he knew how to take portraits, George S. Cook of Charleston. It was an ironical choice; Brady was later to be the photographer of the Union, Cook, the photographer of the Confederacy.

The World's Fair was opened officially on the afternoon of May 1, 1851, by Queen Victoria, with her beloved Albert, "father of the enterprise," at her side.

The photographic exhibition was one of the outstanding events of the fair. Of the twenty-four nations represented, six nations (the United States, England, France, Italy, Germany and Austria), exhibited 700 pictures. The Americans, Mathew B. Brady, M. M. Lawrence and John A. Whipple of Boston, won three of five medals. Lawrence received a silver medal for one of his daguerreotypes, Whipple for his famous one-inch daguerreotype of the moon, and Brady for the general excellence of his entire collection.

One comment was, "The United States department is of a very superior character. In the arrangement of the groups and in the general tone of the pictures there will be found an artistic excellence which we do not meet with in many others. This has been attributed to peculiar atmospheric conditions, but we believe it to be due to a great extent also to superior manipulation."

The jury's report declared, "America stands alone for stern development of character, her works, with few exceptions, reject all accessories, present a faithful transcript of the subject and yield to none in excellence of execution . . . The portraits stand forward in bold relief upon a plain background. The artist, having placed implicit reliance upon his knowledge of photographic science, has neglected to avail himself of the resources of art,"53 (apparently a reference to the European fashion of painting in backgrounds of daguerreotypes).

The *Illustrated London News* had this to say: "After a very minute and careful examination we are inclined to give America the first place. Whether the atmosphere is better adapted to the art, or whether the preparation of Daguerreotypes is congenital with the tastes of the people, or whether they are unfettered with the patents in force in England, certain it is that the number of exhibitors has been very great and the quality of production super-excellent.

"The likenesses of the various distinguished Americans by Mr. Brady are notable examples of this style of art. The family of Mr. Churchill is a very pretty group; and the series of views illustrating the falls of Niagara are a very appropriate example of American

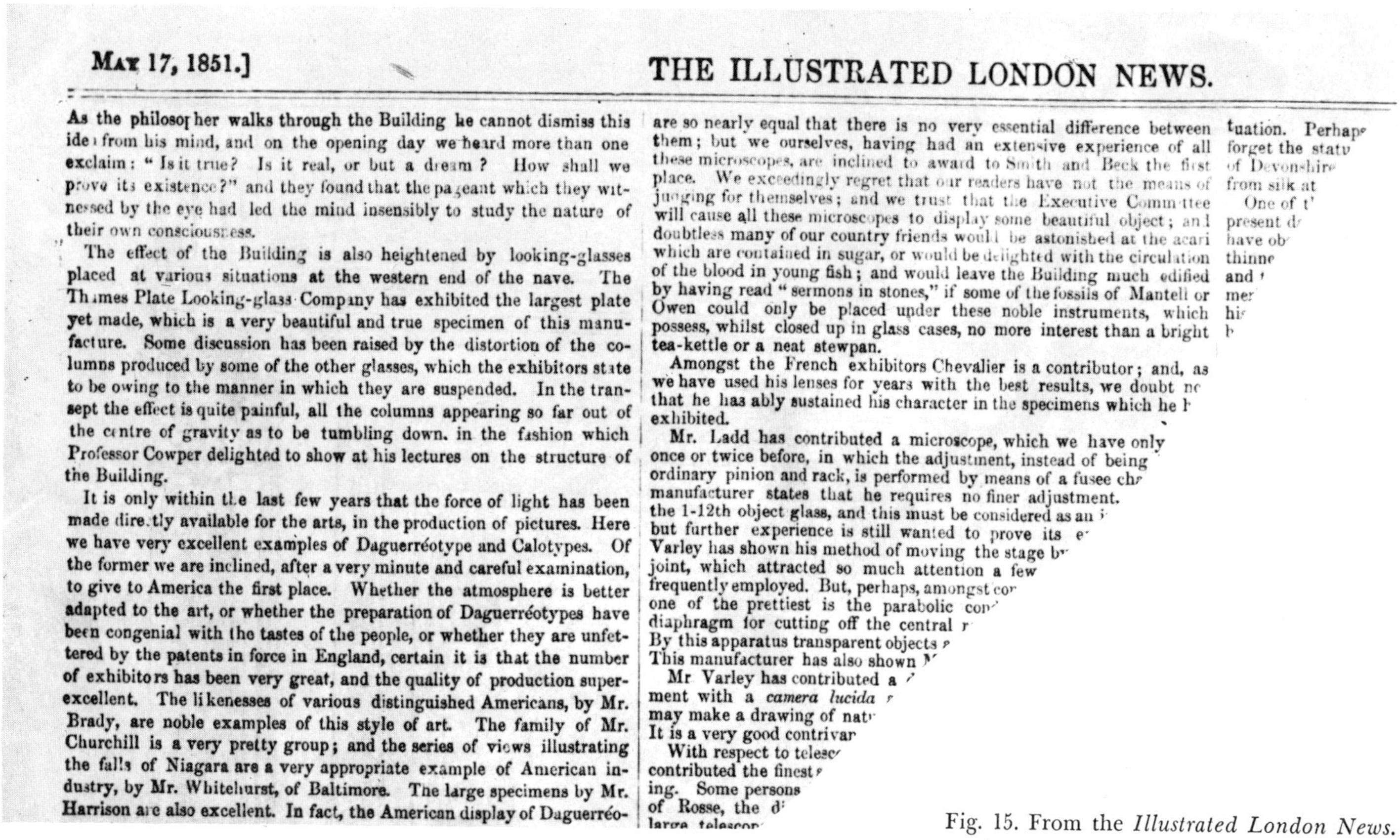

MAY 17, 1851.]   THE ILLUSTRATED LONDON NEWS.

As the philosopher walks through the Building he cannot dismiss this idea from his mind, and on the opening day we heard more than one exclaim: "Is it true? Is it real, or but a dream? How shall we prove its existence?" and they found that the pageant which they witnessed by the eye had led the mind insensibly to study the nature of their own consciousness.

The effect of the Building is also heightened by looking-glasses placed at various situations at the western end of the nave. The Thames Plate Looking-glass Company has exhibited the largest plate yet made, which is a very beautiful and true specimen of this manufacture. Some discussion has been raised by the distortion of the columns produced by some of the other glasses, which the exhibitors state to be owing to the manner in which they are suspended. In the transept the effect is quite painful, all the columns appearing so far out of the centre of gravity as to be tumbling down, in the fashion which Professor Cowper delighted to show at his lectures on the structure of the Building.

It is only within the last few years that the force of light has been made directly available for the arts, in the production of pictures. Here we have very excellent examples of Daguerréotype and Calotypes. Of the former we are inclined, after a very minute and careful examination, to give to America the first place. Whether the atmosphere is better adapted to the art, or whether the preparation of Daguerréotypes have been congenial with the tastes of the people, or whether they are unfettered by the patents in force in England, certain it is that the number of exhibitors has been very great, and the quality of production super-excellent. The likenesses of various distinguished Americans, by Mr. Brady, are noble examples of this style of art. The family of Mr. Churchill is a very pretty group; and the series of views illustrating the falls of Niagara are a very appropriate example of American industry, by Mr. Whitehurst, of Baltimore. The large specimens by Mr. Harrison are also excellent. In fact, the American display of Daguerréo-

are so nearly equal that there is no very essential difference between them; but we ourselves, having had an extensive experience of all these microscopes, are inclined to award to Smith and Beck the first place. We exceedingly regret that our readers have not the means of judging for themselves; and we trust that the Executive Committee will cause all these microscopes to display some beautiful object; and doubtless many of our country friends would be astonished at the acari which are contained in sugar, or would be delighted with the circulation of the blood in young fish; and would leave the Building much edified by having read "sermons in stones," if some of the fossils of Mantell or Owen could only be placed under these noble instruments, which possess, whilst closed up in glass cases, no more interest than a bright tea-kettle or a neat stewpan.

Amongst the French exhibitors Chevalier is a contributor; and, as we have used his lenses for years with the best results, we doubt no that he has ably sustained his character in the specimens which he h exhibited.

Mr. Ladd has contributed a microscope, which we have only once or twice before, in which the adjustment, instead of being ordinary pinion and rack, is performed by means of a fusee ch manufacturer states that he requires no finer adjustment. the 1-12th object glass, and this must be considered as an but further experience is still wanted to prove its e Varley has shown his method of moving the stage b joint, which attracted so much attention a few frequently employed. But, perhaps, amongst co one of the prettiest is the parabolic con diaphragm for cutting off the central r By this apparatus transparent objects This manufacturer has also shown

Mr Varley has contributed a ment with a *camera lucida* may make a drawing of nat It is a very good contrivar

With respect to telesc contributed the finest ing. Some persons of Rosse, the d large telescop

tuation. Perhap forget the statu of Devonshire from silk at One of t present d have ob thinne and mer hi b

Fig. 15. From the *Illustrated London News*.

industry by Mr. Whitehurst of Baltimore. The large specimens by Mr. Harrison are also excellent."

But the reporter could not resist ending his praise with a barb: "In fact, the American display of Daguerreotypes in some degree atones for the disrespect with which they have treated other nations, in having applied for so large a space, and yet at last having left their space comparatively unfilled . . ."[54]

The London correspondent of the *National Intelligencer* stated flatly: "The American daguerreotypes are pronounced the best which are exhibited."

The official report on Brady, Lawrence and Whipple's works reads: "On examining the daguerreotypes contributed by the United States, every observer must be struck by their beauty of execution, the broad and well toned masses of light and shade, and the total absence of all glare, which render them so superior to many works of this class. Were we to particularize the individual excellence of the pictures exhibited, we should far exceed the limits of the space to which we are necessarily confined."[55]

And the official catalogue commented on Brady's works: "The brilliancy and sharpness of some of them are highly remarkable."[56]

The news that the Americans had captured all honors stirred the United States. Horace Greeley editorially rubbed his hands in glee: "In picture-taking we beat the world," he wrote of his friend Mathew B. Brady.

Across the Atlantic the Bradys began a grand tour of

Europe which lasted from the winter of 1851 to the spring of the following year. It was a year of leisure for Brady and rest for his work-weakened eyes. The *Photographic Art Journal* did not quote Brady but stated, "We understand Brady contemplates opening a London Gallery . . ." They added that his health was "improving" and he was proud to find that his pictures had given him "fame before he went to England . . ."[57]

Brady was surprised and pleased to find that his name was well known to the great men of Europe and he had no trouble gaining entree to their homes and offices. When he did he was first the photographer, and secondly the tourist. In England, through Julia, he met and he took daguerreotypes of Cardinal Wiseman and of the Earl of Carlisle, who had visited the United States as Lord Morpeth and had met Henry Clay. He also took daguerreotypes of the French notables Lamartine and Cavaignac. Mr. Thompson, with Brady, took Louis Napoleon, "then freshly Emperor" as Brady recalled.

Wherever he went Brady found European photographers advertising daguerreotypes "taken by the American process," and in the journals in France and England his work was compared with the best of Europe's photographers, with the critics invariably finding their native cameramen inferior when judged against the excellence of Brady's work.

The French correspondent of *Humphrey's Journal*, writing from Paris in 1851, was typical of the critics as he said very bluntly, "The new art in Paris has fallen far behind that of the United States."

Explanations, such as the difference in climate and

sunshine were cited by some experts as the real reason why American daguerreotypers like Brady and Lawrence were able to produce such superior work, but it was American ingenuity and enterprise which brought about the strikingly beautiful daguerreotypes. Brady and Lawrence and the other leading photographers used powerful buffing machines and were experts in applying a high polish to the copper plates.

In Boston, Whipple, whose one-inch picture of the moon had taken a prize in London, used a steam-driven machine for his buffing and, when the temperature rose during the hot summer days, he installed fans to cool off his perspiring customers.[58]

In the spring of 1851 photography took a giant step when Frederick Scott Archer, an English sculptor, announced his method of using collodion—a sticky liquid made by dissolving nitrated cotton in a mixture of alcohol and ether—as an agent to make the light-sensitive image adhere to the glass plate.[59]

The ether and alcohol, evaporating rapidly, left behind a smooth, transparent film which was sensitized by a bath in silver nitrate solution. The sensitivity was lost, however, when the plate dried. This became the famous "wet plate process." To develop the wet plates a solution of ferrous (iron) sulphate with acetic acid was used. The plate was "fixed" by potassium cyanide. The wet plates were capable of unlimited reproduction and were soon found superior. They were soon to make the daguerreotype obsolete.

Meanwhile, during Brady's absence in Europe he was the target for a strange barrage of editorial criticism from a Philadelphia newspaper, which charged that he had helped to organize a meeting of a committee of the Daguerreotypists of New York and Brooklyn for the purposes of publicity for himself.

The *Photographic Art Journal* of November 1, 1851, came to his defense: "Now as Mr. Brady is absent from the city and has been for the last three or four months we consider it our duty to exculpate him from this cowardly, unwarranted and libelous attack. We have no doubt that if Mr. Brady had been in New York at the time of the meeting of the Daguerreotype Association he would have taken an active part in its proceedings; but that this meeting was got up by him for the purpose indicated is a deliberate falsehood and whoever penned the article in question must have known it to be such and had it inserted in a literary sewer for the express purpose of injuring Mr. Brady's business; perhaps with the frail hope that his own—if he is a daguerreotypist—might have profited. If this—as has been suggested to us—is the case, we have not words of abhorrence and censure sufficient to depict his true character. If the editor of the paper inserted the article on his own responsibility all we can say to him is that if he or his

people has the smallest particle of respect or influence in the community where it is printed he may be assured Mr. Brady will insist upon the only reparation a gentleman can lawfully obtain so soon as he returns from Europe, where he is now for the benefit of his health.

"We fear, however, that both the paper and the editor are too insignificant to be noticed by a gentleman and we feel that we are polluting our *Journal* by alluding to the falsifier at all and we should not do so if the attack had not been made on an absent friend, who is unable to defend himself in the manner we have mentioned . . ."

The editorial storm evidently soon died away and in May, 1852, according to the *Photographic Art Journal*, Brady and Julia returned from Europe. It hinted that "Brady has a rich budget to open for his friends . . ."[60]

Refreshed and his health restored, Brady plunged into his work with his earlier vigor and intensity. As he strolled along Broadway with Julia in the warm nights of May and June in the first weeks after his return, he discovered that his biggest rival, Jeremiah Gurney, had moved from 189 Broadway to 349 Broadway and Anthony's National Daguerreotype Depot was now occupying an entire building at 203-05 Broadway.[61]

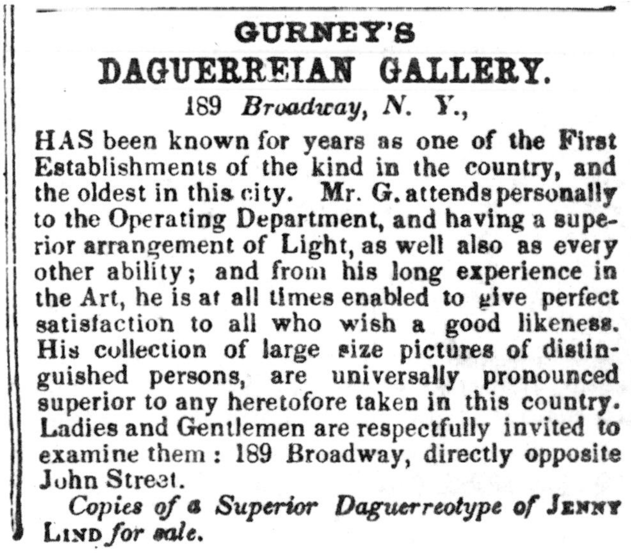

GURNEY'S DAGUERREIAN GALLERY.

189 *Broadway, N. Y.,*

HAS been known for years as one of the First Establishments of the kind in the country, and the oldest in this city. Mr. G. attends personally to the Operating Department, and having a superior arrangement of Light, as well also as every other ability; and from his long experience in the Art, he is at all times enabled to give perfect satisfaction to all who wish a good likeness. His collection of large size pictures of distinguished persons, are universally pronounced superior to any heretofore taken in this country. Ladies and Gentlemen are respectfully invited to examine them: 189 Broadway, directly opposite John Street.

Copies of a Superior Daguerreotype of JENNY LIND *for sale.*

Fig. 16. Gurney's advertisement in *Humphrey's Journal,* January, 1851.

Brady was still at 205 Broadway in 1852, according to the Daguerrean Artists Registry in *Humphrey's Journal,* but the following year he would be located also at 359 Broadway, between White and Franklin Streets, just five doors farther uptown than Gurney. As a street plan of New York City of 1853 shows, Brady had expanded on his theory of "God's sunlight" making better sun pictures; his roof had many skylights, including a few double ones.[62]

There was another young newcomer to Broadway's photography row within the next few months. Brady undoubtedly saw him, S. N. Carvalho, a brisk young man with a short black beard, probably the first American to penetrate America's Wild West with a camera.[63]

Nearly all photographers were experimenting and Brady apparently was trying out a method he might have found in Europe. "Mr. B. has begun experimenting with blue glass in his skylight and has been convinced of its practicability. He also has substituted blue glass in front of his lens with what Mr. B. said was satisfactory results."[64]

It is surprising to find Brady, the expert, who was so shrewd commercially, experimenting with colored glass in his skylights instead of the new wet plate process, one of the greatest innovations in the history of his art. Yet he, like the majority of American photographers, had ignored Archer's process. As a result of their indifference the wet plate had gained enormously in Europe but was almost unknown in the United States.

Finally, after the *Photographic Art Journal* had devoted a long article in 1852 to the new wet plate process, Brady and the other New York City photographers began cautiously experimenting. But the process wasn't easy. As *Humphrey's Journal* noted, to coat a plate with collodion properly required a certain skill, and the writer gloomily observed, after a survey of the city's studios, "results are uncertain, even among the more experienced photographers."

Professor Robert Taft points out that Whipple in Boston appears to have been the first American photographer successfully to master the skill of using the wet plate. His prints sent a ripple of excitement among the country's photographers and by 1853 he was considered the outstanding expert on the use of the collodion wet plate.

Apparently the first wet plate print developed in America was one of Edward Anthony, taken from a daguerreotype. The print, like those of the period, were made from "salted paper"; paper dipped into a common table salt solution. The subject looked flat and gray, but albumen later provided the glossy finished print.

The greatest photographers in America, Brady included, found their way to Whipple's studio in Boston to be instructed in the art of the wet plate for a fee of fifty dollars.

By 1853 it was obvious that the daguerreotype was doomed. In New York, Brady, Gurney and Lawrence found their wet plate business booming. Customers flocked to their galleries by the thousands and with the enormous increase in business, their galleries became larger and more luxurious.

Photography was no longer a fascinating new art; it was now "big business," the forerunner of today's billion-dollar market, and the operators began to promote their wares with paid advertisements, publicity tie-ups with outstanding celebrities of the entertainment world —Brady and P. T. Barnum, for example—and word-of-mouth comment to sell their products. Some of their attempts to steal the spotlight appear ludicrous; if Brady made life-size portraits Gurney made them larger. Then Lawrence topped both of them. Finally, with the dimensions of the prints no longer in inches but in feet, Brady scored the final coup by hanging portraits of Morse, Field and Franklin on a transparency measuring fifty by twenty-five feet, lighted by six hundred candles, outside his gallery.[65]

It was also an age of "types." Leading the list was Whipple's Crystalotype. In 1852 he formed a company of 100 shares, each sold at 250, with trustees who constituted a veritable "Who's Who" in the history of photography. Among them were Samuel F. B. Morse, Caleb Woodhull and the Anthonys. In the April, 1853, issue of the *Photographic Art Journal* appeared a Crystalotype frontispiece of Edward Anthony, the first direct use of a photograph in a magazine in America.[66] Other types were to follow in the years to come; the Ambrotype of Cutting and Rehn, and the Melaintype, or tintype, of Smith and Neff and a hundred others. The tintype, with its thin metal plate japanned black or chocolate brown, could be sent through the mails.

"Imperials," or life-size portraits, next caught the country's fancy and Brady could not produce them fast enough for his customers, even though they were far more expensive than the average oil painting.

Brady's "imperials" on the wall of his gallery became one of the city's attractions and a *Harper's Weekly* reporter who made a tour of the gallery that winter declared, "Photography was born in the United States (sic) and the sceptre has not departed from us. The vocation of the portrait painter is not gone but modified. Portrait painting by the old methods is now completely defunct as is navigation by the stars."[67]

The man from *Harper's* was a bit too enthusiastic. Photography was still in swaddling clothes and the jumbo "imperials" which captivated the reporter were far from perfect because of the long exposure required and the crude printing process.

To polish off the defects an artist's brush was usually used and this raised the price of the portrait still higher. It was not unusual for a customer to pay several hundred dollars for his enormous "likeness." But despite defects the camera portrait had one great advantage over the skilled painter, who could betray truth and make his subject as likeable as he wished. The camera's eye was brutally realistic. As the critic H. H. Snelling remarked in 1857: "The colored [photographic] portrait has an advantage over the best works of the best art masters, for the latter cannot rival the former in truth."[68]

In 1857, the *carte de visite* craze swept across the world with unprecedented speed, to become an important part of the American scene, celebrated in song, story and poetry.

Millions of them were made and a century later the

cards were still so plentiful that several Brady *cartes de visites* could be bought for a dollar without any difficulty.

The tiny portrait photograph intended as a substitute for a calling card, according to Professor Taft, may owe its origin to the Duke of Parma, who started the fashion in 1857. Desderi, who made a picture of Napoleon III in Egypt in 1854, began the fad in France and the fever spanned the Atlantic and swept across America.

A photographer, George Rockford, claimed years later that he brought the fashion to New York City, issuing a portrait of Baron de Rothschild as his first card photograph. His price at the time was three for a dollar.

Brady saw the commercial possibilities immediately and set his staff to producing *cartes de visite* by the bushel. Unskilled labor could cut up a single print, for which only the plate-holder moved, into a half-dozen portraits. Soon there wasn't an average American home that did not have a "*carte de visite* basket" in the hall to collect the cardboard photographs left by friends. Brady, the Anthonys, Gurney and the other photographers begged, pleaded and bribed sitters—actors, actresses, statesmen, outlaws, foreign visitors, freaks, clergymen—anyone who was famous or infamous. The usual inducement was a small fee or a few copies of the print.

In the late fifties there was a brief lull in the *carte de visite* craze, but with the outbreak of the Civil War the fashion became more feverish than before, with soldiers and generals clamoring for pictures of themselves to send home to their wives and sweethearts, and vice versa.[69] Lights burned late in Brady's gallery as his operators prepared thousands of the cardboard pictures. Sometimes, when a new "issue" was announced, crowds would flock to Fulton Street, push their way up the stairs to the gallery and clean out Brady's stock within a matter of hours. At one time, the Anthonys later recalled, they were printing as many as 3,600 cards a day.

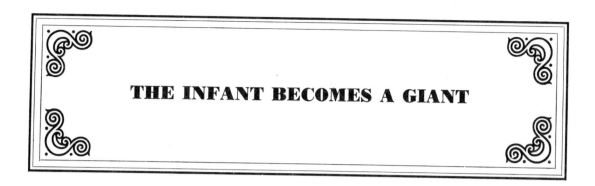

THE INFANT BECOMES A GIANT

PHOTOGRAPHY was growing up with almost unbelievable speed. The squalling infant, sired by Daguerre, spanked in a lusty childhood by Draper and Morse, Brady, Anthony and Gurney and others, had grown into an awkward, bumptious giant. With the advent of the wet-plate process the new art had found its destiny; in the hands of Mathew B. Brady and his assistants the fragile pieces of glass coated with sticky collodion would soon imprison for history the violence, the savagery and the havoc of the American Civil War. But that was yet to come; it was now 1853 and the self-appointed aristocracy of American photography were more concerned with photographic exhibitions, one sponsored by the Anthonys and another in New York's Crystal Palace, Cutting's Ambrotype process and Brady's luxurious new gallery at 359 Broadway, the showplace of the city's studios.

It seems proper that the bumptious new art should grow up amid the gusto and extravagance of a lusty, brawling America. Its home, New York on July 4th: six miles of roast pig lining Broadway in booths, champagne popping like firecrackers, the sky exploding with rockets, and women wearing white leghorn hats as big as windmills; of P. T. Barnum's "newest and greatest show on Earth!"; a $100,000 mansion on Thirty-fourth Street built by Dr. Samuel P. Townsend, the sarsaparilla king; August Belmont's "thoroughbreds worth $25,000 without trappings" and $1,500,000 spent annually at Saratoga. . . .

These were the years when the world's great figures were coming to America, some of them to hurry to Brady's gallery to inspect, sneer and smile at this strange Democracy. Some left behind their memoirs and impressions of the young land in which Brady lived and worked.

The haughtily bred Mrs. Trollope wrote that in America "any man's son may become the equal of any other man's son." Mrs. Trollope might have been thinkings of Mathew B. Brady, the farm boy who was now sought out by princes, emperors and presidents.

Anthony's announcement that he was offering $500 for "the best photographic invention of the year" was the first big event. But inventors were slow to respond, so Anthony bought an elaborate pitcher and two small goblets which he offered as prizes for "the four best pictures submitted by an American operator." The closing date for entries was November, 1853.[70]

It was an important contest, with much prestige attached to the award, and every important photographer in the country carefully selected his subjects and perfected his entries. All but Mathew B. Brady, one of the most famous.

In December seven winners were announced, with Jeremiah Gurney, one of Brady's top competitors, named as the winner of the cup and goblet.

Brady at the time was a slim young man in his early thirties, contentedly married, well on his way to amassing a $100,000 fortune, on friendly terms with the world's great and near-great and with ambition still strong in him. He had taken one of the top prizes in London, why not the Anthonys'? Was he too busy with his own business to bother? Was he embittered against Gurney for some reason? We don't know.

It is also a mystery why he did not attend the meeting in Gurney's studio when Anthony made the award and where a gay party followed the speeches. *Humphrey's Journal* gives a detailed account of the affair and lists the names of the guests. Brady's name is not among them.

It must have been a wonderful night in the gaslit studio with the liquor flowing and with much chatter of shop talk and the latest gossip of fellow operators.

As the *Humphrey's Journal* reporter wrote:

"The light lamps held out until one o'clock and everybody had something to say . . ."[71]

But Brady closed his gallery and walked home—alone.

Why this strange loneliness, this separation from the men of his fraternity? Was it because this "gentle, shy and modest man who was never known to his fellow photographers" felt ill at ease with them, perhaps inferior?

His pitifully few "papers," the faded, brittle newspaper clippings and the three letters written by other men about him, do not tell us.

The exhibition at the New York Crystal Palace followed in 1854 and this one Brady entered and won a bronze medal. As *Humphrey's Journal* reported, "News has been received that Mr. B has won the premiums for the Daguerreotypes he submitted at Crystal Palace. If true, that is not surprising."

A brittle newspaper clipping that fell apart at the author's touch describes very briefly Brady's collection which won the prize:

"Brady's 30 group (sic) of portraits which for uniformity of line, sparkness and boldness we have never seen surpassed. Two or three of these we noticed especially as very fine. The head of Mr. J. Perry, a group of females and the head of the eccentric (sic) Carman of John Street. Mr. Brady's reputation will be much enhanced by these pictures . . ."[72]

Brady took his honors lightly; he was more concerned with his new gallery at 359 Broadway, over Thompson's Saloon. A reporter for *Humphrey's Journal* was sent to tour the new studio in the winter of 1853.[73] From his article one can visualize the luxurious interior.

At the front entrance was a large glass case filled with "specimens" of Brady's fine daguerreotype work, each picture framed in rosewood or gold leaf. After climbing the stairs to the second floor one faced two large folding doors made of glazed glass etched with figures of flowers "artistically arranged."

The largest photographic reception room in the city—26 feet by 40 feet—was also a room of quiet beauty. "The floors are carpeted a deep rose and velvet drapes embroidered with gold threads hang to the floor. The wallpaper is rich and conservative. The ceiling is frescoed and in the center hangs a glittering glass chandelier from which "prismatic drops sparkle like stars" in the gaslight. Curtains of imported needlework hang at the window. The furniture is of rosewood, the deep rich wood imprisoning the glow of the chandelier. The reception desk is large and off to the left of it are easy chairs and marble-topped tables with showcases of pictures." And, "gazing down at the luxurious rooms from the frames of gold and rosewood are the kings, statesmen, emperors and American leaders, living and dead," who sat for Brady and for History.

In the smaller "Business Room" were clusters of pictures on a few tables, inviting the guests to buy their likenesses. One popular display was of "ladies' lockets," which the gallants of the day purchased to give their sweethearts—with a picture included, of course.

The walls of the "Ladies' Room" were papered in green and gold. Here the ladies could preen like peacocks in front of a wall of solid mirrors, to pat a hat in place or fluff a curl before they entered the "Operating Room."

One flight up, it was a large room, sunshine streaming through the skylights, covered with mesh to diffuse the light. Two connecting rooms about 150 feet deep were filled with "all of the very best equipment. There is nothing in Brady's apparatus of second quality." On the fourth floor were the Plate Cleaning Room and the Electrotype Room; on the fifth a spare Operating Room and Chemical Room, where Brady stored his wares and plates.

It was, as the reporter called it, "a prince of a gallery."

While Brady's new gallery enjoyed a brisk business, an innovation was introduced by James A. Cutting in Boston called the Ambrotype. It was a thin glass negative which, when placed on a black background, produced a positive picture if viewed by reflected light. Brady experimented with Ambrotypes but he soon abandoned Cutting's invention to return to the wet

Fig. 17. A sketch of Brady's Photographic Gallery at 359 Broadway, "over Thompson's saloon," in 1859. *Courtesy New York Historical Society.*

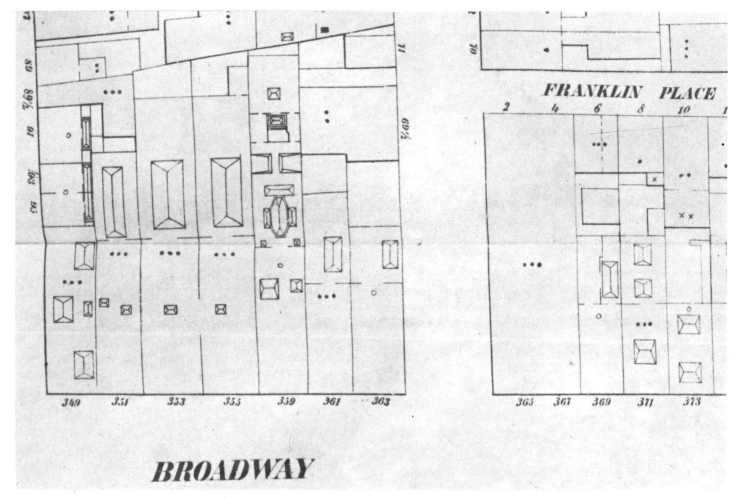

Fig. 18. A New York City street map, 1854, showing Brady's studio at 359 Broadway, near Franklin Street. Note the numerous skylights. *Courtesy New York Historical Society.*

plates. There are only a few ambrotypes among his plates.

It was clear, at least to Brady, that the Ambrotype had produced no violent revolution in photography as the wet plate process had done. It flared up only briefly, apparently shining just a bit brighter than the other "types' had done, to catch the eye of the American photographers. But soon their attention waned and again they turned to give all their love, daring and energy to their first love, the wet plate. Brief was the hour of glory for Cutting's Ambrotypes.

And what of the proud daguerreotype, first born of the new art? By 1854 the shiny copper daguerreotypes were still in demand but their popularity had been overshadowed by the cheaper and cruder paper prints, although in that year, the peak, there were about three million daguerreotypes taken at prices of anywhere from two dollars and fifty cents to five dollars.

The *carte de visite* photographs were being reproduced by the millions and the only effort required of Brady and the other photographers was to obtain new subjects before their cameras.

There was another year of triumph for Brady. The Washington studio was progressing excellently and a number of valuable pictures of American and European statesmen had been added to Brady's Gallery of Illustrious Americans. We still know little of Brady himself—a line or two in *Humphrey's Journal* or the *Photographic Art Journal* or in the New York *Herald*. He had his portrait painted by Charles Loring Elliott during this year and long cherished it, lending it to the Metropolitan Museum of Art in New York for an exhibition of American artists, the last year of his life.

On August 10, 1855, a child was born to Julia's brother's wife and the Bradys were to attend the christening in Washington. A few days later Brady and his wife watched the infant in its lace dress being given the waters of baptism and the name of Levin Handy.[75]

History and Brady would know much of Levin Handy.

1858. The eyesight of the prince of photographers was fading worse than ever. The long nights in the darkroom were extracting their toll. The lenses of his spectacles were now blue and even thicker. Brady still could be found behind the camera, but on rare occasions. He was still attracting the great men of America and the world to his busy galleries in New York and Washington, but other men were now doing most of the actual photography work.

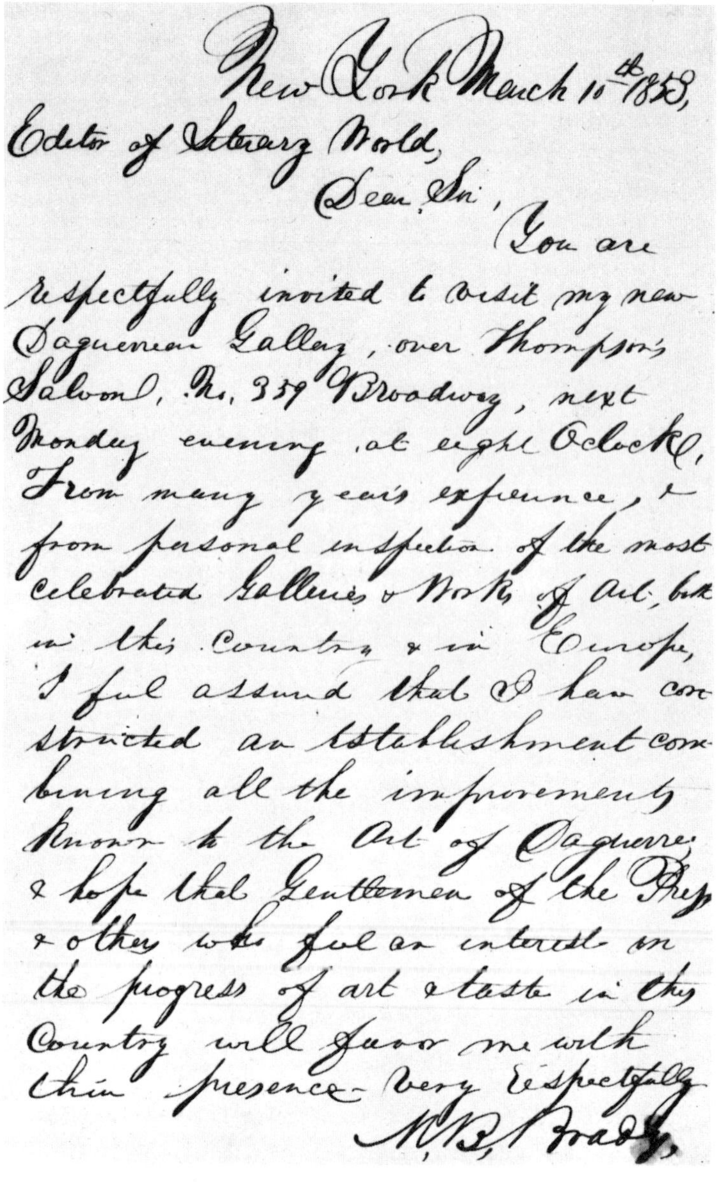

New York March 10th 1853,
Editor of Literary World,
Dear Sir,
You are respectfully invited to visit my new Daguerrean Gallery, over Thompson's Saloon, No. 359 Broadway, next Monday evening at eight O'clock. From many year's experience, & from personal inspection of the most celebrated Galleries & Works of Art, both in this Country & in Europe, I feel assured that I have constructed an Establishment combining all the improvements known to the Art of Daguerre; & hope that Gentlemen of the Press & others who feel an interest in the progress of art & taste in this Country will favor me with their presence. Very respectfully
M. B. Brady

Fig. 19. A Brady invitation to his new gallery. Not written by Brady. *Manuscript Division, New York Public Library.*

One was an Englishman named A. Berger—or Burger. A photographer with that name appears in *Humphrey's Journal,* in articles picked up from London papers or the *Journals of the Royal Society,* and one mentions that he was on his way to New York. It is pure speculation but this may be the Berger of Brady's New York studio, and the A. Berger who was to become the manager of Brady's Washington Gallery.

There was another assistant in Brady's New York gallery destined to become one of the great American photographers. Like Brady, Alexander Gardner, the Scot, would document the devastations of the Civil War. And after Appomattox, while Brady remained in Washington and New York, Gardner's restless feet would carry him to the frontier where his camera would record for history the opening of the West.

Gardner, part dreamer, part artist and journalist, was born in Paisley, Scotland, on October 27, 1821. His father came from a well-to-do family of ministers, physicians and landowners. Little is known of his mother, but evidently she was an educated and courageous woman. After her husband died she raised Alexander and his three brothers and kept them all in school while she worked as a schoolteacher.[77]

When he was fourteen, Gardner left school to take a job as a jeweler's apprentice. He had an intensive yearning for knowledge and for eight years worked from dawn to dusk in the jeweler's shop, ate a hurried meal, then spent the rest of the evening studying chemistry and astronomy.

When he was twenty-one he left the jeweler's shop for a job on the Glasgow *Sentinel* as a reporter. The man who sat next to him was Buchanan, father of the famous Scottish poet.

Gardner's favorite dream was of a "cooperative society" where men would work and live in brotherhood and peace. There were long discussions about "the society" in the kitchen of his Glasgow flat and finally his friends urged him to write an outline of this mythical society of which he had talked so long and earnestly. Whether he did write such a pamphlet is not known. But he did show a flair for writing and editing and after only a year of reporting he was appointed editor of the *Sentinel.*

A short time later several of his friends formed a "cooperative society," such as Gardner dreamed of, and migrated to the Iowa frontier. Later, members of his family joined them and as enthusiastic reports came back to Glasgow on the society's progress in the wilderness, more went out to join them.

[Advertisement.]

We call attention to the card of Mr. Braby, published in another column announcing a new feature in his business. It will supply the necessity so long felt by the public, of a place where really good and enduring likenesses may be obtained at a cheap price, as all pictures taken by him are executed in the highest style of the art.

[Advertisement

ADDRESS TO THE PUBLIC.—New-York abounds with announcements of 25 cent and 50 cent Daguerreotypes. But little science, experience or taste is requisite to produce these, so called, cheap pictures. During several years that I have devoted to the Daguerreian Art, it has been my constant labor to perfect and elevate it. The result has been that the prize of excellence has been accorded to my pictures at the World's Fair in London, the Crystal Palace in New-York, and wherever exhibited on either side of the Atlantic. Art has always suffered when the public have been deceived by unfounded assumptions of economy. A valuable invention is no sooner presented than its counterfeit is paraded at half the price. By such deceptions art has at all periods deteriorated.

My new Gallery, No. 359 Broadway, over Thompson's Saloon, combines every facility for the production of first-class pictures; but for the accommodation of such persons as may desire cheap likenesses, I take this opportunity of announcing that I am prepared to furnish Daguerreotypes at fifty cents and upward, at my old establishment, No. 205 Broadway, corner of Fulton-st., where specimens may be seen with the prices affixed; and I will demonstrate that I can produce a better picture for four shillings than any adventurer. Being unwilling to abandon any artistic ground to the producers of inferior work, I have no fear in appealing to an enligtened public as to their choice between pictures of the size, price and quality, which will fairly remunerate men of talent, science and application, and those which can be made by the merest tyro. I wish to vindicate true art, and leave the community to decide whether it is best to encourage real excellence or its opposite; to preserve and perfect an art, or permit it to degenerate by inferiority of materials which must correspond with the meanness of the price.

M. B. BRADY.

Fig. 20. A Brady advertisement in the New York *Tribune,* April 10, 1854.

BRADY'S DAGUERREOTYPES

WAS AWARDED AT THE

WORLD'S FAIR, IN LONDON,

1851,

THE PRIZE MEDAL,

For the Best Daguerreotypes in New York.

BRADY'S DAGUERREOTYPES have invariably commanded the highest prizes whenever offered for competition.

The proprietor has no hesitation in claiming for his new Gallery, 359 Broadway, advantages possessed by no similar establishment either in this country or in Europe. The facilities for the production of

First Class Pictures,

are unrivaled. An additional building has been erected, by which the Reception Saloon, Ladies' Dressing Room, and Operating Rooms are on the same floor, thus forming a new and most desirable arrangement.

This Gallery, in connection with the Old Establishment, 205 Broadway, corner of Fulton Street, contains a collection of American and European celebrities unrivalled on this continent.

BRADY'S DAGUERREIAN GALLERRIES,

359 & 205 BROADWAY, NEW YORK.

Fig. 21. Another Brady advertisement.

Curiously, Gardner, the champion of the cooperative idea, did not join it. He advanced in the newspaper profession and became well known in Glasgow as the writer of pamphlets dealing with man and his destiny. His thirst for knowledge drove him back to school and in a short time he had mastered Pitman's new shorthand system.

Scott Archer's announcement of the wet plate process captured Gardner's imagination and he determined to master the new art. In 1856 he sailed to America to join Mathew B. Brady.

How did Brady know of Gardner? How did he persuade him to come to America as his assistant? Perhaps Brady met him in London during the World's Fair and approached him there. This may be true, but Gardner's closest friend, who read a long memorial after his death, makes no mention of it.

It is not true, as one account says, that Gardner was employed mainly to coat the collodion plates in the New York studio. The Scot was an "accomplished photographer" by the time he met Brady. It is logical

to assume Brady would not pay the fare to America for an amateur. Gardner was not only an expert in the wet plate process but also an accomplished photographer in producing "imperials."

They made a fine team. Both were quiet, modest men and indefatigable workers. Brady soon recognized Gardner's master touch with the camera and appointed him manager of the Washington gallery in 1858.

Before he left for Washington, Gardner copied a small piece of paper and did the bankers of New York a good turn.

One day while experimenting with copying documents he decided to find out how to make a photographic copy of a check so perfect that it would fool a banker. After some hours of work he made a perfect copy and brought it to the local bank.

The cashier cashed it without question. Gardner asked: "Is the check good, sir?"

The cashier smiled and replied, "It's perfect, Mr. Gardner."

"Very well, please summon the president."

The surprised clerk called for the president of the bank and Gardner asked for his check.

"Is anything wrong with this check, sir?" he asked.

The president examined it. "If it isn't genuine, Mr. Gardner, I'll eat it."

"You had better start eating then," Gardner said. "This is a photographic copy and here is the real check."

That afternoon the banker summoned several other New York bankers, explained Gardner's technique and proposed a plan "to produce a check that could not be photographed." The plan was followed "and soon a check which could not be reproduced photographically, was issued by all New York banks."[78]

The following year photography joined hands with law enforcement in its fight against the underworld and crime.

The country's first official Rogues' Gallery, forerunner of today's gallery of 680,000 criminal records, was opened in New York City's Police Department.[79]

A century separates today's New York's gallery and the crude one of Brady's time; a large efficiently run bureau with a file of more than 80,000 pictures of world-wide criminals as compared with a small, grimy room in the rat-infested Police Headquarters Building at Grand and Crosby Streets. It had 450 daguerreotypes with only one-line descriptions of the subject.[79]

It is amusing to take this small tour with the reporter for *Humphrey's Journal* who wrote the story of the founding of the gallery, surely a "first" for students of criminology.

We are met at the door by a Mr. Van Buren, the official photographer, accompanied by, appropriately enough, a giant of a policeman, with enormous sideburns and a night stick dangling from his belt, who was stationed in the room to help Mr. Van Buren to deal with "fractious customers." The walls are covered with the daguerreotypes classified as to their "professions." "The Leading Pickpocket," "The German Shop Lifter." We find as the man from *Humphrey's* does, that the pictures are "life-like" and the most noticeable feature the "absence of self-satisfied smirks." Small wonder: the iron clasp of the photographer's "immobilizer" necessary in those days and the glare of the camera's lens were enough to freeze any man, pickpocket or president.

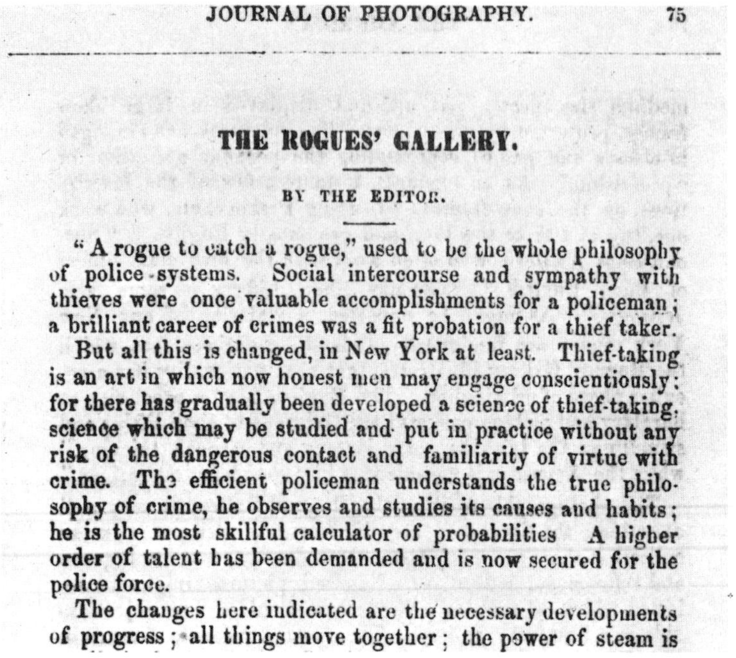

JOURNAL OF PHOTOGRAPHY. 75

THE ROGUES' GALLERY.

BY THE EDITOR.

"A rogue to catch a rogue," used to be the whole philosophy of police systems. Social intercourse and sympathy with thieves were once valuable accomplishments for a policeman; a brilliant career of crimes was a fit probation for a thief taker.

But all this is changed, in New York at least. Thief-taking is an art in which now honest men may engage conscientiously: for there has gradually been developed a science of thief-taking, science which may be studied and put in practice without any risk of the dangerous contact and familiarity of virtue with crime. The efficient policeman understands the true philosophy of crime, he observes and studies its causes and habits; he is the most skillful calculator of probabilities A higher order of talent has been demanded and is now secured for the police force.

The changes here indicated are the necessary developments of progress; all things move together; the power of steam is

Fig. 22. The first announcement of the establishment of a Rogues' Gallery. From the *American Journal of Photography,* 1859, Vol. 9.

The furniture in his new gallery had scarcely lost its polish when Brady discovered that the volume of his business had increased so rapidly he was forced to seek additional quarters. This time he was determined to establish the largest and most luxurious photographic studio in the world.

During the waning days of March he found the ideal location; in a building at the corner of Tenth Street and Broadway. Because "much had to be done to make it the most ornate gallery this side of the Atlantic," Brady leased still another building on the corner of Broadway and Bleecker Street and turned the former offices of the well-known importers, Nunn and Clark, into a temporary gallery.[80]

On March 2, 1860, Brady moved "uptown to Bleecker Street," joining what the *Herald* reported as "the general business movement uptown." Brady's move was significant of the rapidly expanding photographic business which had mushroomed from a few tiny downtown "on the side" studios to the uptown "big business." As the *Herald* pointed out, in the early days there had been scarcely a gallery above Canal Street, but when Brady moved from Fulton Street his competitors followed him like eager sheep, "and there are none below St. Nicholas . . ."

Brady's announcement that his new studio was to be located at Tenth Street and Broadway was big news. Horace Greeley sent a reporter to the building to inspect the new quarters, echoing with the hammers and the saws of carpenters.

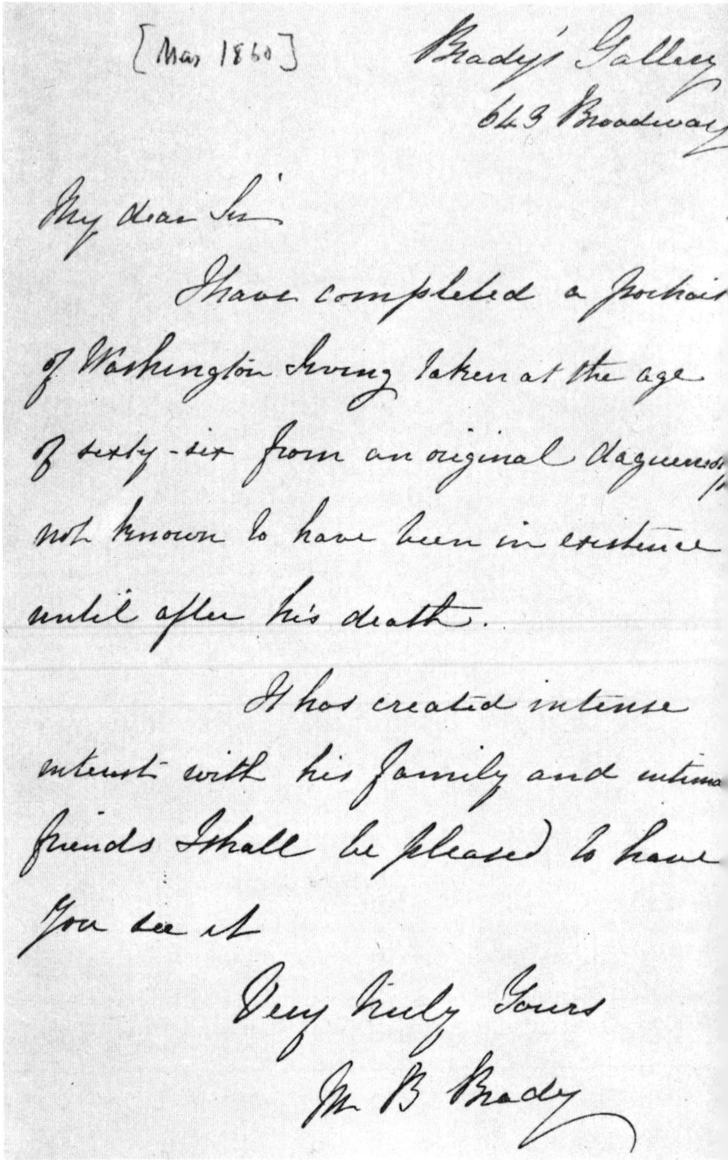

[Mar 1860]

Brady's Gallery
643 Broadway

My dear Sir

I have completed a portrait of Washington Irving taken at the age of sixty-six from an original daguerreotype not known to have been in existence until after his death.

It has created intense interest with his family and intimate friends I shall be pleased to have you see it

Very truly Yours
M B Brady

Fig. 23. A March, 1860, Brady letter about his picture of Washington Irving, sent from his gallery on Broadway near Bleecker Street. Not written by Brady. *Courtesy New York Historical Society.*

The reporter wrote: "The situation is the most commanding on Broadway, and with the alterations Mr. B. has in contemplation, his new gallery in point of accommodation and elegance will be the most complete establishment of its kind on either side of the Atlantic. This will also allow more space for his historical collection which is without rival."

The reporter had also inspected Brady's collection of historical plates, and like most spectators who saw the striking daguerreotypes of the great Americans for the first time, he was impressed: "When this collection is finally brought together it will occupy the foremost place among the local attractions in New York."

When Brady's plans leaked out, other photographic studios tried to overshadow the new establishment. Jeremiah Gurney refurnished his studio and C. D. Fredericks & Company, later in partnership with Gurney, moved to a new Broadway location and summoned the reporters. The whole front was what one reporter called a "crystal front." The windows were filled with daguerreotypes and life-size portraits in oil and crayons and the walls of the ornate reception room, in imitation of Brady's studios, were covered with daguerreotypes and painted prints of celebrities. A gallery which ran around the reception room enabled the visitors to "obtain a general view of the salon, the *haut ensemble* of which was magnificent."

But all the photographic galleries in America and Europe were overshadowed that winter when Brady opened his newest and largest studio at Broadway and Tenth Street. The studio extended down Tenth Street for one hundred and fifty feet, and was opposite Grace Church and A. T. Stewart's new store (later John Wanamaker's). The interiors shimmered with elegance. The floors were covered with costly carpet "and luxurious couches abound in liberal profusion." The gallery itself was lighted by artistic gas fixtures made by Morgan L. Curtis, who was in great demand by the millionaires of the day. Littlefield Heaters, the most modern of heating equipment, was a talked-about feature of the new studio, but the vast collection of historical pictures, which covered every inch of the gallery's wall space, was the major attraction for the visitors who crowded the studio on the opening day.

For the ladies there was a private or "ladies' entrance" on the Tenth Street side, which led directly into the "operating rooms," all lined with "eye-soothing glass."

It was truly the most glamorous studio in the world. After a tour of the building one reporter from *Leslie's Illustrated Newspaper* summed up his impressions: "If Brady lived in England his gallery would be called the Royal Gallery."[81]

The news of Brady's gallery was followed by another great event in the history of photography: the taking of the first aerial picture in America. The pioneer aerial photographers were Professor Samuel King and J. W. Black, one of the partners of the camera supply house of Black and Batchelder. Curiously, this great event went unnoticed by New York's great dailies. But there is no doubt that Brady heard of the tiny aerial picture which was exhibited for a week in Boston, attracting hundreds who stared unbelievingly at Boston taken from a swaying balloon. Fortunately the Boston *Herald* recognized the importance of the flight and devoted a long article to it on October 16, 1860, a few days after the flight.[82]

After an unsuccessful attempt in Providence, "where the clouds threw a shade upon the earth," King and Black then went to Boston, where they hired a balloon and recruited a number of husky friends to hold on to the thick cable which held the balloon on the ground. The day was bright and clear as they climbed swiftly in the sleepy autumn sky. At 1,500 feet Professor King waved a handkerchief, the agreed signal, and the men below stopped the ascent.

Professor King began to operate the camera with Black's help. But disaster struck.

"Professor! The gas is fogging the plates!" Black cried suddenly.

King stared at the plates Black held up. While their attention had been occupied by the swaying balloon and the picture-taking, they had not noticed the gas hissing out of the neck of the balloon. Each plate had turned a dark brown and was ruined.

"The gas was filling the atmosphere," King later recalled, "fogging the plates, several of which were destroyed and we lost precious time."

They worked swiftly to repair the leak. But the sun was beginning to set and the light was dimmer. Now Black took the camera "and, working with a celerity that was astonishing," he used up the remainder of the plates.

A brisk breeze had come up and the basket was swaying violently despite the taut cable. Below them, King and Black could see the doll-like figures of the men staring up at them. Several times the pair in the balloon thought they could hear faint shouts.

At last the plates had been used up. They did not yet know whether Black's latter attempts had been successful, but the day was fine, the sky unblemished by a single cloud, and a wind, fresh but not too strong, was tugging at the basket, eager to send it soaring across the sky.

Black and King looked at each other. Then, as if by mutual consent, one of them leaned over, unloosened the cable and the balloon, now free, flew like a coasting bird over the city. After the photographic pioneers had passed over the village of East Weymouth, "the balance of the voyage was devoted to leisure." The trip finally ended when the balloon sank earthward and was trapped in a tree. They had been aloft two hours and fifteen minutes and had traveled thirty miles.

In Boston the plates were developed and one historic air view emerged. It was a remarkably clear picture of Boston with sharp details of church steeples and rooftops.

Professor King wrote, "The time has come when what has been used for only public amusement can be made to serve some practical end . . ."

Each thunderous blast from a jet-propelled reconnaissance bomber as it roars through the atomic age underscores his prophetic remark.

The picture was the sensation of its day. Large crowds gathered in front of the window of Black and Batchelder. Newspapers and magazines sent special feature writers, one Oliver Wendell Holmes, who wrote in the *Atlantic Monthly*: "One of the photographs is lying before us. Boston, as the eagle and the wild goose see it, is a very different object from the same place as the solid citizen looms up its leaves and chimneys. The Old South and Trinity Church are landmarks not to be mistaken . . . windows, chimney, and skylights . . . attract the eye . . ."[83]

In England, James Glaisher, president of the Photographic Society of Great Britain, tried to duplicate the American aerial expedition with terrifying results. Equipped with the finest of photographic cameras and plates, he climbed into his balloon and soared skyward without a cable. It rose like a rocket, climbing higher, finally reaching the height of six miles. Choking and gasping for air, the Englishman fought to remain conscious as he struggled with his cumbersome camera. But the lack of oxygen felled him and he slipped into unconsciousness.

The pilotless balloon soared still higher. Glaisher lay on the bottom of the basket, bleeding from his mouth and nose. Finally the balloon began to descend slowly. Glaisher awoke, coated with ice and almost frozen to death, in pitch blackness. Hands and feet frozen, he tried desperately to save his plates by thrusting them inside his clothes. The wind screamed through the wires of the balloon and the basket rocked back and forth like a frenzied pendulum. At last the downward speed accelerated. Glaisher, "light-headed and with his fingers coated with ice tried to work his spectroscopic camera," but, as he later reported, the swaying of the basket was too violent. Blue with cold and numb to the bone, Glaisher left the frozen heavens to return to a world of riotous June flowers and meadows rippled by the lazy breeze of a warm summer's day . . .[84]

He had failed.

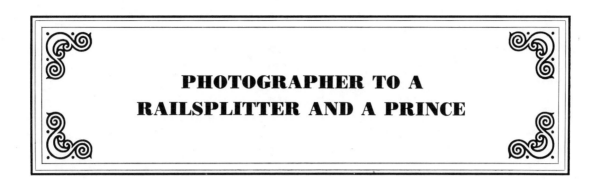

PHOTOGRAPHER TO A
RAILSPLITTER AND A PRINCE

IN 1860 a royal prince and a onetime railsplitter visited Mathew B. Brady's luxurious gallery on Tenth Street and Broadway; the prince gave Brady an ivory-headed rosewood cane, the railsplitter gave him a glimpse of his own greatness.

In a curious way the photographing of both men signified the end and the beginning of an era in Brady's life. The photograph of the prince marked his peak and his end as America's premier fashionable photographer; the railsplitter introduced him to war, death, bankruptcy—and immortality—for his camera.

Lincoln came first. In February, 1860, Lincoln arrived in New York to address the congregation of Beecher's Church in Brooklyn. However, several prominent Republicans persuaded him to talk at the Cooper Institute instead of Brooklyn. It was typical of Lincoln to insist that the Republicans first obtain the permission of Beecher. This was done and R. C. McCormick, in charge of the arrangements, paid Lincoln a visit at the Astor House.

A giant of a man opened the door. McCormick was taken aback when he saw him. He later recalled that the Illinois lawyer, "half alligator, half horse," was wearing a cheap black suit, "much wrinkled from the careless packing in the valise. His form and manner were indeed very odd, and we thought him the most unprepossessing public man we had ever met."

The dubious McCormick and Lincoln strolled down Broadway. They made a strange pair, the bony giant with the wrinkled suit, plug hat and amused brown eyes gazing over the heads of the hurrying New York crowds, and the plump, uncomfortable politician, wondering why in the name of heaven he and his committee had ever asked this bumpkin from Illinois to speak at the Institute . . .

Suddenly Abe saw in the crowd an old acquaintance from Illinois. He pumped the man's hand and asked him how he had been.

The man drawled. "Well, I've lost one hundred thousand dollars since I saw you last, Abe."

Lincoln grinned. "Well, I have eight thousand in the bank, the Springfield cottage, and if they make me Vice President with Seward I'll increase it to twenty thousand and that is as much as any man ought to ask."

We can almost hear Mr. McCormick groan as the two friends shook hands and they continued their leisurely stroll.

They finally reached their destination—Brady's studio.

Brady was in the operating room with George Bancroft, the historian, who hurried up to welcome Lincoln.

"I'm on my way to Massachusetts, where I have a son (Robert) at school," Lincoln said, "who, if the reports are true, already knows much more than his father."

They all laughed, then Bancroft introduced Lincoln to Brady. They shook hands and preparations were made for the "sitting."

Brady put Lincoln before the camera, but somehow he had trouble getting a "natural picture." Finally he asked Lincoln if he would "arrange" his shirt and coat collar.

Lincoln chuckled as he pulled up his loose collar.

"Ah, I see you want to shorten my neck," he said.

"That's just it, Mr. Lincoln," Brady replied.

The little joke seemed to relax Lincoln. He stared into the lens. At the magic second the shutter winked and the calm, beautiful face of the great man was captured on the wet plate.

Within a few minutes Lincoln said goodbye, shook Brady's hand and left with Bancroft and McCormick.[85]

Lincoln's speech at the Cooper Institute demonstrated that the backwoods lawyer was a man of ability and dignity. Still there was the wrinkled black suit and his ungainly manners which gave some pause. But Brady's photographs dissipated the doubts. The newspapers used the portrait for their wood engravings and Currier and Ives made some striking lithographs from it. Francis B. Carpenter, the artist, remarks in his diary: "The effect of such influence (the photograph) though silent is powerful."[86]

Years later when Brady and Lincoln met at the White House, Brady recalled that when Marshal Ward Hill Lamon said, "I have not introduced Mr. Brady," the President remarked, "in his ready way," "Brady and the Cooper Institute made me President."

On a bright October day in 1860, the Royal Prince came to the Tenth Street gallery. In October the Prince of Wales, later Edward VII, arrived from Canada for a tour of America with his royal entourage. One member was a handsome, aloof man, with bristling sideburns, whose principal task was to protect the royal morals, Lord Lyons, who would acquit himself with honor in Washington during the war years.

New York gave the charming young man a typical Manhattan welcome. There was a torchlight parade by the Fire Department past the Fifth Avenue Hotel at Twenty-third Street, where crowds gathered nightly to cheer the Prince whenever he appeared on the balcony, a fireworks display and a band serenade outside his window. The great "Diamond Ball" was held and Edward danced the night through, tumbling into bed at dawn.

It was known that the Royal Party would be photographed and behind the scenes the city's photographers fought a savage skirmish every day for the prestige of being the "prince's photographer."

Brady did nothing. He went his quiet way photographing his customers and lulling them into a relaxed pose with his endless fund of stories.

On October 16, 1860, the prince announced he was ready to be photographed by an American photographer and the royal party set out in their carriages. When word sped about the city a crowd followed behind the carriages, in groups and smaller crowds like a large rolling human snowball, blocking Broadway from curb to curb, cheering and shouting. The prince, who seemed to enjoy his popularity, waved and tipped his hat.

It is almost anticlimactic to say that the carriages drove in the direction of Brady's studio.

Soon Brady and his assistants could see the horses, black and sleek, as if they had been greased, with feathers and plumes nodding in the fresh October afternoon. The carriages turned into Tenth Street and the prince led his party through the Ladies' Entrance with one last wave of his top hat to the crowd who cheered him again.

Brady greeted him and the royal tour of the gallery began immediately. A reporter from *Leslie's Illustrated Newspaper* observed: "The Prince immediately began inspecting with curious interest the portraits of the statesmen and the other celebrities of this country."[87]

After a preliminary look the party was escorted by Brady into the operating rooms. The Prince first posed alone, then with his party, then in pairs. Three "imperials" were taken of the entire group, a full length portrait of the Prince, and a number of *carte de visite* portraits.

With Brady and the prince in the lead, the grand tour began. The colored photographic section of the gallery interested the prince and his party, and they stayed there for some time.

"This is indeed the *chef d'oeuvres* of art, Mr Brady," the Prince at last told Brady.

The Duke of Newcastle devoted most of his tour to examining the portraits of American politicians and both he and the prince ordered several. One copy they asked for "immediately" was of President Buchanan and his Cabinet. Before they left the gallery Brady produced his "register" and asked for the royal signatures. The prince was first: Albert Edward. Then the others: Lyons, Newcastle, St. Germans, Hinchingbrooke, Charles G. I. Elliott, G. D. Englehart, Hugh W. Ackland, G. F. Jenner, Robert Bruce and C. Teasdale.

As the last signature was written with a flourish Brady brought up an old man "tottering with his years."

"Your Grace," Brady said, "this gentleman has asked to be presented to you. He was present in your household when you were born."

The prince shook hands with the old man, listened to a few words from the old gentleman, shook hands once again and was ushered out by Brady.

The crowd was so great by this time that the police were called to hold it back. A loud cheer arose as Brady came out with the royal party. Before he stepped into his carriage the future King of England leaned down and "shook hands with Brady for the last time, expressing great gratification and satisfaction from the inspection of his collection."

As each man in the party passed he shook Brady's hand. In a few moments the carriages rolled down the street, followed by the cheering people who couldn't get close enough to see a real prince of England.

The visit of the prince raised Brady's prestige considerably. The day after the royal visit crowds streamed in and out of the gallery, "not only to have their picture taken by the prince's photographer, but to shake the hand of the man he visited."

Brady modestly recalled his royal honor years later, "I was surprised amidst such competition that they came to my gallery and repeatedly sat." He ventured to inquire of the Duke of Newcastle: "Your Grace, might I ask to what I owe your favor to my studio? I am at a loss to understand your kindness."

The duke's reply was, "Are you not the Mr. Brady who earned the prize nine years ago in London? You owe it to yourself. We had your place of business down in our notebooks before we started."

PART TWO

The War Years

···›·——◆›●‹◗——·‹···

"Men who were not backward in furnishing means; and to a score or less of workers—men who were not afraid of exposure and who could laugh at fatigue and starvation; men who could face danger in all shapes and were at all times ready to march, often between two armies, in the trenches, on the ramparts, through the swamps and forests, with the advance guard and back again at headquarters—not a flank movement but the willing and indefatigable artist at his post of danger and adventure.

"The public does not and cannot realize the part that the camera served in bringing down the facts of the late war for future history; one cannot look back but with wonder and admiration on these few, industrious, painstaking men . . ."

—"Photographic Reminiscences" by Captain A. J. Russell in *Anthony's Photographic Bulletin.*

"It is so nearly like visiting the battlefields to look over these views that all the emotions excited by the actual sight of the stained and sordid scene, strewed with rags and wrecks, came back to us, and we buried them in the recesses of our cabinet as we would have buried the mutilated remains of the dead they too vividly represented."

—Oliver Wendell Holmes

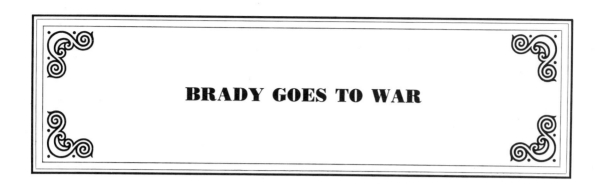

BRADY GOES TO WAR

To photograph the Civil War. This was Brady's ideal and it burned fiercely in his heart, refusing to be quenched by the pleas of his wife and his "most conservative" friends. In the end this ideal would destroy him but, at the same time, give his work a permanent niche in history.

The ideal glowed, flickered, then burst into flame sometime in 1860-61 as the roar of war grew louder in the ears of the Republic. Brady knew, from rough calculation, it would be enormously expensive to photograph a war, even the "six months' war," as most Northerners thought of it in those early days. It would also be dangerous. To get good pictures a cameraman would have to be in the thick of the fighting, and cannons and rifle balls know no neutrality.

Why this intense drive, this desire to risk his life and fortune to capture on his wet plates his country at war? Why this departure from commercial business to pictorial war correspondence?

He explains it simply: "I can only describe the destiny that overruled me by saying that, like Euphorion, I felt I had to go. A spirit in my feet said, 'Go' and I went . . ."[89]

The importance of covering the Civil War was recognized when it began by other men besides Brady. Professor John W. Draper brought up the subject at a meeting of the American Photographic Society on June 10, 1861. And, as president of the organization, he appointed a committee to discuss the matter with the Secretary of War.[90]

Draper's committee, of which Brady was not a member, failed. They filed their suggestions with the War Department and it is not surprising to learn from Draper's report to the members that "little progress has been made in the matter owing to the extraordinary preoccupation of the department . . ."

But Brady tried a different approach, that of personal friendship. He journeyed down to Washington to see his old friend, General Winfield Scott. As he explained, "In the days before the war it was the considerate thing to buy wild ducks at the steamboat crossing of the Susquehanna and take them to your choice friends and I often took Scott, in New York, his favorite ducks."

Scott, so swollen with dropsy that he no longer could mount a horse, heard Brady's suggestion in 1861. Then Scott told him the news that only his aide, Schuyler Hamilton, knew; he was not to remain in command.

"Mr. Brady," he said, "no person but my aide, Schuyler Hamilton, knows what I am to say to you. General McDowell will succeed me tomorrow. You will have difficulty but he and Colonel Whipple are the persons for you to see."[91]

Brady did not go to McDowell or anyone else; at the moment Lincoln's inaugural and his visit to his Washington studio on the afternoon of February 23, 1861, on the day of his arrival in Washington, occupied all his energies.

The portrait painter, George H. Story, who later described to a New York *World* reporter Lincoln's visit to the gallery, said that Lincoln seemed a world away from the bustling of Brady and Gardner, who were hurriedly making preparations by arranging the overhead curtains with poles.[92]

Lincoln, as Story saw him, "seemed absolutely indifferent to all that was going on about him, and he gave the impression that he was a man who was overwhelmed with anxiety and fatigue and care."

Brady asked Story to pose Lincoln in an "artistic" pose. "Pose him?" exclaimed Story. "Never. Bring the camera and take him as he is."

Brady and Gardner needed no further urging. They immediately began to make their exposures. It was a different Lincoln Brady saw that day; in his New York Tenth Street studio, it had been an amiable, beardless giant, dressed in a wrinkled black suit; in Washington it was a weary, troubled, bearded man, whose eyes reflected the anxious hours through which his beloved Republic was passing.

The inauguration followed. The first week of February Brady had asked two of his best photographers, J. F. Coonley and C. N. Barnard to come down from New York to Washington to help him and Alexander Gardner with preparations to cover the inauguration.[93]

According to Barnard's wartime reminiscences, he and Coonley arrived in the capital about the time of the arrival of the Peace Commissioners. This would place them in Washington on February 4, 1861, when the Commissioners, representing thirteen free states and seven border states, met at the request of the Virginia Legislature.

Brady was not one to let history slip from his grasp, so he dispatched Barnard and Coonley to a former Presbyterian church which had been swallowed by the expanding Willard's Hotel, where the committee was to meet. Coonley and Barnard fixed their Anthony & Company camera on the gloomy delegates and the suave, quivering old man who sat in the chair directly beneath the faded oil painting of George Washington. It was the last picture taken of ex-President John Tyler of Virginia.[94]

But the Peace Commission soon departed, to be quickly forgotten in the war hysteria sweeping the nation. The inauguration now occupied all of Brady's attention. It was no easy assignment. Allen Pinkerton, the Chicago railroad detective, had learned of a plot to assassinate the President, and Lincoln had arrived in Washington under somewhat cloak-and-dagger conditions. Whether or not there really was a plot to murder Lincoln will always be debated, but Allan Pinkerton's letterbook and his personal correspondence seem to support the possibility that there was some sort of plot to shoot Lincoln.

In Washington Charles P. Stone, a stern old soldier who was brigadier-general of the United States Volunteers in charge of the inauguration's security measures, took Pinkerton's warning seriously.[95] Sharpshooters were placed on the roofs along Pennsylvania Avenue to watch the windows of the houses across the street and to fire at once if an assassin attempted to shoot Lincoln as he rode to the Capitol. A battalion of District of Columbia troops was to be placed near the steps of the Capitol and riflemen were to be hidden in the windows of the wings of the Capitol.

Washington city, on the eve of the inauguration, hummed with activity, while General Stone slept at his desk among the piles of excited messages and reports which flowed into his office by messengers and telegraph.

In the early hours of the morning a report which Stone described as coming "from a reliable informant" told Stone that a bomb was to be placed under the wooden platform to blow to bits Buchanan and Lincoln, the Chief Justice and the other celebrities, just as Lincoln took his oath of office.[96]

General Stone rubbed the sleep from his eyes, summoned his officers, and sent a company of soldiers to guard the stand. For the rest of the night moonlight glinted on the ring of bayonets which surrounded the inauguration stand and the empty streets echoed with the footfalls of the sentries.

As the first pink shafts appeared in the east, stragglers began to appear to gain advantageous positions. Stone sent another trusted battalion of National Guardsmen to form a semicircle at the foot of the great stairway of the Capitol. Plainclothesmen and policemen were also scattered through the crowd.

Brady and Gardner and their assistants arrived early and took their positions off to one side of the inauguration stand. It appears that Brady was unable to persuade Stone to alter his airtight security arrangements. Brady would surely have preferred to bring his camera up near the stand, but he was forced to take a position at the fringe of the crowd.

It was a drab inaugural parade that moved up Pennsylvania Avenue under a gray sky a few hours later. A strange and uneasy silence hung over the city. Only a few buildings bore gay bunting and flags. Many shops were shuttered and it was whispered that Rebel spies watched from balconies along the way.[97]

It was noon when the word to present arms was passed along the line of infantry and cavalry on the avenue in front of Willard's. "Hail to the Chief" was struck up and Buchanan and Lincoln, according to Stone's plan, came out and stepped into the carriage.

Buchanan sat in silence as the barouche rolled up to the Capitol. Lincoln stared ahead with sad and troubled eyes. There were no loud cheers from the packed sidewalks. A few drunks in front of a tavern held up their bottles and cheered the Confederacy.

The only bit of color in the long column was that of mounted marshals decked in orange, pink and blue. Thirty-four girls, later to be kissed one by one by Lincoln, rode behind them, and coming up, to give the crowd the only laugh of the day, were the New Englanders, whose pegged new shoes made a weird creaking rhythm. And as he rode before the inaugural carriage, General Stone was congratulating himself on nicking his horse so often with his spurs that it would be unlikely that an assassin could get a clear shot at the tall figure of Mr. Lincoln.

The official party entered the north door. Vice President Hamlin and a few senators were sworn in in the Senate chamber and then the party went outside to the stand facing the eastern park, under the steel derricks and ropes of the unfinished Capitol dome.

Senator Edward D. Baker of Oregon introduced Lincoln, and as legend has it, Senator Stephen A. Douglas smilingly took his hat when he looked for a place to put it.

Then Lincoln began to speak, slowly and in a clear voice that swept across a troubled nation on the verge of civil war.

"We are not enemies but friends . . . passion may be strained . . . it must not break our bonds of affection . . ."

At last the great words died away. Chief Justice Taney, a richly dressed living corpse in black silk, tottered across the platform with a Bible bound in cinnamon velvet. In the dead silence of the afternoon Abraham Lincoln swore to defend the Constitution of the United States.

Guns crashed in salute. General Scott, his huge frame clad in scarlet and gold, lumbered to his feet.

And somewhere in the crowd, Mathew B. Brady, who had taken a picture of an Illinois lawyer in a wrinkled black suit much creased from his box valise, clicked his shutter again and took him as President Lincoln.

Uneasy days followed. Major Anderson, commanding Fort Sumter, had sent a note that his provisions were running low and Lincoln ordered the garrison provisioned. Then he prodded Scott into reinforcing Fort Pickens, while rumors swept through the capital that the Rebel ranger Ben McCulloch was ready to capture Washington with five hundred hard-riding raiders.

Seward was the optimist. Peace would continue, he said, and the whole crisis would be forgotten within three months. Lincoln, not so cheerful, posted militiamen about the public buildings. The Chain Bridge, Long Bridge and other approaches to Washington were guarded.

On Friday, April 12, news trickled into the capital that Beauregard had demanded the surrender of Sumter and that Major Anderson had refused. The next day headlines shrilled that the bombardment had begun. Later that afternoon there were reports that Sumter had been surrendered to the Rebels.

Sunday was quiet. Then on Monday morning the news burst over the nation like a giant thunderclap: Civil War! Lincoln called for seventy-five thousand militia for three months.

From sixteen states telegrams poured into the White House offering men and arms. The number of men who volunteered to the colors far exceeded Lincoln's request but six border states sent indignant refusals. Massachusetts, the best equipped for any emergency, notified Lincoln that four regiments under the command of Benjamin Butler were ready. Three regiments were prepared to march into Washington and guard the nation's capital, the governor wired Lincoln.

Just across the Potomac in his white-pillared mansion, Robert E. Lee crossed the Chain Bridge to pay his respects to General Scott, who had summoned him from Texas a month earlier. The old general offered to resign if he, Lee, would take command. The Virginian refused and rode back across the bridge.

On the morning of April 18, Lee stood in Montgomery Blair's yellow house on Pennsylvania Avenue, now Blair House. There in the dining room, Blair, at Lincoln's insistence, offered the Virginian command of the Union armies. Again Lee refused and rode back across the bridge for the last time.[98]

"What will we do for generals?" Seward whispered to Scott when he heard the news.

Scott and General Woll were the only ones who had ever commanded a brigade. "General" Jim Lane, the scourge of Kansas, walked into the East Room of the White House to offer his sword, and Cassius M. Clay, the picturesque Kentuckian, offered his services as a general. Both had fought in the Mexican War.

Troops flooding into the capital soon turned Washington into a war town. Bands and parades were so commonplace that passers-by barely looked twice at the brilliant Zouave uniforms and gave only a quick glance to the bare legs of the Seventy-Ninth, New York, commanded by Secretary Simon Cameron's brother, who dressed his men as Highlanders.

Late in June, on the first payday, the troops ran riot. Drunken Fire Department Zouaves with Navy Colts shattered store windows, terrorized pedestrians, raided brothels, broke up bars "and ran off with gentlemen's carriages." It took two days to arrest the offenders and send them packing off to the provost.

A few days later the Zouaves' drunken brawls were forgotten in the excitement of the news that the first cavalry skirmish had been fought at Fairfax Courthouse. There were the first prisoners, farmboys from Virginia, who marched up the avenue with a great deal of swagger and braggadocio.

Probably one of the busiest men in the wartime capital was Mathew B. Brady. Coonley and Barnard, as they recalled, worked day and night to fill the orders of soldiers who wanted their likenesses on *cartes de visite*. Officers from the rank of general down sat hour after hour in the big reception room, impatiently waiting their turn.[99]

The commercial side of the business was never more profitable, but Brady was devoting most of his waking hours gathering together his equipment to photograph the first big battle of the war which he had heard—as had everyone else in Washington—was now shaping up on the maps of General Irvin McDowell. He had replaced Scott, as the old general had told Brady he would.

Brady had seen both Allan Pinkerton and Lincoln and had placed before them his plan of photographing the Civil War. Pinkerton said he had no objection if

Brady did not get in the way and Lincoln, probably half-humorously, had scrawled "Pass Brady" on a paper.[100]

But it was enough for Mr. B. of Broadway. He knew many of the generals and probably would not need the pass, but he did want Lincoln's permission. The President had told him there was one major requirement he would have to fulfill: the project would have to be financed by himself. The government could not furnish a penny.

While Brady began equipping the black, hooded wagon which would become his famous "What-is-it wagon," a few minutes away from his studio, in a white clapboard house across from St. John's Church, Mrs. Rose O'Neal Greenhow, the Confederate spy, was handing one of her attractive young spies a small patch of black silk. Inside the silk square "The Wild Rose," as the North knew her, had sewed a small dispatch which detailed General McDowell's marching orders. Her courier Betty Duval carried it hidden in her long hair to General Milledge Bonham at Fairfax Courthouse. This was the first of several messages she sent to give vital information to the Confederate command.[101] She would soon be before Brady's camera.

The Confederates on all fronts were closing their ranks. Every commander knew of the Yankee blueprint to drive through Beauregard's lines, split his command and march on to Richmond to end the war even before it began.

July 9th had originally been the date on which McDowell had been scheduled to lead his "rabble" army, as Russell, the London *Times* correspondent, called it, on to Richmond. As he wrote: "They think that an army is like a round of cannister which can be fired off whenever the match is applied . . ."[104]

On Tuesday Washington was in a state of wild excitement. Troops, ambulances, artillery caissons and supply wagons were seen crossing the Long Bridge to Virginia. The army was finally on the move, accompanied by scores on horseback and in carriages. Congressman Alfred Ely of New York hired a carriage and with a beaker of champagne and a cold chicken set off "to see the Rebs beaten."

One of the most talked-about vehicles was a lumbering wagon, hooded with black, which gave it the appearance of a hearse. In it were Mathew B. Brady, dressed in his broadcloth suit, a linen duster and a broad-brimmed hat "like that of a Paris art student," Dick McCormick, a newspaper reporter, Ned House and Al Waud, combat artist for *Harper's Weekly*.[105]

On Wednesday, Brady and his companions straggled into Fairfax Courthouse and twenty hours later into Centerville. It was hot and sticky, and the air was filled with clouds of dust from the marching troops. In the rear were the perspiring sightseeing parties, all clamoring for blood and battle.

Several picket outposts had been driven in and when news of this reached Washington there were cheers for the "major victory" and in Willard's bar cheers were raised for the "retreat" of the Confederate Army.[106]

It was at Centerville that McDowell's army faced the full force of Beauregard's men, intrenched behind the steep banks bordering a small sluggish stream called Bull Run.

A Colonel Tyler, ordered to make a reconnaissance of the lower fords of the stream, needlessly exposed his men and there were heavy casualties as the green troops retreated wildly under sharp-shooting Rebel fire.

On Thursday night the army lay inert in the oppressive heat at Centerville. The supply wagons had failed to come up and the men were desperate for food. On Friday morning the wagons finally arrived and food was distributed. On the 19th and 20th McDowell's engineers carefully examined the position of the enemy and the terrain between them and the Rebel lines.

After they had reported to him, McDowell made up his plan of battle. He selected Sunday, the 20th, as the day he would move and his plan was to turn the enemy's left from his defensive position and if possible, to "destroy the railroad leading from Manassas to the Valley of Virginia, where the enemy has a large force."[107] Unknown to him, the "large force" under Gen. Joseph E. Johnson was already marching into Beauregard's camp.

Meanwhile Brady was getting ready for action. In the early hours of Sunday morning he prepared his equipment and was ready to march into battle. On the hill at Centerville, overlooking Bull Run, the gay crowds from Washington with their picnic baskets were drawn up in their carriages, like spectators ready to view a boat race. Most of them were disappointed. All that could be seen on the wooded plain below were battle smoke, the occasional glint of sunshine on flashing sabres or guns and waving banners.

There was the steady, dry, crackling sound of musketry and the heavier boom of the big guns. Back in Washington a heavy silence hung over the capital. Stores were shuttered, bars were deserted and some of the larger brothels were closed as the "gay ladies" had gone to see the battle.

Again it was Tyler's hesitation that ruined McDowell's battle plans. For two hours his troops blocked off the point on the turnpike where the regiments of Hunter and Heintzelman were to turn off for the flank march and when he finally did move, the Confederates had been alerted to the plan.

In the preliminary battle at nine o'clock, the Confederates were driven back to the Henry House plateau where "the mingled remnants of Bee, Bartow's and Evans command" were reformed under the command of Thomas Jackson, soon to receive his famous nickname "Stonewall."[108]

The pleateau changed hands during the morning's fierce fighting, with the main strength of the Federals being the crack batteries of Ricketts and Griffin. The battle was lost only when they were lost. Mistaking an advancing regiment of infantry for their own, the Federal gunners withheld their fire. A moment later they received "a deadly volley" and were wiped out. When Beauregard advanced, the New York Zouaves who had been supporting the batteries, fled in wild retreat. Panic spread through the whole Union Army and although McDowell and his staff tried desperately to halt them the retreat became a rout.

Flinging aside their guns, the soldiers rushed up the road east of Bull Run, engulfing the carriages, the Congressmen and the gay ladies. Confederate shells began to fall about the road. Horses reared and screamed, soldiers, maddened by panic, cut the reins and rode off on the stolen horses. Ammunition wagons and carts overturned and blocked the bridge over Cub Run. Men fought each other to get through the tangle of reins, wheels and rearing horses.

Brady had followed the army to the high ground by the Matthews house where Evans had taken a position to check Burnside's advance earlier in the day and as he was returning up Bull Run Road he was engulfed by the retreating army.[109]

Brady turned his camera on the frightened mob. Among the pictures he got in those tense minutes was one of the correspondent Russell. These plates have disappeared, but at least one historian recalls seeing a print showing "some people milling about in a country road."

Brady's wagon was overturned, but he managed to rescue some of his wet plates in their heavy wooden plate box. For three days Brady wandered about the forest with other stragglers. Once he bumped into a group of New York Fire Department Zouaves, who gave him a long sword to protect himself. Finally on the third day Brady limped into Washington. After greeting Julia and rushing his plates into the developer, he stepped before the camera, still clad in his dirty linen duster and straw hat.[110]

The hue and cry which rose after the defeat at Bull Run slowly subsided. General Patterson, who had allowed Johnston's troops to join Beauregard, was dismissed, and for a time there was a cloud over Scott's head. But a new star was ascending. All Washington was eager to catch a glimpse of a young (only thirty-five) major-general named George B. McClellan, who had been summoned from western Virginia to succeed McDowell.

There was more of interest. Congress put aside a large appropriation for repairing Long Bridge, and also voted the men and money to carry on the war. Mc-

Clellan set about forging his Army of the Potomac after putting down two rebellions in the unruly Seventy-Ninth and the Second Maine. In his Pennsylvania Avenue studio, Mathew B. Brady began the extensive preparations he realized were needed to cover what the whole nation now realized was no longer "a six months' war."

His venture at Bull Run had been highly praised and his prints had a large sale. As *Humphrey's Journal* stated:

"The public is indebted to Brady of Broadway for numerous excellent views of 'grim-visaged war.' He has been in Virginia with his camera, and many and spirited are the pictures he has taken. His are the only reliable records at Bull's Run. The correspondents of the Rebel newspapers are sheer falsifiers; the correspondents of the Northern journals are not to be depended upon, and the correspondents of the English press are altogether worse than either; but Brady never misrepresents. He is to the campaigns of the republic what Vandermeulen was to the wars of Louis XIV. His pictures, though perhaps not as lasting as the battle pieces on the pyramids, will nonetheless immortalize those introduced in them.

"Brady has shown more pluck than many of the officers and soldiers who were in the fight. He went—not exactly like the 'Sixty-Ninth,' stripped to the pants—but with his sleeves tucked up and his big camera directed upon every point of interest on the field. Some pretend, indeed, that it was the mysterious and formidable-looking instrument that produced the panic! The runaways, it is said, mistook it for the great steam gun discharging 500 balls a minute, and immediately took to their heels when they got within its focus! However this may be, it is certain that they did not get away from Brady as easily as they did from the enemy. He has fixed the cowards beyond the possibility of a doubt.

"Foremost among them the observer will perhaps notice the well-known correspondent of the London *Times;* the man who was celebrated for writing graphic letters when there was nobody to contradict him, but who had proved, by his correspondence from his country, that but little confidence can be placed in his accounts. See him as he flies for dear life, with his notes sticking out of his pockets, spurring his wretched-looking steed, his hat gone, and himself the picture of abject despair.

"But, joking aside, this collection is the most curious and interesting we have ever seen. The groupings of entire regiments and divisions, within a space of a couple of feet square, present some of the most curious effects as yet produced in photography. Considering the circumstances under which they were taken, amidst the excitement, the rapid movements, and the smoke of the battlefield, there is nothing to compare with them in their powerful contrasts of light and shade."[111]

Eleven days after the battle the *American Journal of Photography* praised Brady, the "irrepressible photographer, who, like the war horse, sniffs the battle from afar." Brady, the article said, got as far as the "smoke of Bull Run and was aiming his never-failing tube at friends and foe alike, when with the rest of our Grand Army they were completely routed and took to their heels, losing their photographic accoutrements on the ground, which the Rebels no doubt pounced upon as trophies of victory. Perhaps they considered the camera as an infernal machine. The soldiers live to fight another day, our special friends to make again their photographs . . . when will photographers have another chance in Virginia? . . ."[112]

With everything quiet on the Potomac Brady started to recruit his photographic teams. Before the war would be finished, he would have his What-is-it wagons in almost every theater of war, working with the Armies of the Potomac, Tennessee, Red River, Cumberland and the Gulf. He later recalled that he spent over $100,000 and "had men in all parts of the army like a rich newspaper."

Brady of course, did not take all the battlefield pictures, which have been credited many times to him alone. It is obvious that such a task would have been physically impossible. He was the organizer both in the field and at home. Little is known of some of the men who worked for Brady photographing the war, though some of their names can be gleaned from Alexander Gardner's two-volume *Sketchbook of the Civil War,* which he published shortly after the war. There was no method of reproduction at the time, so he pasted in the actual photographs with a credit byline under each print.[113]

On Brady's staff were Lewis H. Landy, Alexander and James Gardner, David Knox, William R. Pywell, Timothy N. O'Sullivan, D. B. Woodbury, J. L. Rockey, J. F. Coonley, T. C. Roche, Samuel C. Chester and four other men, a Mr. Wood, a Mr. Gibson, a Mr. Fox and a Mr. Berger.

O'Sullivan and Gardner took extensive battlefield pictures, and Gardner is credited with having made three-quarters of the scenes with the Army of the Potomac. It was O'Sullivan who made the memorable "Harvest of Death" picture at Gettysburg. Both men are a major part of Brady's story and we shall return to them.

After Brady had demonstrated to the army how valuable photography was in a war the War Department hired photographers to accompany the army, copy maps and photograph the terrain and enemy installations. Stanton may have given the order for the employment of photographers, for Coonley rushed his battlefield pictures back to Washington, "where they were hurried to Secretary of War Stanton for his examination."

The Confederacy had George Cook of Charleston, who had been in charge of Brady's New York studio in 1851. There was also S. R. Seibert of Charleston, Edwards of New Orleans, Vannerson and Miley. Another Southern photographer was A. B. Lytle of Baton Rouge, who covered the war for three years through several campaigns, not only as a photographer, but as history's first camera-spy. In 1911 Mr. Lytle's son told historian Henry Wysham Lanier that his father used to signal with a flag and a lantern from the observation tower on the top of the ruins of the Baton Rouge capitol to Scott's Bluff, from which point the coded message would be relayed to the Confederates near New Orleans. He discontinued this relay system after the Yankee sharpshooters began lining him up in their sights and the bullets began pinging off nearby rocks.[114]

The Anthonys were not idle while Brady was collecting his small army of photographers, assistants, drivers and printers. After Bull Run they had seen the obvious and now, in addition to selling their photographic supplies, they also equipped teams to send out to the battlefields.

The competition was keen and the Anthonys were not beyond raiding Brady's staff. Thomas C. Roche was the first to leave Brady and join the Anthonys, who hired him to make[115] stereo views of the war. The Anthonys also supplied chemicals and glass to cameramen on both sides. The Confederate photographer Lytle recalled that the chemicals did not run the blockade but were sent south marked "orders to trade" with the iodides and bromides going under the guise of quinine. Some orders-to-trade were actually signed by Lincoln.[116]

One wonders how Brady and his assistants accomplished so much with such cumbersome equipment. Imagine the toil to get to the scene of action with a heavy wagon, a darkroom tent, several hundred fragile glass plates, whose destruction meant utter failure, along back country roads ridged with iron-like ruts in winter and turned into impossible morasses in spring thaws, with the constant danger of sharpshooters perched in trees, cavalry raiders or bushwhackers.

The troops at first derided Brady's What-is-it wagon, but later they came to respect this strange breed of men who carried no sidearms or rifles, but cameras, and who could amaze combat veterans by scrambling to the top of redoubts even when the firing was the heaviest.[117]

But getting to the scene was only the beginning for Brady and his men. Consider the steps that were necessary to take the pictures one sees in this book. George G. Rockwood, a Civil War photographer, recalled in 1912: "First, all the plain glass plates in various sizes, usually 8 x 10, had to be carefully cleaned and carried in dust-proof boxes. When ready for action, the plate was carefully coated with 'collodion' which carried in solution the 'excitants'—bromide and iodide of potassium, or ammonia, or cadmium. Collodion is made by the solution of gun-cotton in about equal parts of sulphuric ether and 95-proof alcohol. The salts above mentioned are then added, making the collodion a vehicle for obtaining the sensitive surface on the glass plate. The coating of plates was a delicate operation even in the ordinary well-organized studio. After coating the plate with collodion and letting the ether and alcohol evaporate to just the right degree of 'stickiness,' it was lowered carefully into a deep 'bath holder' which contained a solution of nitrate of silver about 60 degrees for quick field work. This operation created the sensitive condition of the plate, and had to be done in total darkness except subdued yellow light. When properly coated (from three to five minutes) the plate was put into a 'slide' or 'holder' and exposed to the action of the light in the camera. When exposed, it was returned to the darkroom and developed."

Mr. Rockwood described Brady's What-is-it wagon as an "ordinary delivery wagon of the period, much like the butcher's cart of today" with a "strong step attached at the rear and below the level of the wagon floor. A door was put on at the back, carefully hung so as to be lightproof. The door came down over the step, which was boxed in at the sides, making it a sort of well within the body of the wagon rather than a true step.

"The work of coating or sensitizing the plates and that of developing them was done from this well, in which there was just room enough to work. As the operator stood there the collodion was within reach of his right hand, in a special receptacle. On his left also was the holder of one of the baths. The chief developing bath was in front, with the tanks of various liquids stored in front of it again, and the space between it and the floor filled with plates.

"With such a wagon on a larger scale, large enough for men to sleep in front of the darkroom part, the phenomenal pictures of Brady were made possible. Brady risked his life many a time in order not to separate from this cumbrous piece of impedimenta.

"On exceptional occasions in very cold weather the life of a wet plate might be extended to nearly an hour on either side of the exposure, the coating or the development side, but ordinarily the work had to be done within a few minutes, and every minute of delay resulted in loss of brilliancy and depth in the negative."

Mr. F. M. Rood, who went through the war in New York's Ninety-Third regiment, knew how delicate the operation was.

"The plate 'flowed' with collodion was dipped at once in a bath of nitrate of silver, in water also iodized, remained there in darkness three to five minutes; still in darkness, it was taken out, drained, put in the plateholder, exposed, and developed in the dark-tent at once. The time between flowing the collodion and developing should not exceed eight or ten minutes. The developer was sulphate of iron solution and acetic acid, after which came a slight washing and fixing (to remove the surplus silver) with solution of cyanide of potassium; and then a final washing, drying, and varnishing. The surface (wet or dry), unlike a dry plate, could not be touched."[118]

J. Pitcher Spencer remembered, "We worked long with one of the foremost of Brady's men, and here let me doff my hat to the name of M. B. Brady—*few today are worthy to carry his camera case*, even as far as ability from the photographic standpoint goes. I was, in common with the 'Cape Codders,' following the ocean from 1859 to 1864; I was only home a few months—1863—and even then from our boys who came home invalided we heard of that grand picture-maker Brady, as they called him.

"When I made some views (with the only apparatus then known, the 'wet plate'), there came a large realization of some of the immense difficulties surmounted by those who made war-pictures. When you realize that the most sensitive of all the list of chemicals are requisite to make collodion, which must coat every plate, and that the very slightest breath might carry enough 'poison' across the plate being coated to make it produce a blank spot instead of some much desired effect, you may perhaps have a faint idea of the care requisite to produce a picture. Moreover, it took unceasing care to keep every bit of the apparatus, as well as each and every chemical, free from any contamination which might affect the picture. Often a breath of wind, no matter how gentle, spoiled the whole affair.

"Often, just as some fine result looked certain, a hot streak of air would not only spoil the plate, but put the instrument out of commission, by curling some part of it out of shape. In face of these, and hundreds of minor discouragements, the men imbued with vim and forcefulness by the "Only Brady" kept right along and today the world can enjoy these wonderful views as a result."[119]

BATTLES AND BUSINESS AS USUAL

IN the fall of 1862 Brady photographed the battle at Antietam, Md., one of the most picturesque and also one of the bloodiest battles of the entire war. The pictures Brady, Alexander Gardner and their assistants made that stirring September day did much to bring the grim reality of war into the American home.

The campaign which Lieutenant General James Longstreet described as "the keystone of the arch upon which the Confederate cause rested," began with Lee's army of fifty thousand crossing the Potomac at Leesburg, concentrating around Frederick, less than forty miles from Washington.[120]

As McClellan moved to meet him, Lee ordered Stonewall Jackson to take Harper's Ferry at the junction of the Shenandoah and the Potomac rivers. Stonewall marched through Frederick and crossed the Potomac, reaching Bolivar Heights on the 13th. Two days later Jackson's guns forced Harper's Ferry to surrender. But on the 17th, "Fighting Joe" Hooker, advancing to seize high ground, discovered a large part of Jackson's Corps in a cornfield three-quarters of a mile from the Hagerstown Pike. Hooker set up his guns and raked the Confederates with close-range canister shot, inflicting terrible losses.

Before long the cornfield was literally soaked with the blood of Jackson's men, who died before yielding up the cornstalks behind which they crouched, firing until their rifles grew too hot to handle. In the afternoon the Federals had pushed them back to a stone wall which stretched along the pike. Here they died in one last desperate rally.

Brady and Gardner, advancing with Hooker's forces, photographed the Confederates shortly after the Union forces had rolled over them in a series of wild charges. The dead lay sprawled on their backs, flung there only a short time before by Union bullets, their rifles, haversacks and bits of personal belongings strewn about the ground.

Brady's camera covered the campaign from the time the first covered wagons creaked across the low stone Antietam bridge to the wall on the pike where the last of Jackson's men died after fourteen hours of battle in which one hundred thousand men and five hundred pieces of artillery fought across the three miles of gentle valley and low hills.[121]

One of the best pictures of the battle was the scene at Dunker Church taken by Gardner. Burnside's men had pushed up Sharpsburg's Main Street and Shepherdstown Road, leaving behind several Confederate artillerymen sprawled about their pieces. The battered white church, the dead men stiffening in the chill air—everything that is war, is plain to see. One can almost sense the strange quiet which some veterans remembered, that followed in the wake of the fierce battle.

The poignant pictures stunned Americans. In the *Atlantic Monthly*, Oliver Wendell Holmes said of them: "These terrible mementoes of one of the most sanguinary conflicts of the war, we owe to the enterprise of Mr. Brady of New York. We ourselves were upon the battlefield upon the Saturday following the Wednesday when the battle took place. The photographs bear witness to the accuracy of some of our sketches . . . the 'ditch' encumbered with the dead as we saw it . . . the Colonel's gray horse . . . just as we saw him lying . . . let him who wishes to know what war is, look at these series of illustrations . . ."[122]

After Antietam Brady returned to Washington and Julia. While his assistants roamed the battlefields he prepared a group of prints to be submitted to an international photographic competition to be held that year in London.[123]

Brady's selections were inferior to the group of daguerreotypes he took to London in 1851. Perhaps this was because he had little time, between directing his vast enterprises, now rapidly consuming his fortune, and making tours of the battlefields, to devote to peacetime exhibits, which now seemed less important.

Trade journals and art critics pummeled him unmercifully. Only one voice was raised in his defense, that of the London correspondent of the New York *Express*, whose report in *Leslie's Illustrated Newspaper* of April 5, 1862, declared: "The three best and best known experts in this modern and money making art are Brady of Broadway, Nadar of Paris, and Silvy of London; and I name them, I think, in their order of merit, for I have not seen anything in London or Paris superior, if equal, in the shape of the sun pictures, to those done under the practiced hand of Brady.[124]

But Mr. B. of Broadway had little time to consider the critics' complaints. His friend, Major General Ambrose Everett Burnside, a West Point graduate who had invented a breech-loading rifle, possessor of the proud side-whiskers which would later become part of the American language as "sideburns," had been given command of the Army of the Potomac and another battle was shaping up on the maps. Brady decided to join his friend and be ready to bring his camera to war again.

The unfortunate battle of Fredericksburg was evidently planned—as Baldy Smith once irreverently observed—before the fireplace by Burnside and his favorite servant, Robert, with whom he had long talks about the war, "while crack cavalry units kept guard at the front door."[126]

One bright fall morning the disheartened Army of the Potomac rose to its feet and ponderously started in pursuit of Lee, who had massed his entire army along Stafford Heights on the east bank of the Rappahannock opposite Fredericksburg. At the time Burnside did not believe the Confederates would put up much of a fight for the town, and he permitted the crossing of the river to be delayed for nearly a month while the Rebels dug in. By October their lines stretched for five miles along the range of hills which spread like a brown and gold crescent in the autumn sun, around the lowland where the city lay. The strongest Confederate position was on the slopes of Marye's Heights, which rose in the rear of the town. Along the foot of the hill was a four-foot stone wall bounding the eastern side of Telegraph Road, running north and south. It was here that Tim O'Sullivan and Brady would make some of their most memorable pictures.

Lee placed a large force behind the wall while higher up, stretching along the hills, was massed the main army. Brady stayed at headquarters with Burnside and

before the army moved one of his assistants took a picture of him seated outside a tent with Burnside.

Then at Warrenton, on the eve of the big attack, Brady took a picture of Burnside as he stared toward the Confederate lines and the low stone wall behind which lay the sharpshooters in gray.[127]

We can only guess what Brady and his assistants did on the bright cold morning of December 11. Probably all were up before dawn, his assistants busy coating the plates in the dark, uncomfortable What-is-it wagon, while Brady prepared his camera and prepared to follow the army.

On the other side of the river, Lee's men, stamping their feet to keep warm in the early morning cold, peered through the river fog for a glimpse of the enemy. When the sun came out to lick away the mist they could see Burnside's blue legions and thousands of white patches—tents, wagons and ambulances. Somewhere along the line an officer's sword flashed downward and the siege guns and field artillery, wheel to wheel, crashed into a solid sheet of flame. As the hours passed, Fredericksburg was methodically reduced to a rubble. As Brady's later pictures showed, every house was a target; every street was pockmarked with shell holes.

For two days Union troops poured across the swaying pontoon bridges. Attack; retreat. Again, attack; retreat. On December 13, General Thomas F. Meagher's famous Irish Brigade stormed Marye's Heights. The riflemen behind the wall watched the gallant blue wave move up the hill in a crouching run. Each rifleman on the wall picked off a blue coat. The Irishmen came on. Men fell, rose and fell again. Others silently slumped over.

The first wave broke and retreated, still firing. The second attack swept back up the hill. Confederate rifles spoke; again the Union blue covered the trampled grass. Again they fell back, this time to the pontoon bridges. Across the river, only two hundred and fifty men, out of a thousand-odd, now answered the beat of the drum. Brady found a few survivors and gathered them together for their last picture. The next morning some would be dead.[128]

Six times during the two days Burnside sent his troops to storm Marye's Heights and each time the assault was blunted and broken by Lee's riflemen kneeling behind the wall. The losses were horrible. The tall dry grass caught fire and as the survivors of each charge retreated they left the wounded men screaming in agony in the flames.

The nights were worse. The temperatures fell below zero and at sunup, as the troops moved upward for another attack, they were saluted as they passed by blue arms, frozen in their death agonies.

Brady and his assistants took many pictures of the battle, but at last they were ordered to return to their wagons to pack their equipment; Burnside had called off the attack. His casualty list was long—12,653 dead. Lee's loss was 5,377.[129]

The campaign over, Brady hurried back to Washington, sending Gardner back to the field to take a picture of Lincoln on October 8, 1862, when the President visited the camps at Antietam.[130] After Lincoln had spoken at length with John McClernand, soon to be an unhappy bridegroom-general with Grant at Vicksburg, he posed with McClernand and Allan Pinkerton, in a bowler hat and checked shirt. Not long before, Pinkerton, the mysterious "Major Allen," had arrested the Confederate spy, Rose O'Neal Greenhow. He had gathered evidence against her by standing on the shoulders of one of his operatives and peering into her Washington living room where she was entertaining a Federal officer who had just given her a number of maps.[131] Brady, learning of this, had hurried over to the Old Capitol Prison to pose the spy with her daughter in the courtyard.

In the late summer of 1862 a collection of Brady's best war views and portraits found its way to England. The unusual photographs stirred at least one writer on the London *Times* to a perceptive critical analysis of Brady's work, later reprinted in the *Photographic Times*, September 15, 1862.

The unknown author of the article, in discussing the role of the war photographer, also disclosed that Roger Fenton was not the first photographer to take his camera to the battlefield in the Crimea: "Mr. Simpson was out before him (Fenton) in the Crimea and it is no disparagement to the former to say that the scenes in the trenches were much more interesting than the likenesses or groups or other works of the photographer though they were more ideal or less actual."

The article continued:

"We have before us a collection of photographs by one of the best known of American photographers, Mr. Brady of New York, which includes, however, not merely war scenes but a number of interesting portraits of the most eminent Americans and of some strangers.

"First there are two plates of the *Monitor,* one showing her deck, which seems raised a vast distance above the water, whereas it is only a few inches, and the cupola or revolving tower with the shot marks upon it from the *Merrimac's* guns. . . . The other represents the crew on the deck in easy groups . . . a set of stout, brawny fellows in no particular uniform and rather unkempt of whom a few have the air of the genuine 'old salt.'

"For guns and the like the lens is well adapted in experienced hands and here we have a striking 'picture of the effect caused by the bursting of a 100-lb. shell' on board the Confederate gunboat *Teazer* which was captured by the Federals, deck stove in, iron stanchions gone, a great crater in the hold, machinery torn into ribands . . . with its engines exposed on deck and frail scantling.

"Mr. Brady's artist went down to Richmond and has sent us some views which are of interest, but generally the sun of Virginia was too powerful and the appearance of snow is produced on most of the photographs and a whiteness of color diminishes the effect.

"Groups of wounded out in the open sun at Savage's Station, on the railroad to Richmond, 'the house where Washington wooed his Martha,' burnt by the Federals when they abandoned the line of the Pamunkey; Virginian family wooden houses; the Confederate works at Yorktown; the ruins of Hampton, destroyed by Magruder; batteries of artillery, horses and all, which should be a very close object of study to our Horse Guards, who might get an idea of what the Federal cavalry are like, by examining the appearance, state, equipment and horses of the field artillery which are unquestionably the best part of the Federal army. These and the last are all very worthy of attention. It can be seen from them that the work executed by the Corps at Yorktown was very slovenly but that nothing that was ever seen of the most slovenly European soldier can equal the utter want of military smartness in the Federal army. Men with unbuttoned coats and open collars and all sorts of headgear are seated, with their overalls gathered halfway up the leg, in their saddle, with an attempt to fall in line, which renders their shortcomings more obvious.

"The most agreeable subject in the volume perhaps is one of a Confederate lieutenant of the Washington family and name—for all the representatives of the *Pater Patriae* are and were Secessionists—who was taken prisoner, sitting beside his original friend and relation, Captain Custis, of the U. S. Army, while a negro boy, barefoot, with hands clasped, is at the feet and between the knees of his master, with an expression of profound grief on his shining face. The captive, in his close gray uniform, sits up erect with a pure, direct fighting face and head; The Federal, a fair-haired, thoughtful-looking man, looks much more like a prisoner; the *teterrima causa belli,* who appears to think only of his master, is touching enough.

"We can see here that the houses in which the better sort of people live in this part of the old Dominion would not content the humblest of our tenant-farmers or yeomen; that the Federal soldiers do not improve in appearance during the war and that their attention to the uniform is of the smallest, and we form some idea of the difficulties of fighting in such a country when we perceive that every view is fringed by woods.

"Continuing to the volume of portraits the eye is first arrested by Mr. Lincoln, sitting in company with an inkbottle, at a table which does not conceal that foot, which he is so often said by the papers 'to put down' on various questions—an odd, quaint face, sagacious notwithstanding the receding brow and kind despite the coarse heavy-lipped mouth but with such capillary arrangements that in combination with the long-limbed narrow body and great extremities there is a gorilla expression produced by the *ensemble*.

"Next is Hannibal Hamlin, Vice President, who is chiefly interesting on account of what he might become. Turn over and Mr. Stanton gives a sitting for his head alone, the lines of which do not stand comparison very well with the clear outline of Mr. Seward's features next to it. Why did not Mr. Brady give the full face of Mr. Seward so that one could see his eye? In other respects, the likeness, though it does not convey that air of 'cunning and conceit' which Prince Napoleon's attaché attributed in his *feuilleton* to the Secretary of State, is characteristic and true.

"Pass over Mr. Bates and we come to Mr. Chase, who is standing with one hand outside his coat, over his breeches pocket, and the other on a plaster of Paris pedestal, looking as though he were waiting for someone to lend him a little money and expecting it too. He has one of the best heads of the Cabinet, though one cannot help remembering he has a defect in his eye and oddly enough so has General Butler and so has Mr. Jefferson Davis.

"It is not too much to say that any stranger would be struck by the immense superiority of the heads and expression of Mr. Davis, of General Polk, of Beauregard, of Stonewall Jackson and Lee to most of the Federal chiefs of whom few are striking in any way. McClellan looks small and anxious and unhappy; Blenker stands like a soldier and has an air of being one, and Burnside seems calm and self-possessed and capable. Halleck's head is intellectual but the vision is tricky and the lower jaw feeble; Pope is a stout, florid, sanguine-looking man, like a German bass singer in fine condition; and there is no other to speak of, except perhaps Meagher and McDowell in the list of soldiers worth looking at a second time, after we have passed Banks, the unhappy recipient of Stonewall Jackson's favours. The few naval men in the book contrast advantageously with many of the soldiers but some of the best of the latter are not here. 'Stonewall' Jackson's likeness is something like that of Ney. . . .

"From the Confederate soldiers there is but a thickness of cardboard to the Federal journalists of whom the most remarkable thing is that they all seem to be above the age for liability to conscription. Literary men follow a group of the clergy and the fine faces of Longfellow and Motley are among the best in the collection. Jefferson Davis, who comes after a batch of Federal politicians, is back to back with Jerrit Smith and Mr. Stephens, the Vice President of the Southern Confederacy, supports Mr. Charles Sumner. The portrait of Chief Justice Taney attracts one not merely on account of the air of the venerable old man but because it is the likeness of the Judge who will in all probability prove the last that ever sat on the bench as head of the Supreme Court of the United States and in whose person was demonstrated the complete worthlessness of that palladium of the American Constitution when the storm arose and the sword was unfurled by violent and unscrupulous men.

"*Place aux dames.* In the photograph of Mrs. Lincoln the loyalty and skill of Mr. Brady are as conspicuous as his gallantry in adapting the focus to the subject, but he has treated the wife of the President, who is of course the 'first lady of the United States,' much better than he has Miss Lane, who did the honors of the White House for President Buchanan and who won such praise for her discharge of them. . . .

"But the portraits are of lasting attractiveness, though we were too apt when looking at them now to forget that we are scanning the features of men who will be famous hereafter as actors in the greatest drama which the world has seen in these later ages."

One of Brady's wartime sitters, a twenty-year-old officer, left for history a charming account of President Lincoln posing for a "standing" at Brady's Washington gallery on a wintry day in 1863. His little-known story of that day is an amusing picture of Lincoln posing for Brady's camera.[132]

The young officer, John L. Cunningham, of the 118th New York Volunteer Infantry (Adirondack Regiment), was then in charge of the guard at the Old Capitol Prison, where Brady had photographed Rose O'Neal Greenhow.

On February 12, 1863, he was assigned to provost duty at Camp Adirondack, near Findley Hospital north of the Capitol. Cunningham was a friend of Congressman-elect Orlando Kellogg from his district. When Kellogg paid a visit to the capital he stayed with Cunningham and then took him to see President Lincoln, whom he knew.

They stayed "at least a half hour," with Lincoln, his feet on the desk, spinning yarns and reminiscing of past and happier days. More than once Kellogg made a move as if to go, but Lincoln made him stay. The young officer noticed that Lincoln, although he looked "pleasant," did not laugh so heartily as Kellogg. In fact, the President "scarcely smiled."

His secretary, John Nicolay, kept bringing in calling cards and looking sternly at the visitors. Lincoln would glance at the cards, then lay them aside. When Kellogg protested he said, "These gentlemen can wait—they all want something. You want nothing and I enjoy your visit."

Cunningham's visit to Brady's gallery when Lincoln was present must have taken place the week of February 13th, for Cunningham notes in his diary that he had received orders to move on the 20th. He and his fellow officer Riggs went off to Brady's gallery "just before we left Washington and when we were under orders to be ready to move."

When they arrived at Brady's they received numbered cards. While they were waiting for their numbers to be called Nicolay came into the reception room and "said to the man in charge that the President had been asked by Brady to pose for a standing full-length photograph and that he was in his carriage outside and would come in if the matter could have immediate attention."

Here is what happened, as Cunningham noted in his diary:

"We waited no longer, but bounded into the operating room to be there when the President came. Shortly after, the office man appeared with President Lincoln and requested that we waive our priority in his behalf.

"Lieutenant Riggs replied, rather dramatically, 'Certainly, our Commander-in-Chief comes first everywhere.'

"Mr. Lincoln thanked us and said in substance, 'Soldiers come first everywhere these days. Black coats are at a discount in the presence of the blue and I recognize the merit of the discount.'

"The operator was a Frenchman with a decided accent. He said to the President that there was a considerable call for full-length standing photographs of him. The President, joking, inquired whether this could be done with a single-sized negative.

" 'You see I am six four in my stockings,' he said.

"The operator said it could be done and left to arrange for the 'standing.'

"The President said to us that he had lately seen a very long, or rather a wide landscape photograph and that he wondered if there was a camera large enough to take in such an area, but on close examination he found that it had been taken in parts and nicely joined together, and he thought, perhaps, this method might be necessary for his 'full-length landscape.'

"The operator announced he was ready and then went into the camera room but the President stood where he could see and hear him. He asked [the operator] if he should stand as if addressing a jury, 'with my arms like this,' stretching out his right arm.

"The operator came to him several times, placing the President's arms by his side, turning his head, adjusting his clothes, etc.

" 'Just look natural,' said the operator.

" 'That is just what I would like to avoid,' Mr. Lincoln replied.

"In the meantime each of us had tried on the President's hat and it fitted Lieutenant Riggs finely.

"The President came back to us and told us of a custom-sawmill built in the early days out in his part of the country, a very up-to-date, single-gate mill, of which the owner was proud. One day a farmer brought from some distance an oak log, by ox-team, to be sawed into planks, and he waited for the product. The log was adjusted and the saw started and all went lovely—for a while. A crash came! It happened that in the early days of the oak tree an iron spike had been driven into it and covered from sight by later growth but the saw found it.

"The saw was broken and other damage done to the mill, to the grief of the owner. He shut off the water and while sorrowfully investigating the cause of the disaster, the farmer anxiously inquired, 'Say, yer ain't spiled the plank, hav yer?'

" 'Goldarn yer old log—just look what it has done to the mill,' replied the mill man.

" 'That camera man,' continued the President, 'seemed anxious about the picture, but, boys, I don't know what might happen to the camera.'

"The operator came back from the darkroom, holding up the negative to the window, and asked the President to look at it, and suggested that it was very natural.

" 'Yes,' said the President, 'that is my objection. The cameras are painfully truthful,' saying this with an assumed solemnity.

"Two other negatives, with little change in pose, were taken, and the President was asked if he had any choice. He replied, 'They look alike as three peas.'

"The operator then mentioned that Secretary Seward had recently visited the Gallery for a sitting and the President asked, 'Did he tell you any stories?'

"The operator said he did not and the President said, 'I did not suppose he did, for Mr. Seward is limited to a couple of stories, from which repeating he believes are true.'

"He then said that he had recently heard a story about Mr. Seward that, whether true or not, was 'a good one on him.' He related it in substance to the effect that during the then last presidential campaign, Mr. Seward was engaged to speak at a 'pole raising and mass meeting' affair and was asked to make a later date because the pole could not be ready for the raising; the point being that they considered the raising of the pole of more consequence than Mr. Seward's presence and speech.

"He told the story with some animation and with bits of interspersed humor.

"Mr. Lincoln seemed happy and carefree that morning and we thought he really enjoyed his hour or so at the Gallery. Mr. Nicolay, who had driven away with the carriage, returned for Mr. Lincoln. Mr. Lincoln again thanked us for our courtesy in waiving our first claim to gallery service, and gave us each a hearty handshake and departed.

"We went to the window and looking upon the street, saw him seated in quite a common-looking barouche with his secretary and drive away. Nothing to indicate that this man, President of the United States, Commander-in-Chief of its Army and Navy, was other than an ordinary citizen. . ."

The winter passed into spring with Brady having little reason for peace of mind. Day by day he lived under a gradually mounting burden of debt and trouble, climaxed when Alexander Gardner notified him he was leaving to open his own gallery.

It had been four years since Gardner had been brought from Glasgow by Brady and some sort of a warm friendship must have sprung up between these "shy and gentle" men.

We don't know the reason for their break, nor can we in our imagination reconstruct the scene from a few scraps of information which have passed down through the years by letter or legend. There is reason to believe that Gardner left Brady's service because of a dispute over wages or because Brady simply could not pay him. This is borne out by the fact that Brady gave Gardner a duplicate set of his battlefield wet plates, possibly in lieu of past wages.[133]

There was plenty of opportunity for both to exchange harsh words, but it is to their credit they remained silent. Perhaps they even remained casual friends, someone in Brady's studio, either Brady himself or one of his assistants, thought enough of Gardner's new studio to take a picture of it.

This was a crucial year in Brady's life, yet we know little of his personal affairs. It is frustrating to attempt to investigate them. We know Edward Anthony had given him "unlimited" credit to keep his photographic teams on the battlefields, we know his own money, if not already exhausted, dwindled fast, yet we have no knowledge of the inner man. Was he discouraged, disheartened, embittered? And what of Julia, who waited for him patiently in their apartment at the National Hotel in Washington? Did she plead with him each time he returned from the front, to abandon this foolhardy venture before it destroyed them both? Did she write him tender, fearful letters and did he read them with a full heart by the light of the campfires at Burnside's headquarters while his assistants were storing away the wet plates with their images of the dead across the river before the stone wall at Marye's Heights. . . ?

We do not know. Though generals and privates paused in the fighting to write letters home or to pen memoirs, Brady was silent. In the fifties he was a trim, goateed shadow standing, with his camera, against the background of a lusty young Republic; in the sixties he was the same shadow, wearing a linen duster and a straw hat, moving, with his camera, against a backdrop of battlesmoke.

This we do know. Physical and financial hardship and an intimate acquaintance with war and death did not deter him from his ideal of documenting the American Civil War with a camera. If anything, he redoubled his efforts.

In the spring he and his assistants again joined the Army of the Potomac, now under the command of "Fighting Joe" Hooker. In Washington, while convalescing from his foot wound, Hooker had played his political cards neatly.[134]

On January 26, after a great deal of behind-the-scenes maneuvering, Hooker had been appointed Commander-in-Chief of the army with this advice from Lincoln: "Beware of rashness; with energy and sleepless vigilance go forward and give us victories. . ."

Hooker's strategy was to deploy a portion of the army as decoys for Lee while the rest of his men occupied the vicinity of Chancellorsville, a little over two miles south of the Rappahannock River and about ten miles west of Fredericksburg. Brady, Tim O'Sullivan, Alexander Gardner, and Captain A. J. Russell probably joined the army sometime in April. Before the big movement began Brady and his men were busy taking staff pictures; Hooker on his horse, General George Stoneman and his staff, just before he led his ten thousand sabres on a daring but futile raid to cut Lee's railroad communications with Richmond; Major General John Sedgwick and his staff, who were to win undying glory in a few days before Marye's Heights, and many others.[135]

Then, on the morning of the 27th, Hooker's campaign was put in motion when Sedgwick was sent east of Fredericksburg to distract Lee's attention.[136] Cook fires were left burning in the camp and a force left behind to give the idea that the main army was still there; instead, it was moving to Chancellorsville. The strategy was partially successful. On the 30th, except for Sedgwick's First, Third and Sixth Corps, Hooker's army was planted on Lee's left flank. But Lee and Jackson were helped by Hooker's strange command of May 2nd to Meade and Slocum, on Lee's left and right flanks, to pull back to their old positions after a day of furious fighting in which they had pushed Lee back. The Confederate master of strategy, "Stonewall" Jackson, promptly moved into the abandoned Federal works and, in defiance of all accepted theories of military strategy, divided his force in the face of the enemy. Jackson led his foot cavalry in what Hooker thought was a retreat. But Old Jack promptly swung about and made for the right flank of the Federals at a point where the Eleventh Corps was commanded by General Oliver Howard.

With the Rebel battle cry shrilling in their throats, Jackson's troops burst out of the woods to cut Howard's lines to pieces. Nightfall closed in over a battlefield littered with the dead and dying and in a small farmhouse near Guinea Station the great Stonewall Jackson lay dying with A. P. Hill's name on his lips, "Tell Hill he must come up."

That night Sedgwick received his orders from a

troubled Joe Hooker. Between him and the main army stood the Confederates, flushed with victory. Immediately before him was Fredericksburg and the terrible Marye's Heights, which had destroyed Burnside the previous winter.

Sedgwick moved at once. He told his officers he was going to strike at Fredericksburg. Apparently Brady accompanied the Sixth Corps, as most of his pictures of the battle were made on the ground recaptured by the Confederates only a few hours after the pictures had been taken.

At eleven o'clock the Sixth Corps crossed the river and assaulted Marye's Heights; twenty thousand men, wave after wave, swept up the slope, slippery with blood and trampled grass, toward the wall where Lee's riflemen, packed in ranks of four by four and six by six, met them with a deadly fire.

The first assault crumbled less than twenty-five yards before the wall, with thirty-six per cent of the Fifth Wisconsin and the Sixth Maine wiped out within six minutes. Then a flanking attack was launched. With a roar on "On, Wisconsin" and "Maine, forward," the blue waves rushed upward, wavered, buckled, gathered strength, then rolled over the wall with bayonets flashing brightly one moment, dull and red the next.

The wall was won. The Confederates, fighting like madmen, were driven back. The guns must have been still smoking when Brady and his assistants appeared early that afternoon in the creaking What-is-it wagon. Brady evidently was surveying the battlefield with General Herman Haupt, Chief of the Bureau of Military Railroads, and W. W. Wright, superintendent of the Military Railroad, who are in his pictures.[137]

Here he captured the grim reality of the battle's aftermath: the Confederate dead as they had fallen, one young trooper, his head thrown back, staring with open eyes at the clear sky; his young comrades, hunched against the wall; the dead horses and smashed guns of the famous Washington Artillery, which had raked the assaulting Federals, shown after they had received a direct hit from the Second Massachusetts siege guns planted across the river at Falmouth to support Sedgwick.

We don't know how long Brady and his men stayed on the Heights, but if it was overnight surely they hurried back down the slope the next afternoon when another force, detached by Lee from the main army at Chancellorsville, dislodged Sedgwick's men on the afternoon of May 4th.

Gardner was now in the field, the Anthonys had T. C. Roche and other fine cameramen in their employ, but it was "Brady's pictures" which held the country spellbound. As *Harper's Weekly* pointed out, "Again we are indebted to the enterprising Mr. Brady. . ."

The Tenth Street gallery in New York was still a big part of Brady's life and business during the war years, especially in 1863, when many a notable figure found his or her way to Brady's of Broadway for a photograph.[138]

Among them was a bemedaled admiral and several muscular seamen of the Russian Imperial Navy, which sailed into New York harbor one fall day in 1863, to startle the country and bewilder the admiralties of England and France.[139]

It was shortly after the Federal disaster at Chickamauga, September 19-20. Sixteen thousand Union casualties and Brady's battlefield pictures had cast a deep gloom over the country. Four days later New Yorkers strolling along the Battery were astounded to see a huge screw frigate, bristling with fifty-one guns, her rigging black with seamen, steam up the bay and drop anchor in the Hudson River, in line with the Trinity Church spire. She was the *Alexander Nevski*, flapship of the Russian Atlantic squadron, commanded by Rear Admiral Lisovski.

She was soon followed by the *Peresvet*, a forty-eight gun frigate. They were followed two days later by the *Variag*, a slim and beautiful sloop of 2,100 tons and fourteen guns. Within three weeks the *Almaz* and the *Osliaba* steamed past the Battery and anchored. The *Osliaba* had reached New York with a crew of 450 seaman and marine artillerymen after a voyage of three months. The others had sailed from Kronstadt. While the Atlantic squadron was sailing into New York, Russia's Pacific squadron was dropping anchor and moving into San Francisco Bay.

On September 23, 1863, Secretary of the Navy Gideon Welles welcomed the Russians to New York in a letter to the Russian minister: ". . . The presence in our waters of a squadron belonging to his Imperial Majesty's Navy cannot but be a source of pleasure and happiness to our countrymen. . ."[140]

Welles, a conscientious diarist, also jotted down his personal impressions: "In sending them [the ships] to this country there is something significant. What will be its effect on France and the French policy we shall learn in due time. It may moderate; it may exasperate; God bless the Russians. . ."[141]

Harper's Weekly described the warships off the Battery: "The frigate *Osliaba* is unlike the other two; she has more the appearance of one of the first of the heavy screw ships built in the European dock yards. Her bluff bows and counter do not give evidence of great speed; but she is doubtless a fair goer and fine sea boat. The two steam corvettes, or sloops, as we term them, *Variag* and *Vitiaz*, are apparently very superior vessels. They are fully equal in tonnage to the steamers in our service of the class of the *Brooklyn*, *Richmond* and others, and carry very serviceable batteries. They are evidently constructed for speed and have engines of full power. All these vessels are ship-rigged and are heavily sparred, so much so that if their smokestacks were out of sight you would hardly suppose them to be propelled by steam.

"The batteries of these ships are of formidable character, although all smooth-bored guns. They are of one caliber, throwing a solid shot of sixty pounds' weight, and of two classes, the long and medium, weighing about sixty and eighty hundredweight."

On Thursday, October 1, the City of New York gave the Russians a royal reception. At ten o'clock the Committee of the Common Council went down the Bay in the steamer *Andrews* to present the resolutions adopted by the city to Rear Admiral Lisovski. As they set off from the foot of West 23rd Street a band "regaled the ear with performances of popular airs."[142]

It was a bright day and the city fathers intended to make the most of it. They ordered the *Andrews* to make a circuit south of Governor's Island and to come up on the west side of the French and English squadrons. As the *Andrews* passed the French they struck up the first chords of "The Marseillaise," but as there was no recognition from the French the council ordered the band to stop. The English squadrons were greeted with "God Save the King," but again the irritated city fathers shouted to the band to stop after a lack of response from the English band.

The Russian men-of-war were the next to be visited. As the *Andrews* came up they could see the rigging filled with curious seamen. As they drew near a Russian rendition of "Yankee Doodle" came across the water and the captain of the *Andrews* hailed the Russians.

A sixteen-oared gig, "manned by sinew and muscle acquired on the steppes of Tartary," brought the city fathers to the Russian flagship, which had a deck, as one man later recalled, "large enough to accommodate a fair-sized army and with ordnance heavy enough to blow up Fort Sumter."

The guns, incidentally, were American-made, out of Pittsburgh. The admiral, wearing his many decorations, and speaking in broken English, welcomed the city fathers and escorted them on a tour of the ship. After a seventy-one gun salute had shaken the entire lower part of the city, the committee with the admiral and his officers returned to 23rd Street, where they landed for the parade.

From a *Harper's Weekly* reporter, "perched in Brady's front window," we know it was a typical New York Broadway reception. The buildings were decorated with colored bunting and Russian and American flags. The admiral and his officers and some of the crew rolled along in carriages, bowing, waving and gesturing to the cheering thousands. After a reception at City Hall Read Admiral Lisovski and his officers and several members of the crew were taken to Brady's Tenth Street gallery. Here the admiral posed for several pictures alone and then some members of the crew were lined up to be photographed. The pictures are believed to have been taken by one of his New York "operators." Brady, at this time, was busy in Washington.

Weeks of celebrations were climaxed by a gigantic reception given in honor of the Russians by the City of New York. It was held at the Astor Irving Hall, next to Delmonico's, who prepared and served the dinner. The New York *World* reporter who covered the event was impressed with the gargantuan capacity of the czar's officers. "For the sake of history" he listed what was consumed that evening: twelve thousand oysters (10,000 poulette and 2,000 pickled); twelve monster salmon (30 pounds each); twelve hundred game birds; two hundred chickens; a thousand pounds of tenderloin; a hundred pyramids of pastry; a thousand large loaves and three and a half thousand bottles of wine.[143]

The Russian fleet stayed in the New York and San Francisco harbors for seven months. It was assumed that as traditional allies, they had come to the aid of the United States to frighten off any major powers who might be tempted to step in on the side of the Confederacy. Actually, this was far from the truth. Russia was afraid that because of her treatment of the Poles, France and Great Britain might join forces and bottle up her fleet. Down through the years there have been legends of sealed "secret orders" held by Lisovski which he was to break open should France and England join the Confederacy. In no official documents yet unearthed has there been the slightest hint of such orders. Lincoln, his two secretaries, Secretary Welles and Cassius Clay, who served as minister to Russia (1861-62 and 1863-69), knew nothing of them.[144]

Brady's "register" of his New York gallery during the war years gives the names of other celebrated customers during that period. Brady apparently spent little time in New York, evidently preferring to let the business he had established so firmly go along on its own momentum, while he devoted his time and energies to the project closest to his heart—photographing the Civil War.[145]

The New York gallery had no difficulty in attracting customers. From February, 1863, to April, 1865, the month of Appomattox, a total of five thousand, four hundred and twelve pictures were taken of the world-famous and ordinary citizens.[146]

On February 14, 1863, the Harper Brothers, James and John, the Long Island farm boys who started the famous publishing firm in 1817 as J. & J. Harper, and the other two brothers, Joseph Wesley and Fletcher, who later joined the growing business, marched four strong into Brady's studio and had their picture taken.

The portrait symbolizes the unity of the four brothers, who referred to themselves as the Cheeryble Brothers after *Nicholas Nickleby*, which was published in 1839.

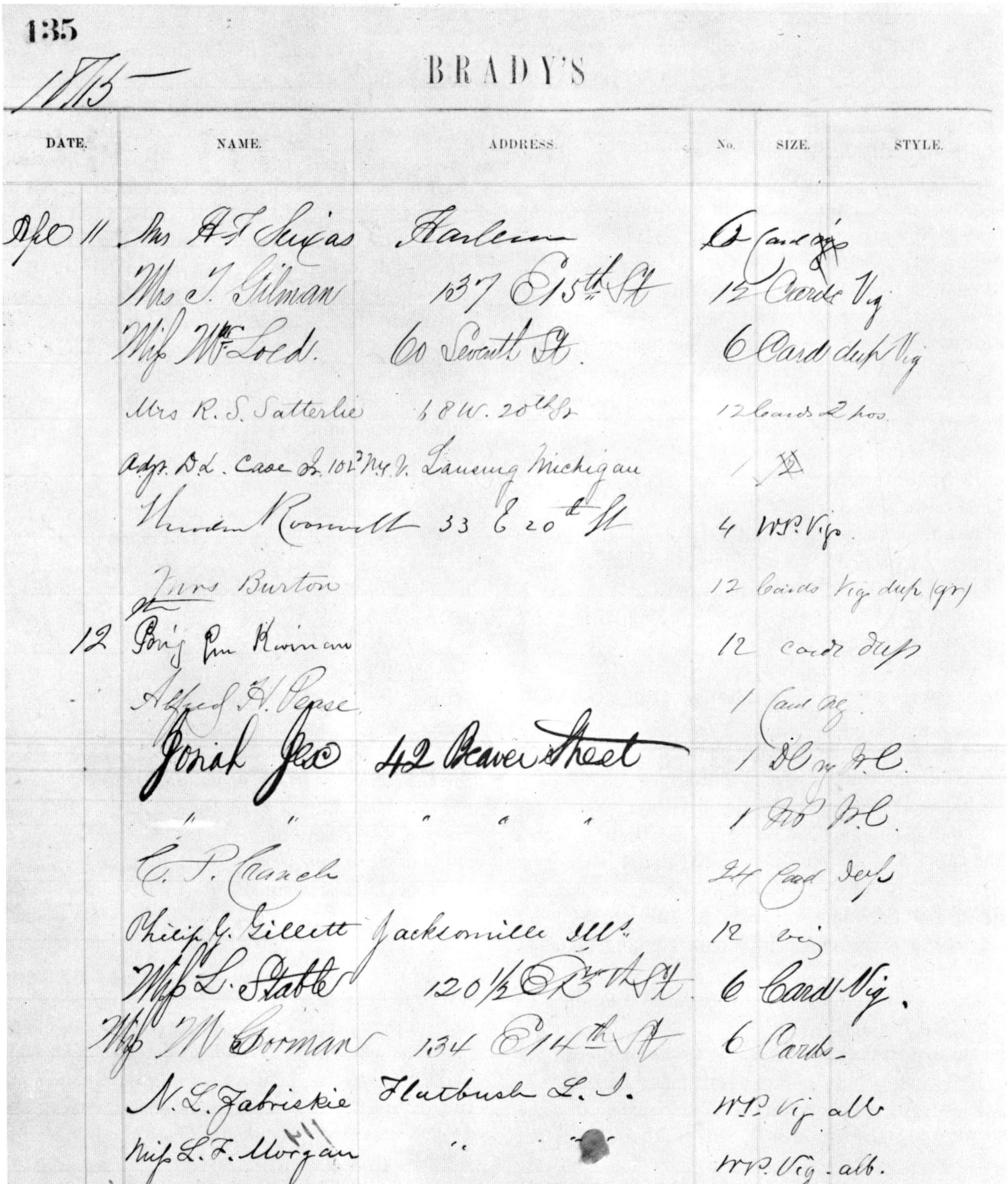

135

1865—

BRADY'S

DATE.	NAME.	ADDRESS.	No.	SIZE.	STYLE.
Apl 11	Mrs A. F. Seixas	Harlem	6	Cards	
	Mrs J. Gilman	137 E 15th St	12	Cards Vig	
	Miss Wm Lord	60 Seventh St	6	Card dup Vig	
	Mrs R. S. Satterlie	18 W. 20th St	12	Cards 2 pos	
	Adjt. D. L. Case Jr. 102 N.Y.V.	Lansing Michigan	1		
	Theodore Roosevelt	33 E 20th St	4	W.P. Vig	
	Mrs Burton		12	Cards Vig dup (gr)	
12			12	cards dup	
	Alfred H. Pease		1	Card Vig	
	Josiah Lee	42 Beaver Street	1		
	"	"	1		
	C. T. Church		24	Card dup	
	Philip G. Gillett	Jacksonville Ills	12	vig	
	Miss L. Stable	120½ E	6	Card Vig.	
	Miss M. Gorman	134 E 14th St	6	Cards	
	N. L. Zabriskie	Flatbush L. I.		W.P. Vig alb	
	Miss L. F. Morgan	"		W.P. Vig. alb.	
	Mrs J. T. Bigelow	Montreal	6	Cards dup.	
	Mrs J. M. Storey	74 West 11th St	1		
	Mrs C. A. May	259 Fifth Ave	1		
	Mc Ryan		12	cards	
	M Cochrane	64 W. 19th St			

Fig. 24. From Brady's New York *Register,* 1865. Note signature of Theodore Roosevelt, probably the father of President Theodore Roosevelt, who was then only seven years old. Note also the Brady signatures at the bottom. *Manuscript Division, New York Public Library.*

FRAME.	ENGAGEMENTS. Sit for Artist.		REMARKS.	PRICES.				Printed.	Done.	Delivered.	No. of Negatives.	Charged in Day Book.	PAID.	
	Date.	Hour. Comp'td.		Box.	Frame.	Pho.	Total.						Fo.	C.B.
						3					12640		✓	
			of Child entered before			16					1264	208/19	paid	
			of Capt. Luard		3	4			✓ ✓ ✓			208/19	paid	
			of Lieut Satterlee			6			✓ ✓ ✓				✓	
			Copy of West Point Album sent to H. Rof.										✓	
			copy from Dauret.			13.							✓	
						5							✓	✓
						4							✓	
			For Rosetta, E.A.			—	—				12142		—	
			of Lady	7		10						48/24		
			of Child			30	}14.							
													✓	
						7					12643	210/19	pd	
						5			✓		12644	210/19	paid	
						4					12645	210/19	paid	
						7 }14.						210/19	pd	
													pd	
						4.							✓	
						75.—							✓	
			of Col. May			300							✓	
			Herald											
			M.B. Brady											
			M.B. Brady											

When they walked into Brady's gallery that winter's day their publishing firm was forty-six years old. The last of the brothers died in 1877 and, as in life, they lie side by side in Green-Wood Cemetery, Brooklyn.

Royalty followed literature. Lord Hartington was sent to Brady's New York gallery by Secretary of State Seward. ("Send the bill to Secretary of State Seward as soon as possible.") The government paid $12.50 for seven pictures.

One of the Van Rensselaer girls came down from Albany to pose "and will take a dozen." James Roosevelt, to become the father of Franklin D. Roosevelt, had his photograph taken. George R. Pendleton, who would toss his hat in the presidential ring, put his handsome head in the clasp of the "immobilizer" and bought fifty copies, probably for his admirers and constituents.

Evidently there was always a steady stream of officers and soldiers coming and going at the gallery for *carte de visite* pictures, imperials and portraits. Generals brought their staffs and families; the graduating classes of West Point made annual excursions to Brady's gallery for their class pictures and many a future American general stared stiffly into the lens of Brady's cameras as a cadet.

A banner day for the gallery was November 21, 1864. Grant came to the New York gallery from City Point. There is no doubt that Brady was on hand personally and one can catch a glimpse of the excitement in the studio from the register; on the top of the page for that day is written, "U. S. Grant, City Point, Va." and a line is drawn down the page as if to indicate that the gallery's staff devoted that day entirely to Grant.

Royalty, politicians, diplomats, wealthy women and great generals—all continued to visit Mr. B.'s studio in the war years. In one notation there is a sense of loneliness, of homesickness which reaches across the years. An artillery private, "H. Battery, Valley of the Shenandoah," had his picture taken a few days before Christmas, 1863. Under the listing "When to be Delivered," someone wrote: "Christmas if possible. . . ."

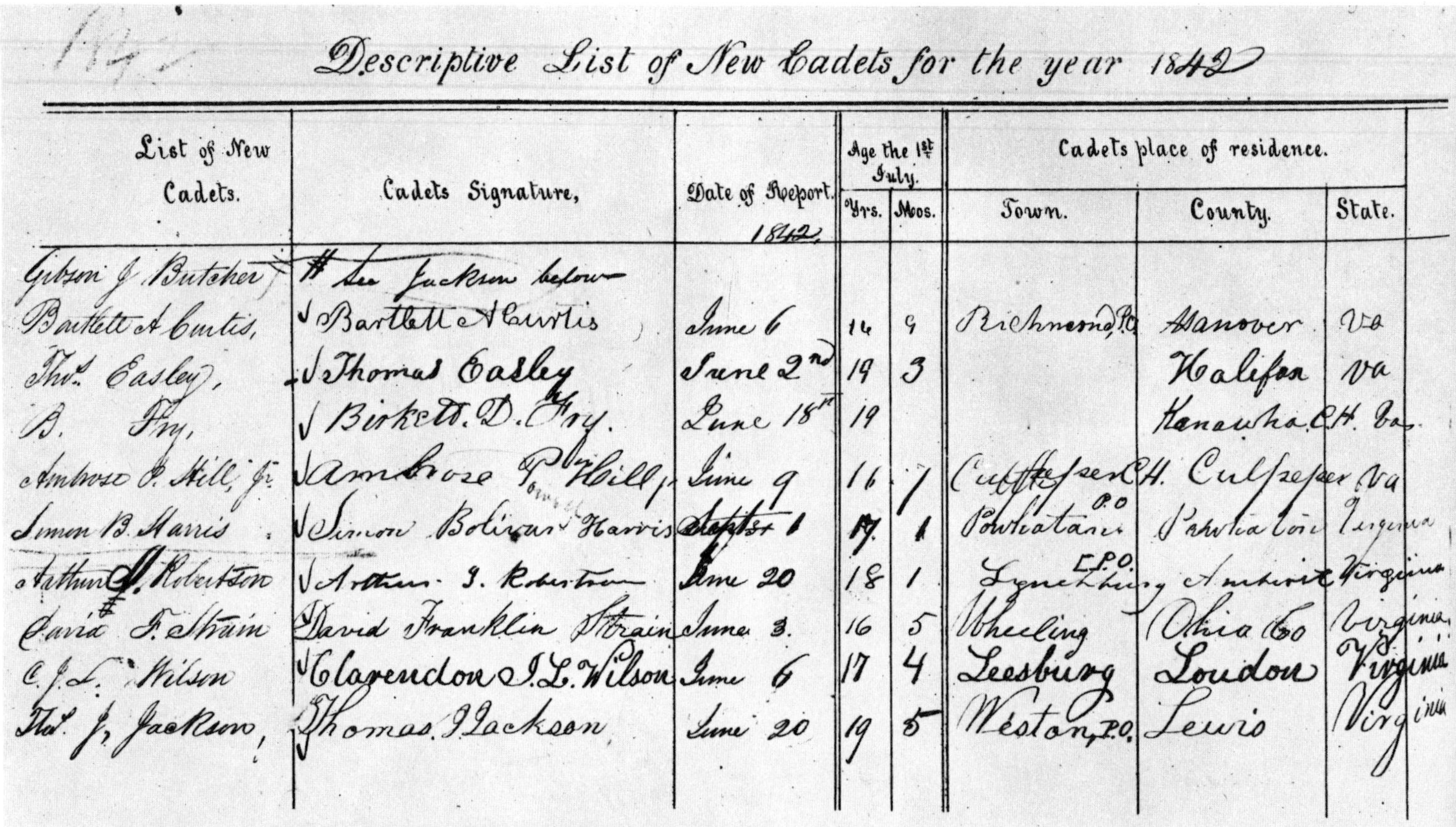

Descriptive List of New Cadets for the year 1842

List of New Cadets.	Cadets Signature,	Date of Report. 1842.	Age the 1st July. Yrs.	Mos.	Cadets place of residence. Town.	County.	State.
Gibson J. Butcher	# See Jackson below						
Bartlett A. Curtis,	Bartlett A Curtis	June 6	14	9	Richmond P.O.	Hanover	Va
Thos. Easley,	Thomas Easley	June 2nd	19	3		Halifax	Va
B. Fry,	Birkett D. Fry.	June 18th	19			Kanawha C.H.	Va
Ambrose P. Hill, Jr.	Ambrose P. Hill, Jr	June 9	16	7	Culpeper C.H.	Culpeper	Va
Simon B. Harris	Simon Bolivar Harris	Septr 1	17	1	Powhatan P.O.	Powhatan	Virginia
Arthur J. Robertson	Arthur J. Robertson	June 20	18	1	Lynchburg P.O.	Amherst	Virginia
David F. Strain	David Franklin Strain	June 3.	16	5	Wheeling	Ohio Co	Virginia
C. J. L. Wilson	Clarendon J. L. Wilson	June 6	17	4	Leesburg	Loudon	Virginia
Thos. J. Jackson,	Thomas J. Jackson	June 20	19	5	Weston, P.O.	Lewis	Virginia

Fig. 25. The descriptive list of the new cadets at West Point in 1842, with Stonewall Jackson's name and signature. Note that among his classmates was A. P. Hill, whose name was on Jackson's lips when he died.

Courtesy West Point Historical Archives.

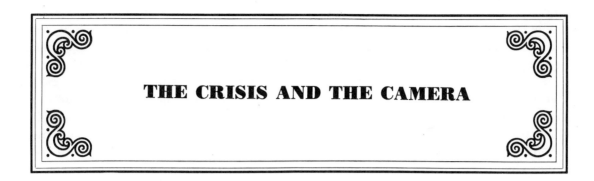

THE CRISIS AND THE CAMERA

IT was a beautiful valley. In the spring the country-side was vivid with color and the rolling farmland warm and brown under the sharp edge of the plow. In summer it brooded in the heat, a blue mist over the swell of the hills, the air heavy with the scent of wild plum and magnolia.

In the center of the valley was a small village named Gettysburg, speared by roads known by the names of the respective towns to which they led. The one leading directly into the town was called Carlisle Road, east was the Harrisburg road and west the Mummasburg Road, which crossed a wooded ridge named Oak Hill. About a half-mile west of the village was a Lutheran theological seminary, situated on Seminary Ridge. Directly south of Gettysburg was Cemetery Ridge.

Three miles from town, Cemetery Ridge culminated into a series of rocky ridges with a peak called Round Top. North of it was Little Round Top. Five hundred yards west of Little Round Top was another rugged peak, an eerie place of thick underbrush and large boulders, strewn about as if by a giant in a frenzy. It bore the apt name of Devil's Den. Crevices were everywhere. The largest, on the slope facing Little Round Top, was a natural fortification "as if fashioned by the devil himself."

Near the northwestern end of Devil's Den was a broad wheatfield and on the July day that Brady saw this gentle valley, it lay motionless in the heat, the tattered tassels waving above thousands of dead in blue and gray.

After three days of fighting here this peaceful valley would be known, in years to come, as a cemetery for more than half a million Americans and the scene of an immortal speech.[147]

For Brady and his men it would mean the imperishable pictures of the battlefield they took there after the first day, with the disordered dead already bloated with the gases of decay; dead horses; smashed caissons and overturned guns and the men beside the broken barrels who stayed at their posts, ramming home a charge; of the gallant four: Winfield Scott Hancock, Francis Barlow, John Gibbon and David B. Birney. It would mean the views they took of Seminary Ridge when a temporary truce was called for both sides to bury their dead; of the gallants of the Irish Brigade who rushed through McPherson's Woods crying, "We've come to stay"; of the field where General Reynolds fell; of the melancholy pastures and acres and acres of dead Union soldiers, all the way from McPherson's Woods to Cemetery Hill; and of the Confederate dead, stripped of their shoes and rifles and ammunition by their comrades who lived to fight another day. . . .

We know Tim O'Sullivan was at Gettysburg, for Gardner in his *Sketchbook of the Civil War* credits him with taking the famous "Harvest of Death" picture on the morning of July 1. A search of *Harper's Weekly* discloses that Brady was also there, both directing his photographers and taking pictures.

Harper's devoted its August 27 issue to Brady's documentation of the great battle. As the article accompanying the engravings—based on his pictures—"Photograph by Brady"—declared:

"Mr. Brady, the photographer, to whose industry and energy we are indebted for many of the most reliable war pictures, has been to the Gettysburg battlefield and executed a number of photographs of what he saw there . . ."[148]

From Brady's collection the editor of *Harper's* had selected the headquarters of Meade and Lee, the breastworks, Gettysburg from the west after the battle, the battered gate of the cemetery, the wheatfield where Reynolds fell and the barn in which he died and some of the dead in McPherson's Woods.

That Brady was at Gettysburg cannot be doubted; one of his men, possibly O'Sullivan, took a picture of him in his famous linen duster, straw hat "like the art students wore" and jackboots, sitting on a shattered tree trunk in the ravaged wooded slope of Culp's Hill, which had been occupied by Lee's men on the night of July 2nd.[149]

Alexander Gardner was also there. *Harper's* later used a full-page battlefield picture and credited it to Gardner. Brady's pictures gained wide distribution, particularly O'Sullivan's grim "Harvest of Death," which cast the nation into gloom.

The dark days of 1864 threw their grim shadow across the Union. In the Midwest the Copperheads were demanding "peace at any cost," gunrunners were crossing the Canadian border with rifles in boxes marked "Bibles" and a secret agent, Captain Thomas Hines, was embroiled in a far-reaching scheme to end the Civil War by internal revolution and terrorism.[150]

They were bitter days for Lincoln. Death warrants, papers concerning men sentenced for life to the Dry Tortugas, crowded his desk. There were such cases as James Taylor: "suspend execution until further notice"; James Whelan of the Pennsylvania Volunteers, who had deserted: "suspend the death execution"; young Joseph Bilisoly: "suspend execution of his death sentence until further orders." Admiral Dahlgren was begging for news of his gallant one-legged son, who lay in his coffin on public display at the Richmond depot; a Mrs. Rumsey was begging to see her folks behind Rebel lines and at last Lincoln granted her and her six children a pass.[151]

In another part of the White House, Francis B. Carpenter, an artist, was spending six months there at work on his painting of the "Emancipation Proclamation." The comments he entered in his private diary show that Brady's studio was visited many times by Lincoln and the leaders of his administration.[152]

Lincoln came to the gallery one blustery day with his beloved Tad; Stanton arrived, irritable from a heavy cold; Seward stamped in, the tip of his bony nose ruby-red from the chill winds; Justice Chase sat for his portrait, and one morning Carpenter called for Justice Smith at his home and they went to Brady's where Carpenter "got a good study."

On February 24, Carpenter asked that Brady make a series of pictures of Lincoln so that he could complete his canvas. The President agreed and arrived at Brady's with Tad. Brady, according to Carpenter's diary, evidently was absent because the pictures, including the familiar one of Lincoln and Tad, were taken, not by Brady, but by Andrew Burgess, then Brady's partner who later went to Mexico and photographed Maximillian.

Of that famous sitting only a fragment of a broken wet plate remains, happily a wonderful likeness of Lincoln. There is also a remarkable feature to this photograph which, up to now, has been missed. Carpenter's handwriting on the back of the plate tells the story. Carpenter remarked, "It (the photograph) was the basis after Mr. Lincoln's death, of the portrait made by Marshall and also the one made by Littlefield; in each engraving the parting of the hair was changed to the left side; as Mr. Lincoln always wore it. His barber by mistake this day, for some unaccountable reason, parted the hair on the President's right side, instead of on his left. . . ."[153]

Probably during the time Carpenter worked on his painting Lincoln regularly parted his hair on the left side. But there are a number of pictures showing his hair parted on the right.

After the series of photographs of Lincoln had been taken, the President posed with his son, Tad, who stood at his side while Lincoln seemingly turned the pages of a storybook—actually a photographic album—as he read to his son.

The journalist, Noah Brooks, in his *Washington in Lincoln's Time,* disclosed that Lincoln was worried that the photograph "was a species of false pretense." "Most people, he thought, would suppose the book a large clasped Bible, whereas it was a big photographic album which the photographer, posing the father and son, had hit upon as a good device . . . to bring the two sitters together . . . Lincoln's anxiety lest somebody should think he was 'making believe reading the Bible to Tad' was illustrative of his scrupulous honesty . . ."[154]

One of Lincoln's best known pictures, "my father's favorite," as his son Robert later said—was taken. This photograph, which is engraved on our five-dollar bill, is known as "Brady's Lincoln."

But was this famous picture taken by Brady or Burgess? Burgess, according to Carpenter, took the series of Lincoln that day and even the famous Tad and Lincoln picture. He makes no mention of Brady being at his studio or personally taking any of the pictures that day.

Another winter day "two of Brady's men" came to the White House at Carpenter's request to take some stereoscopic views of the President's office. As Carpenter wrote, "They requested a dark closet in which to develop the pictures; and without a thought that I was infringing upon anybody's rights, I took them to an unoccupied room of which little Tad had taken possession a few days before, and with the aid of a couple of servants had fitted up as a miniature theatre . . . everything went on, and one or two pictures had been taken, when suddenly there was an uproar. The operator had come back to the office and said that Tad had taken great offense at the occupation of his room without his consent, and had locked the door, refusing all admission.

"The chemicals had been taken inside, and there was no way of getting at them, he having carried off the key. In the midst of this conversation, 'Tad' burst in, in a fearful passion . . .

"Mr. Lincoln had been sitting for a photograph and was still in the chair. He said very mildly, 'Tad, go and unlock the door.' Tad went off, refusing to obey; no coaxing would pacify him. Lincoln suddenly rose and strode off. Directly he returned with the key to the theatre, which he unlocked, and resumed his seat . . ."[155]

Even Presidents, as Lincoln had demonstrated, had their limitations.

The beautiful picture of Lincoln and Tad gained a wide circulation in America and for years copies and lithographs could be found hanging in many a home. *Harper's* gave it an enormous spread in its May 6, 1865 edition, with the credit line "Photograph by Brady." Evidently the picture from the gallery had Brady's official stamp and the editor was not concerned with the individual photographer. The name of A. Berger meant little to Americans, whereas Brady was a household word.

On April 26, a photographer from Brady's studio came to the White House and took more pictures of Lincoln for Carpenter, still hard at work on his canvas. Again, according to Carpenter, it was Burgess, not Brady, behind the camera.[156]

On the battlefields the war moved sluggishly; the talk was not of battle but of the boom for Grant for President which that winter had been gathering strength. Both the Republicans and the Democrats were casting their eyes at the unkempt hero of Vicksburg, trying to lure him into their parties. But Grant would have none of it, as he had assured two of Lincoln's friends in January. He did not want to be a candidate and as a soldier he felt he did not have a right to utter political views.

But Lincoln was not satisfied. He called in one of Grant's friends and questioned him closely about the general's political aspirations. Did Grant want to be President? The friend said no, and Lincoln was satisfied; but, as he said, when a presidential grub got to gnawing at a man nobody could say when it would stop.[158]

On March 4, Grant sent off a note to Sherman that he had been ordered to Washington to receive a lieutenant-general's stars. He added that he would accept the commission, but under no circumstances would he make his headquarters in the political arena of Washington.

When the news broke that Grant was on his way to Washington, *Harper's* and *Leslie's* sent urgent wires to Brady asking for pictures of the first man to wear three stars since Washington and Winfield Scott.

According to the tradition, no pictures of Grant were available, so Brady sent a message to Rawlins, Grant's aide, asking for one of Grant so that he could be identified.[159]

The one he sent showed Grant with a slouch hat pulled over his face. Brady studied the picture and at five o'clock on the afternoon of the 8th went down to the depot to meet him.

A five-foot-eight man in rumpled blue with a ragged, rusty beard and battered campaign hat stepped down from the car. There was no one at the depot to meet the new Commander in Chief of the Union armies, no Congressional Committees, no blaring brass bands, no handkerchief-waving ladies or delegations of small boys running between the legs of the grownups with the unchecked enthusiasm of all small boys at public gatherings, only a slender man with a pointed black goatee.

"General Grant, I'm Mathew B. Brady, the photographer," Brady said, holding out his hand.

Grant smiled and shook Brady's hand. There is no reason why he should have hesitated. Brady was as well known as Grant in those days.

"I've come to see the President, Mr. Brady," Grant said. "Where should I stay?"

"I would recommend Willard's, General," Brady replied.

Grant nodded and walked with Brady to a carriage. Before he left, Grant had promised Brady that he would return to his gallery for a "sitting." Brady hurried back to his studio "to make preparations."

Legend has Grant appearing at Brady's studio "promptly at one o'clock the following day." The appointment might have been for the following day but it wasn't at that particular time. At one o'clock the next day Lincoln gave Grant his commission in a brief ceremony in the room where the Cabinet met. After receiving the official document Grant read his acceptance speech written on a half sheet of notepaper. He read it poorly and stumbled over some of the phrases. Lincoln, who had met him for the first time the evening before at a White House reception, had suggested that he incorporate some points. Grant had listened, nodded, but as he read his speech it was obvious he had passed over the President's suggestions. Nicolay thought to himself that this might be Grant's way of establishing his independence as a new three-star general by disregarding Lincoln's proposals.[160]

Grant undoubtedly drove over to Brady's studio sometime that afternoon or the next day, when the War Department issued orders announcing that Halleck, at his own request, had been relieved as general-in-chief and Grant had been assigned to the command of the Armies of the United States.

Grant appeared at Brady's studio with Stanton. Everything was in readiness. Grant was ushered immediately into the "operating room," where he became the target of three cameras of different sizes; one before him, one at the rear and one at the right. Behind each camera was an artist who moved about at various positions "to get the color of his hair, the eyes, the complexion, special features and to take other notes." Brady himself was to man one of the cameras.

Just as he was about to slide a wet plate into his camera and give the signal for the other cameras to begin, a cloud passed over the sun, and the studio was momentarily darkened. Brady sent one of his assistants hurrying up to the roof to pull back the matting which lay across the glass skylights. The nervous operator began pulling back the matting, but he slipped and his foot crashed through the glass.

A dozen pieces of the heavy glass, some pieces pointed like spears, some heavy enough to fracture his skull, fell about Grant. One passed his face, as one reporter wrote, within "one-sixteenth of an inch, but Grant never flinched."

The impassive Grant showed no emotion, but Stanton's face paled. He pulled Brady aside and whispered to him to keep the incident secret, "and not let out any of the facts for fear the public might think there was a conspiracy afoot to kill the new commander."[161]

Brady promised to keep the incident quiet and went back to his picture-taking. The series he made are the best portraits we have of Grant; the terrible days before Vicksburg, the hours of lonely drinking in his tent to banish unknown fears; the brooding;—all had etched their marks in Grant's face, the mask of war worn by a lonely man.[162]

On March 17, 1864, William Tecumseh Sherman and Grant met at Nashville to arrange for the concerted movement against the two main Southern armies: the Army of Northern Virginia and the Army of Tennessee. Grant, as commander of all the Federal armies, was to take charge of the Army of the Potomac, and Sherman, appointed at Grant's insistence, as head of the Department of the Mississippi, was to move against General Joseph E. Johnson, who had wintered at Dalton, Georgia, thirty miles east of Chattanooga. Both moves were to be made simultaneously in May.

Brady's photographers Coonley and Barnard, who had photographed Lincoln's first inaugural and some early battles, were selected to accompany Sherman's tough and hardened troops, popularly called "bummers" on the famous March to the Sea. However, Barnard, at least, went along as an Army photographer. Photography was now being used extensively by the army after Brady's demonstration of its effectiveness.

Both men were under the jurisdiction of the Quartermaster Department and were ordered to photograph all bridges, trestles, buildings, boats, etc., that were under the control of the department or were being used by them, and also all enemy installations, railroads, bridges, redoubts, etc.[163]

Coonley set out for Nashville where he met Barnard, then "chief photographer for the topographical engineers." It was a brief but hectic reunion. Barnard, a few hours before Coonley's arrival, had been ordered to Atlanta with the rear guard and engineers' corps. They had only a few minutes to swap the latest news about "Mr. B." and other old friends before they shook hands and said goodbye.

Coonley's work was of such a large scope that the Quartermaster Department had fitted out for his exclusive use history's first photographic train. It consisted of an engine and a home-made darkroom fashioned from an old boxcar. In one corner of the room was a barrel made into a watertight tank for the wet plates. In another part of the car was a "field kitchen" consisting of a stove, some battered pots, tin plates, and so on. Along one side were several rough bunks. It was a crowded "apartment," Coonley recalled years later, with the five men who shared the quarters turning the air blue at times as they stumbled in the dim light over pots and the legs of the stove. But there was always room for one more as the "coffeepot engine" chugged its way through the forests to be hailed by some of Sherman's "bummers" or a weary "shoulderstrap" on his way home from the hospital. The photographers gave their guests a chance to wash in the wet plate barrel, a spare meal of mule meat and a few marble-sized potatoes and, to top it off, a free picture by one of Brady's former "picture-makers."

The territory covered by the moving darkroom was from Nashville to Chattanooga and then to Knoxville; also from Chattanooga to Atlanta, Ga.; from Nashville, to Huntsville, Ala.; from Decatur to Johnsonville, Tenn., and from Louisville, Ky. In this way they covered all roads leading into Nashville.

Coonley's work was highly dangerous. The little engine and boxcar were usually more in Rebel-held territory than in their own lines. Some of their assignments were to take pictures of vital installations in advance of the army. Sometimes the high command realized they were sending the little team of photographers into territory which even they grudgingly admitted was in a "super-hazardous location" and detached a company of soldiers to guard the train.

It was a weird sight to see the little train chugging down the rails, drawing behind it the out-sized darkroom, looking for all the world like an old-fashioned super-sized privy, and clinging to its sides, the bearded Sherman's Bummers, tough and dangerous, and armed to the teeth.[164]

The Rebels got to know the darkroom train and cavalry sometimes attempted to capture it by trying to burn the bridges behind it, hoping to prevent a quick retreat. When these tactics failed they tore up the tracks and placed logs across the rails. But their efforts always failed; the train always reached its destination and carried out its assignments.

The engineers who were assigned to it usually carried some spare rails, sledge-hammers and nails—and rifles.

But Coonley refused to play the part of a hero, especially a dead one. When the Rebel cavalry advanced or tried to cut them off, he and his assistants would pile their cameras into the boxcar, grab up a rifle and shout to the engineers to get going. As Coonley said, "We did not wait to inquire what they (the Rebel cavalry) wanted, or to make pictures of them, having pressing business elsewhere about that time. Such interruptions in the accomplishment of our work were frequent . . ."[165]

And what of Brady? He was engaged in publishing a volume illustrating the paintings loaned or exhibited, many of which were sold for the benefit of the Sanitary Commission, entitled *Recollections of the Art Exhibit in the Metropolitan Fair of New York City.*[166]

The book of large handsome photographs of paintings ranged on a wall—"all taken by Brady"—was published in 1864 at his own expense to aid the efforts of the U.S. Sanitary Commission, then trying to reorganize the Medical Corps, improve prison conditions and obtain affidavits from released or escaped prisoners which were to be used later in the trials of war criminals. There is a group picture showing Brady and some of the exhibitors.

There are many "sponsors" listed, including Edward Anthony, but, strangely enough, Brady's own name is misspelled, "Matthew B. Brady."

On June 21, 1864, before Petersburg Brady and Tim O'Sullivan drove up to Battery B, First Pennsylvania, Light Artillery, attached to the Fifth Corps, under General G. K. Warren.[167]

This battery, which had suffered great casualties—twenty-one killed and fifty-two wounded—had been moved up to the front four days before Brady's arrival, and from the first few minutes when the guns were rolled into position, they were dueling constantly with the Confederate batteries near the Avery house, six hundred and fifty yards away.

Brady stepped down from his What-is-it wagon and walked up to Captain James H. Cooper, commanding the battery which was often known as "Cooper's Battery," and asked his permission to take a picture. Cooper agreed and, to make the picture more lifelike, gave the command to load and fire. To the weary gunners his orders were not play-acting. They ran to their positions; cannons were loaded, the ramrods shoved down the barrels and the gunners stood ready to pull the lanyards.

Brady brought his camera in front and just off to the side of the big guns. The gunners, with eyes only on the Avery House, stood by to "thumb the vent." But as

Brady started to make a series of pictures he was spotted by a Confederate lookout who was studying the Federal lines, probably with a spyglass.

Beauregard's batteries, lying across the skyline, opened fire. Shells fell about Cooper's battery, but Brady continued to take his pictures. His horse was more discreet. When the first geyser of earth and debris erupted skyward, the horse bolted, "scattering plates and chemicals" as he ran across the fields, with Brady's driver sawing frantically at the reins. The frightened mount was finally stopped and brought under control and the What-is-it wagon returned to the battery's position. Brady took several more pictures of the battery as it began its duel with the Rebel gunners. As Lieutenant James A. Gardner, gunner, recalled forty-three years later, when shown the pictures, the cannoneers and the corporals who sighted the guns lay flat behind their pieces for protection from the Rebel balls and it "was expected" that the officers would stand upright. In order to take his pictures Brady was necessarily exposed to enemy fire. It was his closest call.[168]

Brady and his assistants covered the entire nine-month campaign, one of the most difficult of the war, which led ultimately to Richmond.

Grant's army had swung around from Cold Harbor. "The Confederate cause was lost," General Ewell said, "when Grant crossed the James." It was a masterful move which "worked like oiled machinery."

Beauregard frantically wired Lee "Where is Grant?" The Second Corps, spearhead of the Army of the Potomac, reached the north bank of the James. By midnight of the 15th, engineers had constructed pontoon bridges and the Second and the Ninth Corps crossed with the Fifth and Sixth Corps and part of the Army of the James on their way by transport from White House Landing to City Point.

The siege of Petersburg, the railroad capital of Virginia, had begun. Sherman's relentless advance continued. It was the beginning of the end and Brady was on hand to record it.[169]

Among the pictures Brady and his men took were the famous 17,000-pound siege gun, "Dictator," which used a charge of fourteen pounds of powder and was drawn on railroad cars; the miner-soldiers who dug the famous Petersburg mine, the crater resulting from the massive charge which erupted skyward at dawn, June 30, 1864, with guns, carriages, and bits of men; the remnants of the colored troops thrown into the breach after the rallying Confederates had swept the Federals back into the smoking crater, where they were torn to pieces by well-aimed Confederate batteries; the ten miles of defenses and salients; Fort Mahone ("Fort Damnation"), Fort Sedgwick and numerous others.[170]

Just before the Federal occupation of Petersburg,

cameraman Roche, who had worked under Brady early in the war and had then gone over to the Anthonys' to take stereoscopic views, was at headquarters visiting a "Captain Russell," who may have been Captain A. J. Russell, Brady's former photographer. His name was sometimes spelled with one *l*.

"Cap'n, I'm in for repairs and want to get things ready for the grand move, for the army is sure to move tonight or tomorrow night. The negatives on hand I wish to send north with some letters. I want to prepare my glass and chemicals; in fact, get everything ready for the grand move, for this is the final one and the rebellion is broken or we go home and commence over again."[171]

Russell could only shake his head at the words of this indomitable photographer. Only a short while before, at Dutch Gap Canal, he had seen Roche risk his life to get his precious pictures.

As he remembered the scene years later, the Confederates had begun shelling the Union lines from Howlett's Point when Roche appeared with his camera. The earth shook from the terrific bombardment of the ten-inch shells, "falling at minute intervals." Disregarding Russell's warning, Roche took his camera beyond the protection of the works and began taking his pictures in the midst of the bombardment.

He had taken several views when he folded his tripod, placed it over his shoulder and ran to a more exposed position. He had almost reached it when there was a banshee wail of a falling shell, followed by an ear-splitting roar. Earth, mud and stones erupted skyward. Roche was momentarily stunned, but in a moment he shook the dust and dirt form his clothes, and wiping the lens of his camera, he moved it to the smoking shell-hole and spread his tripod over it.

Then, as "coolly as if working in a barnyard," he exposed his next plate. When he had taken enough pictures to his satisfaction he folded his tripod, put it over

Fig. 26. A sketch of George N. Barnard, former Brady photographer, as he was traveling with Sherman's Army with his photographic darkroom. From *Anthony's Photographic Bulletin,* 1882.

his shoulder and casually walked back to the Federal trenches. Russell, who had watched him with his heart in his mouth, asked Roche if he had been scared when the shell fell.

Roche arched his eyebrows and grinned. "Scared?" he said with a grin. "Two shots never fell in the same place, Cap'n."

Fig. 27. A sketch of T. C. Roche, former Brady photographer, dodging shells at Dutch Gap. From *Anthony's Photographic Bulletin,* 1882.

Now as they were sitting in the tent before Petersburg their conversation was suddenly cut short by the booming of guns. The roar came from Petersburg. Roche and Captain Russell jumped to their feet and pulled back the flap of the tent. The great Federal bombardment of the city had begun. As they watched, the sky was criss-crossed with the lurid flashes of the guns. Roche turned to Russell and said, "Cap'n, the ball is open. I must be off."

Roche rounded up his assistant and within a quarter of an hour their wagon was hitched to the two horses, chemicals and food packed and Roche, his battered black hat on one side of his head, was passing Russell's tent.

"Goodby, Cap'n," Roche called out, "we'll meet tomorrow at the front!"

It was a wild ride for Roche and his assistant. The night was alive with shellfire and the crash of heavy cannon. For moments there would be complete silence and men who were there remembered they had thought for a moment that they were deafened. Then suddenly another battery would touch off its pieces and again shells would bisect the black sky, leaving trails of fire like meteors.

The road to the front teemed with horses and men. Bugles called from the left and right. Horses screamed and men shouted orders in the darkness. Somewhere in the blackness a man kept his hand on the cord of a locomotive whistle and it added its high-pitched shriek to the din.

Roche fought his wagon down the road. Several times

bouncing artillery caissons flew past, and to save his rickety vehicle he turned off the road. Somehow he got through. Dawn found him on the ramparts taking scores of negatives, many times risking death by inches. Fellow officers reported to Captain Russell that Roche and his camera had been "where the fight was thickest and the harvest of death had indeed been gathered."

When the Confederates finally retreated, Roche, dirty, weary, and still wearing his battered black hat, gathered up his camera and chemicals and drove into the bomb-blasted Confederate works. Another Brady man, Tim O'Sullivan, was there to meet him.

Charleston . . . Atlanta . . . the final March to the Sea . . . Nashville . . . the end in Tennessee . . . the final surrender of Petersburg . . . and finally Appomattox. . . . Because of poor communications Brady missed Lee's surrender to Grant at the home of Wilmer McLean in Appomattox Courthouse. By a strange coincidence McLean's home at Bull Run was Beauregard's headquarters in the first battle of Bull Run. To avoid the war, McLean bought a second home in the quiet, one-street village of Appomattox Courthouse, where he lived for four quiet years. Ironically, the war ended in the home owned by the man who also owned a house in the vicinity in which the war had begun.

Brady and O'Sullivan took a number of pictures of the McLean house after the surrender, but as Brady knew too well, it was only a beautiful white farmhouse, lacking the principals who had played the major roles in the great drama.[172]

Brady set off at once for Richmond, where he took some striking pictures of the gutted buildings. But Lee was the choice prize and he set out to capture in his lens the face of the gallant Southern leader.

Brady went to Lee's home and knocked at the door. He told the servant he wanted to see the General. Lee appeared on the front porch and when he heard Brady's request he said, "It is utterly impossible, Mr. Brady. How can I sit for a photograph with the eyes of the world upon me as they are today?"[173]

Brady then sought out Mrs. Lee and Confederate Exchange Agent Robert Ould, both of whom he had known before the war. The heartsick Lee listened to the pleas of his wife and his friend, put on his gray uniform once more and, with his son and young chief of staff, Colonel Taylor, came out to the basement below the back porch of his home and said to Brady in a weary voice, "Very well, Mr. Brady, we are ready."[174]

Brady later told of this historic picture, which he took "the day but one after he arrived in Richmond. It was supposed that after his defeat it would be preposterous to ask him to sit, but I thought that to be the time for the historical picture. He allowed me to come to his house and photograph him on his back porch, several sittings. Of course I had known him since the Mexican War when he was upon General Scott's staff and my request was not as from an intruder."

Brady took pictures of Lee alone, seated and standing, and with his son and his young chief of staff, Colonel Taylor, also in uniform. Ninety years afterward, Brady's wet plates, despite his dimming eyesight that was the subject of so many gloomy articles in the years before the firing on Fort Sumter, are still clear and the prints from them are superb.

PART THREE

The Postwar Years

—◆>●<◆—

"*Here is a man, who for twenty-five years, has fought to preserve our National Monuments. Some of his men were starved, some wounded in the struggle. . . The government should not take advantage of a man's distress.*"

—Congressman James A. Garfield
in a speech to the 43rd Congress

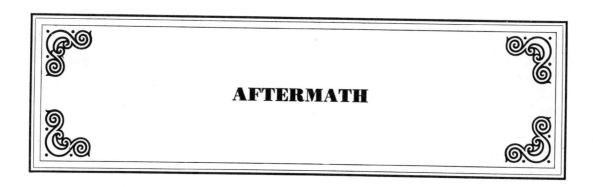

AFTERMATH

THE guns were still. A strange quiet hung over the land. In the South men in gray returned to homes many of which were ruins, while in the North men in blue with limbs missing hobbled, crippled, along city streets. The prison camps were opened and from Andersonville came horrors that were to haunt the North for thirty years or more.

That spring heroes were crowding into Washington for the Grand Review up Pennsylvania Avenue, and Brady and his assistants were out to capture all of them for posterity. The biggest catch of all, besides Grant, was "Uncle Billy" Sherman. When Brady tracked him down to Willard's, the hero of the "March to the Sea" told Brady that he would pose with his staff, "but all my officers are away with their wives, children and sweethearts. It is impossible to get them together, Mr. Brady."

But Brady insisted, "General, if I find them and gather them together at my gallery at two o'clock tomorrow, will you be there?"

Sherman laughed. "Mr. Brady, if you can get them there send me a note and I'll join them . . ."[175]

Brady hurried back to the gallery, where he outlined his strategy to his staff and gave them their assignments. That afternoon and evening, Brady and his men, in several hired carriages, canvassed busy Washington, seeking out Sherman's officers. By nightfall Brady and his assistants had found them all and had extracted a promise from them to be at Brady's at two o'clock. Brady sent the general a note and back came a promise from Sherman that he would be there promptly at two o'clock.

The bearded veterans were as good as their word and at two all were there except General Blair. Sherman and his men began to show signs of impatience and Brady moved among them hopefully, predicting that Blair would arrive within a few minutes

The door opened and a young woman and her three-year-old daughter came in. Brady suddenly remembered that he had made an appointment to take the child's picture. The young mother stood there, embarrassed, while the generals stared or smiled at her.

"Mr. Brady, I didn't realize I was so early," she began.

"General Sherman is waiting for one of his officers," Brady explained. Sherman knelt down and tickled the little girl. The child giggled and Sherman grinned. "You have a beautiful baby."

"Thank you, General," the flustered woman replied.

"We'll wait for Blair," Sherman said to Brady and turned to the little girl.

For one hour, while his astonished generals watched, Sherman—"Crazy Sherman," "Wild Billy" or "Old Sugar-Coated," as they called him in Kentucky—rolled around on the floor, made grotesque faces, walked on his haunches and gave the little girl pony rides on his back "to make the child laugh."

At three o'clock Blair, breathless and full of apologies arrived, and Brady, not wanting to trust his luck too far, hurriedly arranged the famous generals in a row with their red-haired commander in the center.

Sherman's smile faded when he faced the lens. He glared into it, his tousled red hair and stare giving him the look of an angry fighting cock ready to fly at its enemy with slashing spurs.

On the way out General Sherman, who was to succeed Grant as general and commander of the army in 1869, leaned down to tweak the little girl's cheek. But this wasn't unusual for a man who boasted of his large family and who liked Grant at their first meeting because of his obvious love of children.

After Appomattox Brady's entire fortune of $100,000

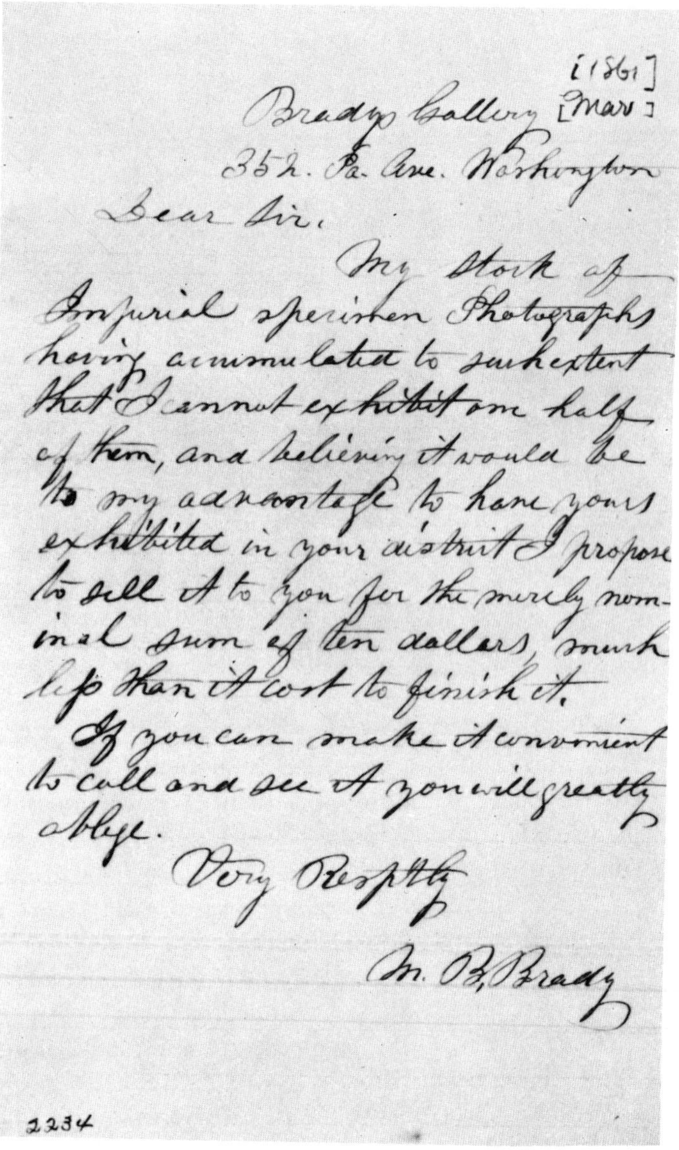

Figs. 28 and 29. Brady letters to Andrew Johnson, not written by Brady himself. *Library of Congress.*

—an enormous sum in those days—was exhausted; his regular business had to be rebuilt; Julia was ill; A. Burgess and Tim O'Sullivan were no longer with him; younger photographers, endowed with his "proverbial enterprise," as one trade journal called it, and better health, were now his competitors; the sale of his "war views" had been far too small to enable him to recoup his lost fortune, and he was deeply in debt to the Anthonys' for supplies long since consumed.

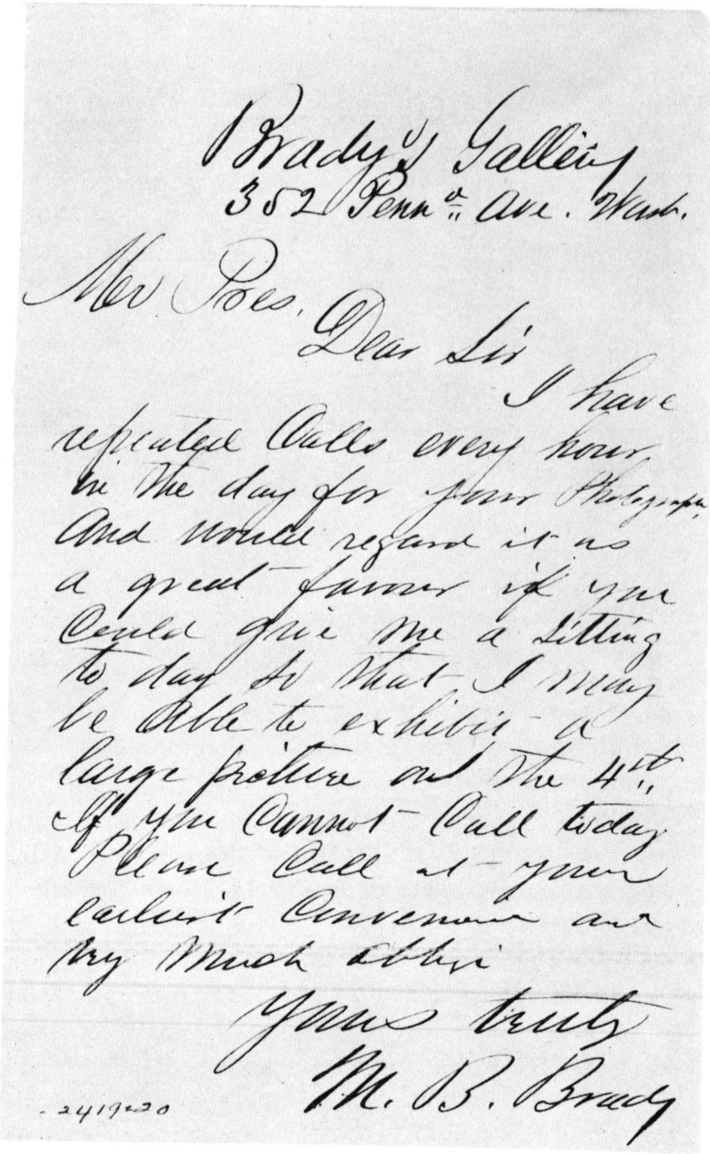

It was almost too much for one man to take. Brady sadly disbanded his twenty-two photographic teams, which, as he said later, he had been operating like "a large newspaper in every theater of war," and stored his spacious collections in Washington and New York warehouses.[176]

From April, when he took Lee's picture in Richmond, until the fall of 1865, Brady was strangely inactive, whether from illness, disillusionment or lack of money we do not know. It was probably a combination of all three.

But History refused to wait for him and rushed on,

sowing momentous events right and left in that tragic year, but it was Gardner's and not Brady's camera which captured them for posterity.

Here was the assassination of President Lincoln; the Grand Review up Pennsylvania Avenue, one of the greatest military salutes to an American victory in our history; the trial of the Lincoln conspirators; the trial of Captain Henri Wirz, commandant of Andersonville Prison, and his execution on the gallows in the shadow of the Capitol dome . . .[177]

Brady took some pictures of Lincoln's funeral cortege May 13 at the New York City Hall. On the same day Gardner was posing Andrew Johnson in his gallery and soon *carte de visite* photographs of the new President, published by Philip Solomon of Washington city, were flooding the country—but with Gardner's name on them.[178]

Gardner in 1865 was as alert and energetic as Brady had been ten years earlier. When the Lincoln conspirators were captured, Gardner hurried over to the basement of the Penitentiary and made a series of pho-

64

tographs which are as clear and revealing as if they were taken today.[179]

The best portrait Gardner made was of the hulking, youthful Payne who almost hacked Seward to death. Gardner, in one pose, showed the wrist irons and in another Payne's rather handsome profile. The raincoat he wore that night is surprisingly modern looking.

Gardner missed Mrs. Surratt, perhaps because she was kept so closely guarded that not even a photographer well placed in high circles, could get in to see her.

The scene of the hanging of four of the Lincoln conspirators have been attributed in many biographies and magazine articles to Brady. Nothing could be further from the truth; Gardner took those pictures, and the large layout of pictures which Harper's devoted to the affair, are all credited "photographed by Gardner."

Brady also missed the fine pictures taken at the dedication of the Gettysburg monument, but Gardner did not. Again it was the restless Scot who got the lion's share of the photographic credit in Leslie's and Harper's. Gardner's camera also caught Sherman's "bummers" swaggering down Pennsylvania Avenue in a splendid victory parade, and when he heard the story of how Jefferson Davis had tried to escape "in woman's clothing," when he was captured on May 10, he hurried over to the War Department and posed an unidentified officer in them. It made a sensational picture and was used by Harper's.

Assuming that Brady was in New York, it is indicative of his inactivity that he did not take a picture—at least of the ruins—of Barnum's Museum, which was destroyed by fire on July 18, 1865.[180]

Jefferson Davis, Jacob Thompson and other Rebel leaders had been captured and thrown into prison and Thaddeus Stevens and his Radicals called for their blood. An eye-for-an-eye fever raged in the land. It was fanned to a white heat by the pictures published in Harper's of the pitiful corpses who stumbled out of Andersonville. To look at them, rotting with gangrene, and starved to the point where bones burst through skin, is to realize the savagery of the American Civil War. Only the living dead of Dachau and Buchenwald can be compared with them.[181]

Here again Brady was given credit for work he never did. The pictures were taken at "Geer's Hospital," Wilmington, Del., on June 17, 1865, probably by a government photographer working with the U.S. Sanitary Commission, whose members during the war had expedited the exchange of food packages, investigated the stories of returned Union prisoners, and collected their affidavits for future war trials.

The series of pictures was gathered by Chaplain J. J. Geer, of the One Hundred and Eighty-Third Ohio Volunteers. They were published in Harper's on June 17,

1865, "the exact facsimile of photographs," with Chaplain Geer's name the only one mentioned. Obviously, if the editors of Harper's, who had used hundreds of Brady pictures in the past and were only too eager to use his name, had been given the pictures by Brady or his gallery, they would have credited him with taking them and certainly would have mentioned his name in the article which accompanied the engravings.[182]

After the pictures were published and the stories began circulating, the cry "Hang Wirz" echoed on street corners, in meeting halls and in Congress. There was a loud demand for a public blood-letting. The Congressional Committee trying Jacob Thompson, who had worked with Captain Hines in Canada to spread terrorism and revolution, thought they had a perfect case against the former Secretary of Interior who had supposedly helped to engineer the Lincoln murder, but the government case crumbled when the chief Congressional witness was proved to be a liar, blackmailer and thief.[183]

Still there was Andersonville, and Captain Wirz, the Swiss commandant, was in jail. The government hurriedly gathered together its evidence; former inmates of the prison were interviewed. Rebel guards were located and ordered to testify, along with Union surgeons and prisoners. Boston Corbett, who supposedly shot John Wilkes Booth in a flaming barn, came forward and said he would be willing to testify about his term in Andersonville. His offer was gratefully accepted.

On August 21, 1865, Wirz was brought to trial on a charge of inflicting "wanton cruelty" upon Union soldiers at Andersonville. The first charge linked him with General Robert E. Lee, General Winder, the provost marshal of Richmond, Confederate Secretary of War James Seddon and other Rebel generals and statesmen with "conspiring to injure the health and destroy the lives of United States soldiers held as prisoners by the Confederate States."[184] There was a second charge of murder, "in violation of the laws and customs of war." Under the second charge there were thirteen specifications.

The trial began at one o'clock in the well-furnished room equipped "with a dozen lounge seats" before a military commission headed by Major General Lew Wallace. Two side windows overlooked a cool, leafy park, and it was noted during the long hot days that the members of the commission studied it longingly many times.

Wirz, born in Switzerland, and said to have been a physician, was of medium height, slender and stoop-shouldered. The man's outstanding characteristic, which more than one reporter noted, was his "gray and restless eyes." He sat before the commission, flanked by an impressive battery of attorneys, which included James Denver, Charles J. Peck, Louis Schade, and an ex-circuit court judge named Hughes.

The following morning the court announced through

Wallace that it had been "dissolved" by President Johnson to allow for a new indictment to be drawn up charging Wirz alone with the crime and eliminating the names of Lee and all the other statesmen and generals. It was obvious Johnson realized that the gallant Lee and the Confederacy's leaders could never be found guilty of such charges, but the man they now held in custody could be.

Judge Hughes and Peck immediately resigned as defense counsel and the courtroom was thrown into an uproar with Wirz standing up and shouting in a high, shrill voice that without counsel he would surely die on the gallows. The shadow of the noose was already swaying on the courtroom's sunny walls.

Schade and another well-known Washington attorney, O. H. Baker, later that day formally listed themselves as the defense battery and the trial was put off until the following day, following a formal plea of "not guilty."

The government's first exhibit was a curious one; a letter written by Wirz to Confederate headquarters in Richmond was read and introduced and accepted as evidence. It actually was a score for the defense, for the brief note described the shortness of rations and then went on to describe himself "as the tool in the hands of my superiors."

Several witnesses followed, one a former commandant of the prison and an assistant Confederate surgeon. They all agreed as to the terrible conditions and the lack of medical supplies and proper housing in the camp where 33,000 men, many with gangrene and scurvy, and crawling with lice, existed on chunks of cornbread unfit for hogs, an ounce of rotting beef and a small cup of weak rice water.

The courtroom stirred with anger and Wirz clenched and unclenched his fists as Doctor A. W. Barrows, physician to the Twenty-Seventh Massachusetts Regiment, described how seven hundred men, nearly all naked, died during the bitter days of the winter of 1864, as they huddled in old coats under strips of canvas, or burrowed like rats in their holes. In the stockade, he added, "they were like ants and bees."

The doctor's vivid description of Wirz moves through his testimony, like figures in another and more terrible war crimes trial ninety years in the future.

The physician told how Wirz, on horseback, followed by a pack of vicious hound dogs, inspected the camp every day, warning the Union officers and men that if any prisoner escaped, "I'll starve every damn Yankee for it . . ."

Barrows also told horrible stories of torture and inhumanity at Andersonville; of human skeletons strung up until only their toes touched the ground; of naked men spread-eagled on the frozen ground; of the "dead line," the wooden railing encircling the interior of Andersonville beyond which a prisoner could not stretch his hand on the threat of being shot; of boys fifteen and sixteen years old who lay in mud holes while their gangrenous limbs rotted away.

Boston Corbett recalled how he had had to lie among Wirz's hound dogs to keep warm during an unseasonable cold spell. When asked by Wirz's counsel why the dogs had not bitten him as they had other prisoners, Corbett thundered: "The same power that kept the lions from biting Daniel to pieces is the same in whom I trust!"

The trial went on for ten days. Wallace and his fellow commissioners must have engaged in heated courtroom battles with Wirz's counsel, because on several occasions there are indications in the record of the trial that the attorneys had resigned despite Wirz's pleas, but, by the time the court reconvened, had evidently relented and returned.

In October the trial was adjourned when Wirz fell ill. The government treated him with extraordinary kindness, allowing him a "grate fire and a tumbler of whiskey." When Wirz protested he was unable to go to court because of his illness, Wallace ordered him brought into court on a stretcher.

It was a dramatic moment when Wirz, his pinched fetures appearing as sharp as a fox's, was brought into the room and placed on a couch before the commission's table. He lay there motionless, his restless gray eyes jumping from witness to witness.

He was found guilty on November 6, and sentenced to hang on the morning of the 10th. On Thursday, the eve of his execution, Wirz wrote a long and detailed "memoir" which has apparently been lost to history, while the government distributed two hundred and fifty cards for "spectators' seats."

At dawn of the 10th, those not lucky enough to have tickets fought for choice seats in the elm trees surrounding the courtyard. The gallows had been erected in the same yard where the Lincoln conspirators had died and there were the same fatal thirteen steps for Wirz to climb. Four companies of soldiers marched into the yard at nine o'clock and formed a human square. From eight until ten o'clock, Andersonville was "the lively topic between the soldiers and the spectators." A large crowd of newspaper correspondents, dressed in top hats, were ushered in at nine to take an unmerciful ribbing from the soldiers and the civilians.

Before he left his cell, Wirz said goodbye to General Winder, begged him to "wipe this awful stain from my character" and to take care of his wife and children. Winder, badly shaken and himself under the shadow of the noose, took Wirz's hand, promised to fulfill his last wishes and turned away.

At 10:15 A.M. Wirz, "his face flushed from the copious draughts of whiskey" he had downed in his cell, walked across the courtyard. He was accompanied by two Catholic priests, Fathers Boyle and Wiggett.

His appearance was the signal for one of the most

violent demonstrations in the history of public executions; the spectators in the trees shouted curses and jeered, others in the yard hooted and whistled while the soldiers, standing at attention, began to chant: "Wirz, remember Andersonville . . . Wirz, remember Andersonville . . ."

Wirz, his face impassive, walked slowly up the thirteen steps, to face a Major Russell, who was to read the death warrant. The officer had to shout the official words above the tumult, then held out his hand and said that he "deplored this duty." Wirz smiled and said dryly, "I know what orders are, Major."

As Russell turned away Wirz called out: "And I am being hanged for obeying them."

As they tied his hands the priest asked if he wished to make a confession. Wirz shook his head.

"No, I am not guilty, Father."

When they tied his legs he again called out, "I go before my God—the Almighty God—who will judge between us. I am innocent and I will die like a man."

He then thanked his jailers, the black hood was slipped over his head, and the noose was adjusted. The priests and the others stepped back. A spring was touched, the trap opened and Wirz plunged down.

The fall, however, failed to break his neck, and he flopped on the end of the noose like a fish on a line. As he slowly strangled to death, in his ears was the terrible chant: "Wirz, remember Andersonville . . . Wirz, remember Andersonville . . ."

Gardner, from an elevation, probably on a wall, took a series of memorable pictures of that execution, showing in vivid detail the entire scene including the figures of the morbid spectators clinging to the trees against a background of brooding majesty—the nation's Capitol.

Wirz undoubtedly was an "evil man," as one account described him, and there is also no doubt that he received a fair trial, although he might have been an "unfortunate scapegoat," as Thaddeus Stevens described him in a speech before the House. Stevens declared that if anyone should die for the horrors of Andersonville it should not be Wirz, "that wicked fellow," but those responsible for the acts of the entire Confederate government.

Yet one has only to read the official transcript of the Wirz trial to realize that it would have been a travesty of justice to have let Wirz go. The evidence of his sadistic cruelty is overwhelming.

It must also be recalled that Federal prisons claimed the lives of thousands of Confederate prisoners through starvation and disease.

Jefferson Davis, just before he died, attempted in a series of two articles published in *Bedford's Magazine* in February, 1890, to justify the conditions at Andersonville and described Wirz as a "martyr." But General N. P. Chipman, Judge Advocate General at the trial, published a book the following year, tearing to shreds Davis's defense by the evidence he presented. It is interesting to note that Chipman in 1891 tried to find the pictures of the Andersonville victims published here, but as he reported in a footnote, "they cannot be found."

THE YEARS OF THE BLOODY SHIRT

THE greatest pictorial essay of Brady's time—and our own—lay gathering dust in warehouses. The finest of modern cameras of the future would achieve results no finer than the results Brady and his assistants obtained, under great difficulty, with their cumbersome equipment.

In the summer of 1865, Brady, the chronicler of an epoch, the delineator of the manners of his time, had to return to the florid society of New York and Washington city which he had deserted for the battlefields.

He had lost everything except a few parcels of property near Central Park in New York, which he was forced to sell in 1869. Bankruptcy, Julia's health and his own and new competition, plagued him. (The records of Brady's bankruptcy proceedings in the National Archives bear his signature. These proceedings took place in the U. S. Southern District Court on January 11, 1873.) If he was embittered at his country's peculiar talent for withholding deserved aid until it was too late, we do not know. We do know that the doors of his Pennsylvania Avenue gallery were open and his camera again was ready. Twelve tragic years followed Lincoln's assassination. They were years of revolutionary turmoil, violence, unbelievable corruption, broken homes, hearts and heads. It was a time in which the honor and glory of many men would be tarnished, and when others, thought to be lesser men, emerged as giants in the land.

If a dramatist were to use this era as a play, the theme would be one of tragedy. But offstage he would find much bawdy humor and farce.

The principal characters were figures in our history who were regarded as men of honor and integrity, but their actions showed them to be hypocritical and corrupt as they made a doormat of the Constitution of their country, a mockery of their Supreme Court, of freedom, liberty and justice, while they looted and plundered with the relish and enthusiasm of eighteenth-century freebooters.

It was drama with terrible violence and corruption swirling about the feet of its two leading figures: Andrew Johnson, seventeenth President, and Thaddeus Stevens, who waved a bloody shirt to lead one of the most violent political insurrections in the history of the country.

There were beautiful women among the belles of their time, tragic Kate Chase Sprague, Peggy O'Neal Eaton, a "fading rose" which still charmed men's hearts, Madame Constantine Catacazy, her complexion as "delicately tinted as the heart of a seashell," Mary Todd Lincoln, a sorrowing widow.

The sets for the melodrama were magnificent, ranging from pavilions floored wth golden damask carpets and glowing with the lights of hundreds of flawless wax candles to the paneled dining room of Ben Butler's mansion, where men lingered over their cigars and brandy and plotted the destruction of other men, and the House, where the dying Thad Stevens managed the Impeachment Committee he had formed with loving hands.

But to tell the whole fascinating story would take a thousand manuscript pages, countless actors, and in the end it would all sound make-believe.

Yet it all did happen. Newspapers of the time, confidential diaries, incriminating letters, memoirs and government reports tell us of the way it was. But it is Brady's camera which brings the people of the day back to life. As they passed before his camera his genius caught the slyness, the arrogance and the beauty and the dress of the men and women who played the leading roles in the pageant. And through his camera we see the outsized frontier Capitol, with its muddy streets and stately buildings, where it all took place.

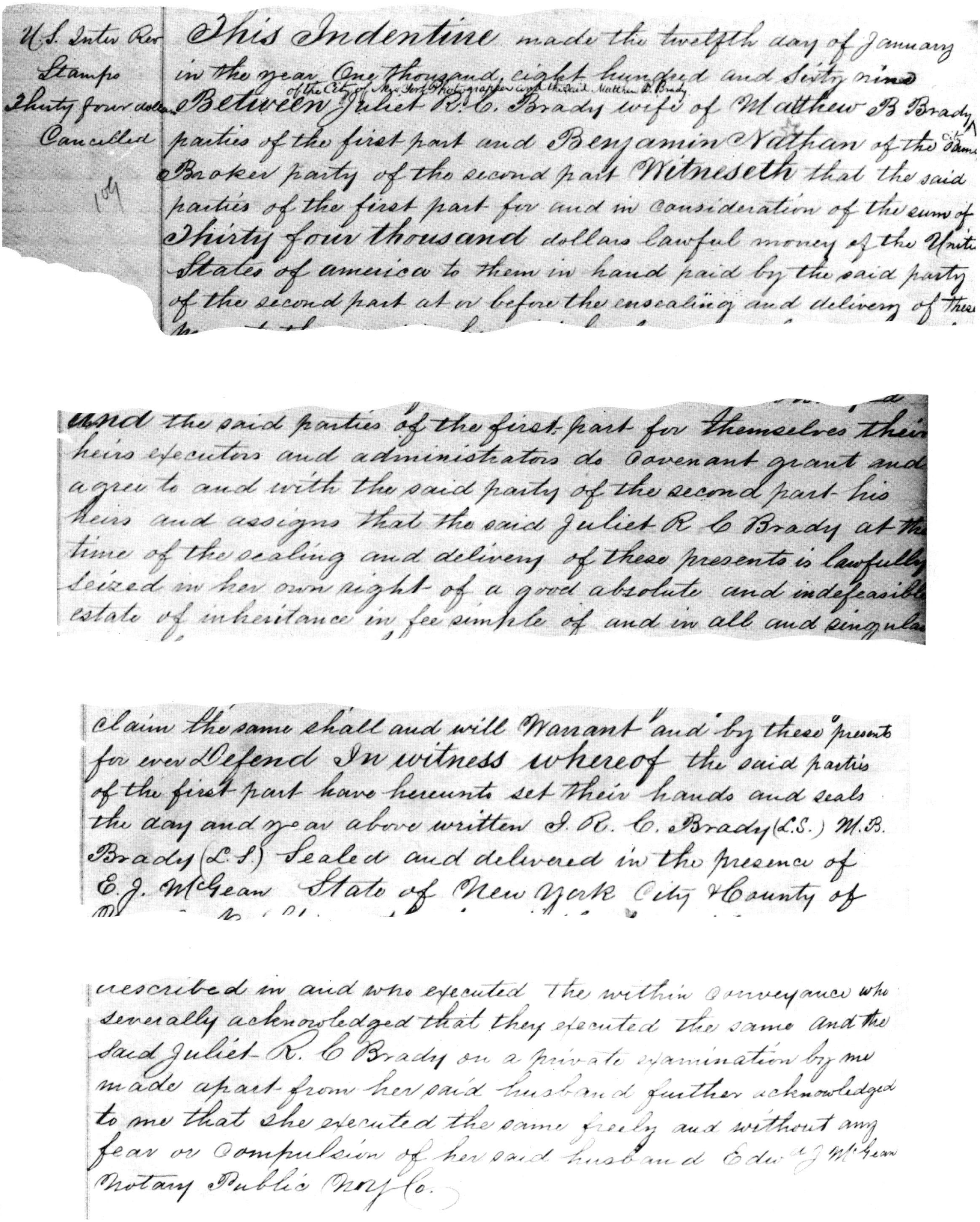

U.S. Inter Rev Stamps Thirty four dollars Cancelled 109

This Indenture made the twelfth day of January
in the year One thousand eight hundred and Sixty nine
Between Juliet R. C. Brady wife of Matthew B Brady of the City of New York Photographer and the said Matthew B. Brady
parties of the first part and Benjamin Nathan of the Same City
Broker party of the second part Witnesseth that the said
parties of the first part for and in consideration of the sum of
Thirty four thousand dollars lawful money of the United
States of America to them in hand paid by the said party
of the second part at or before the ensealing and delivery of these

and the said parties of the first part for themselves their
heirs executors and administrators do covenant grant and
agree to and with the said party of the second part his
heirs and assigns that the said Juliet R C Brady at the
time of the sealing and delivery of these presents is lawfully
seized in her own right of a good absolute and indefeasible
estate of inheritance in fee simple of and in all and singular

claim the same shall and will Warrant and by these presents
for ever Defend In witness whereof the said parties
of the first part have hereunto set their hands and seals
the day and year above written J. R. C. Brady (L.S.) M.B.
Brady (L.S.) Sealed and delivered in the presence of
E. J. McGean State of New York City & County of

described in and who executed the within conveyance who
severally acknowledged that they executed the same and the
said Juliet R. C Brady on a private examination by me
made apart from her said husband further acknowledged
to me that she executed the same freely and without any
fear or compulsion of her said husband Edwd J McGean
Notary Public N.Y. Co.

Fig. 30. Extracts from the record of the sale of the Bradys' real estate at 105th Street and Fifth Avenue, New York City. Note that Julia Handy Brady's legal name was apparently Juliet R. C. (Handy) Brady, and that the property was hers, by inheritance. The curious statement at the end was a legal formality. *Hall of Records, County of New York.*

The Washington city to which Brady returned after the war was a dirty, brawling, lusty city, one step removed from the frontier. In the summer of 1865 living quarters were impossible to find and too expensive. A house which rented for three hundred dollars a season before the war now brought twelve hundred to its owner. The city itself was shabby and rundown. One carpetbagger, between gulps of Monongahela whiskey, was heard to say in Willard's that the White House should be torn down "because it was just too plain and cramped for visitors."

Even Cabinet members grumbled that now the time for sacrifices was over, they should not be compelled to live in "such shabby dwellings."

In July a *Herald* reporter made a walking tour of the homes of the government officials and was "horrified" to find that Admiral Dahlgren lived in a two-story brick house on 4½ Street. He wrote indignantly: "No naval hero should be forced to live on a street with such a vile name."[185] The reporter must have forgotten what the *Herald* had called Lord Lyons during the days of '64 when it seemed that the exploits of the Confederate iron rams would bring England into the war, for he wrote that the fact that such a great European diplomat had to be confined to a "dingy gray barn on Eighth Street is an outrage."

The reporter found only one consolation in his entire tour: notorious F Street, which every spring was a quagmire of mud and potholes, was at least being paved. It was on this street that a foreign diplomat in lace and gold found his carriage sunk to the wheel hubs and had made the rest of the journey down the street on the back of a husky government servant.

During the summer of 1865, President Johnson and Preston King of New York were "keeping bachelor quarters" in the Hooper House on 8th Street and 15th Street.

Charles Dickens saw Johnson that summer and found him "a man with a remarkable face, indicating courage, watchfulness and strength of purpose. I would pick him out of anywhere as a character of Washington."[186]

As for Thaddeus Stevens, whom Brady photographed for history, his enemies bitterly detested him; his friends had an everlasting love for him. One man thought he looked as if he had swallowed a pickle, another said he looked like "Old Scratch" ready to end the world. They could be apt captions for any of Brady's portrait studies of Thaddeus Stevens.

Stevens hated the Confederates and the South and said so on more than one occasion. In July, 1867, while discussing the Military Bill he told the House how he would treat Jefferson Davis and the leaders of the Confederacy. Eyes blazing, his voice trembling, he shouted that if he had his way he would organize "a military tribunal under military power which would put Davis and the others on trial for murder for the Andersonville prison camp deaths and the cold-blooded shooting of Federal prisoners . . ."[187]

When Brady took Stevens' picture he was about seventy-four. His long, pallid face was framed by a rusty brown wig. Keen eyes of an uncertain color glared out from beneath the beetling eyebrows at the flat chevalier lens, and his underlip protruded defiantly.

Brady never caught Stevens smiling for the simple reason that few men ever saw him smile. When he walked into Brady's operating room he walked slowly and with great difficulty, favoring a deformed leg. When he spoke it was in a deep, hollow voice, almost sepulchral.

When Brady took Stevens' portraits, the leader of the Radicals was dying. E. B. Callender recalled that when Stevens rose to speak, two of his friends had to support him. For the first few minutes his voice could barely be heard, but as time passed it grew stronger. When he had been "stung" by a Democrat, he would glare about the room, his eyes burning in his pale face and his voice would rise in volume until it boomed into the remotest corners of the domed roof.[188]

The gentle Carl Schurz knew and was awed by Stevens' sardonic sallies. Once when a Democratic opponent rose to speak Stevens said with a twist of his lip, "I now yield to Mr. B., who will make a few feeble remarks."

The "hot stove" story is also attributed to Stevens.

"You don't mean to say Simon Cameron would steal, would you?" Lincoln once asked him.

"No, I don't think he would steal a red-hot stove," Stevens replied with his customary deadpan face.

Lincoln, who found the joke too good to keep to himself, repeated it to Cameron, who demanded a public apology. Stevens hurried back to the White House.

"Mr. Lincoln, why did you tell Mr. Cameron what I said to you?" he demanded.

Lincoln replied, "I thought it was a good joke and wouldn't make him mad."

Stevens replied, "Well, he is very mad and has made me promise to retract. I will now do so. I believe I told you he would not steal a red-hot stove. I now take that back."[189]

In the summer after Appomattox Stevens usually was carried to the House by two stalwart Negro boys. Once Schurz overheard him say to them as they lifted his frail body into his seat, "Thank you, my good fellows." Then as an afterthought he added, "What shall I do when you are dead and gone?"

In his last year Stevens lived for one ideal. It blazed at white heat in his embittered heart and dictated his every action; he wanted the largest possible Republican majority in Congress and he said that to accomplish it he would seat Beelzebub in preference to the Angel Gabriel had he believed that Beelzebub could help him more than Gabriel in defeating Johnson's Reconstruction Program.[190]

Stevens, for all his bitterness, was an absolutely honest man, who hated hypocrisy and who never asked for mercy from his enemies. Stern, unbending, arrogant, he is a striking figure on the canvas of history.

Brady met Thaddeus Stevens and many other American political leaders and actors and writers in the salon maintained by a journalist-politician, John Forney, on the first floor of the Mills House, where every three months Forney held open house for his friends. There were other photographers on the Washington scene now but Forney recalled that Brady was the only one he invited.

Forney himself left an account of those evenings.[191]

It is the summer of 1865, and the night is warm and ablaze with gaslight. For a larger "meeting" than usual Forney would rent the entire Mills House.

Charles Loring Elliott, who had painted a portrait of Brady, was wont to discuss the "new art" of photography and Brady probably talked with him there.

Thaddeus Stevens, looking like a living corpse, might be there, playing whist with John Law of Indiana. Schuyler Colfax might be discussing politics with George D. Prentice, of the Louisville Journal, and Joseph Medill of the Chicago Tribune, Ben Wade and Oliver Morton.

Edwin Forrest, no stranger to Brady's camera, might come in after the theater, dramatically tossing aside his black cloak and demanding to know where his host might be.

The men would crowd about him, leaving space for a sort of stage in the center of the room on which he could perform: an imitation of a deaf old North Carolina clergyman who thought everyone else in the world was deaf, an account of his meeting with Lafayette in Albany in 1825 and the grand old actor Edmund Kean.

Past midnight was still early for Forrest, "who comes early and stays late." The surprise of the evening, announced by Forney, might be the recital by Forrest of "The Idiot Boy."

Forrest's magnificent voice, soaring and swelling in the hushed room, made the men weep unashamedly before joining in the vigorous applause and shouts of "Bravo."

The evening ended with the singing of "The Star Spangled Banner."

"Goodnight, Mr. Brady," was no doubt heard through the night air as Forney saw his guests to their carriages. Brady might have leaned back against the leather cushions, smelling faintly of cigar smoke and horses, and as the horse clip-clopped back to the Na-

tional Hotel along the silent street, with a smile remembering some of the men he met and the way they looked as they sat in his studio before the unblinking eye of the camera.

It was Schuyler Colfax, dubbed the "Smiler" by the press, who touched off the Radical Revolution. He was an advance man, sent to the capital before the opening of Congress. His voice would be the dictum of Thad Stevens, who had fashioned his thunderbolts that summer in the quiet of his beloved Lancaster.

Colfax, eternally smiling, suave, debonair, with the edge of his political sword always razor sharp, swept into Washington. A crowd gathered at once outside the National Hotel, where Brady and Julia lived, and surely they also heard Colfax's seemingly impromptu speech.

It was a declaration of war between Congress and the President. Congress and not the President would decide the future of the conquered states. It was a violent pro-freedman speech declaring Johnson's Reconstruction program to be invalid. Also incorporated was political proscription for the natural leaders of the South, another point on which Stevens insisted.[192]

Charles Sumner of Massachusetts, who had been photographed by Brady, was pained by Johnson's "prejudices, ignorance and perversity." The president had "had the gall" to ask Sumner about the roll call of murders in his state when Sumner wanted to know when Jefferson Davis and the rest of the Confederate leaders were going to be sent to the gallows for murder.[193]

Congress opened under the iron rule of Stevens. If we could have looked down for a moment from the crowded galleries we would recognize them from the pictures in Brady's gallery; there was scarcely a man in the room who already had not been, or would not soon be photographed for history by Brady.

There was Stevens, "looking so quiet, men stopped to see if he had died in his seat"; Ben Wade, who once kept a loaded horse pistol at his desk; Oliver Morton, stricken by disease and, like Stevens, carried into the chamber, seated in a chair, but always eager to grapple with the hated Democrats; Colfax, smiling, standing behind the speaker's platform and waving to Ben Butler, once called the "Beast" by the ladies of New Orleans; Frederick Douglass, the mulatto orator was there, and hurrying down the aisle dressed in the height of fashion was Henry J. Raymond, Republican chairman and founder of the New York Times, temporarily a champion of Johnsonian policies. He would soon feel the party whip and join the Radicals.

They listened to Johnson's message which Welles, in a diary entry, thought had been polished by Seward, but actually had been written by George Bancroft, the historian, who had introduced Brady to Lincoln in his

Tenth Street Gallery in 1860.[194]

On December 18, Stevens rose to answer Johnson. It was a historic moment in which the future destinies of a people were to be decided, and as Claude Bowers put it, spoke "with the decision and force of an absolute monarch laying down the law to a cringing parliament."

The Committee of Fifteen was appointed, which pointedly ignored Johnson. The Freedman's Bureau Bill was passed, along with the Civil Rights Bill, which made the freed slaves citizens, and finally Congress passed the Fourteenth Amendment and sent it to the states for ratification.

The battle between Stevens' Radicals and President Johnson continued to rage. Congress took away his powers of proclaiming a general pardon for political offenders, command of the army and the right to remove officers. Johnson vetoed each bill but they were railroaded through over his vetoes by two-thirds majorities.

He removed Secretary of War Stanton, who had been double-dealing with the Radicals, but Stanton refused to yield his office and the Senate supported his position by passing a resolution to impeach the President for violating the Tenure of Office Act.

The decision had been made by Stevens on January 6, 1867, when he presided over his revolutionists with the remark: "Yes, sir. I think he ought to be impeached."[195]

There were other stirring events: Mrs. Lincoln, mentally unaccountable, had horrified the country by announcing the sale of her wardrobe; the Democrats had swept Connecticut; Ben Butler had hired detectives to trail Grant, who had turned down the Radicals' offer of the Presidency, and the New York *World* published a sensational story on page one that Thad Stevens was living with a pretty mulatto.[196] Lydia Smith, mother of two children, was Stevens' housekeeper and had known him for many years in Lancaster.

Editor Drake, who wrote the story, pulled no punches. He charged the Radical leader with "living in open adultery with a mulatto woman whom he seduced from her husband, a full blooded Negro. The woman manages his household both in Lancaster and in Washington, speaking of Stevens and herself as 'we.'"

The country waited breathlessly for a typical Stevens roar but there was not even a whisper of protest. It was the talk of Washington and the larger cities but in the few days remaining to him, Stevens never referred to the *World's* story.

When notice of Johnson's second removal of Stanton (Grant had served as Secretary of War for an interim) was relayed to Stevens he gleefully declared, "Didn't I tell you? If you don't kill the beast it will kill you."[197]

He called for Johnson's impeachment, in one of the most dramatic moments in our history. He rose slowly, gripping a heavy cane and standing a moment in silence,

savoring the drama which hung in the crowded chamber. His old voice could be barely heard; sometimes his lips moved but no sound came out. At last he handed his speech to the clerk to read and sat down, "with a half-smile of triumph."

The roll was called—strictly a party vote—and Colfax named a committee to draw up the impeachment papers. The Impeachment Managers presented eleven articles, nine revolving about Stanton's dismissal, and the tenth concerning Johnson's extemporaneous public statements and behavior.

That morning the articles were read. Ben Butler called the President a "criminal," and the Senate refused a forty-day recess but granted ten. The most impressive figure in the courtroom was no stranger to Brady's camera: Chief Justice Salmon P. Chase. His black robes seemed to make him taller, his huge head leaned against the backrest of the chair and his gray eyes constantly swept the chambers. But Stevens dominated the room; the flame of life was flickering low in his breast, but Brady's camera would catch his image before it fluttered and died.

On the morning of the second day Stevens' servant found him staring intently, unable to recognize him. Doctors were called and Stevens recovered. Later that same day—even before they sat to go over the evidence against the President of the United States—the Impeachment Committee hurried to Brady's to have their pictures taken! George W. Julian, in his unpublished diary, used by Bowers in his book, *The Tragic Era*, declared that Stevens was too ill to join the committee at Brady's but the group portrait found in the Brady-Handy collection shows that he did get there.

While the Impeachment proceedings were going on, crowded Washington was enjoying Maggie Mitchell in her favorite roles such as "Jane Eyre," listening to Fanny Kemble's dramatic readings or Ole Bull's violin. Hotels were crowded and Brady's gallery temporarily enjoyed a brisk business.

Then the great day came. A great silence fell over the chamber as the roll was called.

"Not guilty."

The place became a bedlam. Men shouted, jeered and fought each other, while Chase vainly pounded his gavel for order. Suddenly through the waving arms a strange figure emerged; Thaddeus Stevens was being carried out on a stretcher borne aloft by his two faithful Negro boys.

As he appeared outside the crowd roared: "The verdict, Thad . . . the verdict . . ."

Stevens held high his pipestem arms. His face was twisted with rage.

"The country is going to the devil," he croaked. "The country is going to the devil."

Then he lay back, exhausted. Thaddeus Stevens had lost and was going home to die.[199]

The Impeachment over, Washington gradually slipped back to routine. The visitors departed and Brady's temporary boom collapsed. He was again in desperate straits, forced to send several thousand negatives to New York as security against his debts to the Anthonys. Several thousand negatives were in a Washington warehouse gathering dust, and storage fees which Brady could not pay were mounting.

In an attempt to recoup his losses, Brady opened an exhibition of prints from his collection in 1866 at the New York Historical Society. The exhibit was praised by the press, critics and historians but the general public, satiated with blood and death and war, was apathetic. Again failure and debt stalked the great photographer.[200]

On January 29, 1866, the Council of the National Academy of Design adopted a resolution in which it acknowledged the "extensive and valuable Collection of Photographs by Mr. M. B. Brady of Scenes, Incidents and Portraits connected with the late Rebellion and other material of historic interest as one of great value, as a nucleus of a National Historical Museum, as reliable authority for Art and illustrative of our history." It strongly recommended the proposal to secure for it a safe and permanent place in the keeping of the Historical Society. But no action was taken.[201]

On February 3, 1866, Grant wrote to Brady from "Hd. Qrs. Armies of the U. S., Washington, D. C.": "I am glad to learn that you have determined to place on permanent exhibition . . . your Collection of Photographic Views of Battlefields taken on the spot while the occurrences represented were taking place.

"I knew when many of these representations were being taken, have in my possession many of them and I can say that the scenes were not only spirited and correct but also well chosen.

"The Collection will be valuable to the student and the artist of the present generation; but how much more valuable it will be to the future generations."

Admiral David G. Farragut sent Brady a note on November 1, 1866, from his New York City residence: "I have had the pleasure of seeing many of the Photographic War Pictures in your collection and have admired their spirit and truth.

"The intention of transferring permanently this Collection to . . . is one that must meet the approval of every lover of Art and History."

But not even the personal and sincere endorsements of the great general and admiral could move Congress.

It was about this time that Brady had a young visitor in his Washington gallery. It was Julia's nephew, Levin Handy, just twelve, a bright-eyed lad with a small bowler hat.

Young Handy came in one afternoon bouncing a ball. "I've come to work for you, Uncle Mat," he said. "I want to be a photographer like you."

Brady chuckled. "Go back to school, boy."

Young Handy shook his head. "I can't, Uncle Matt, until the teacher sends for me." He then explained what had happened. On his way to school he had found a small hollow rubber ball and at the noontime recess had filled it with water at the school pump.

It was a warm spring day and the windows were open and he was dozing, bored with whatever lessons were being taught, when a classmate "made a face" at him. Young Handy took aim with the ball and squeezed it. The stream hit the boy in the face. He let out a squeal and the teacher rushed down the aisle, confiscated the ball and told young Handy to go home "and not come back until I send for you."

"How did I know he was going to squeal?" young Handy asked innocently.

Brady chuckled and sent his nephew to a back room to coat some plates. The following day Brady was out. The third day he saw young Levin and asked, "What are you doing here instead of being at school?"

Young Handy looked him in the eye and said unsmilingly, "She hasn't sent for me, Uncle Matt, so I guess I had better stay here."

The teacher never sent for him and Levin Handy stayed at the Pennsylvania Avenue gallery. At first he coated plates, but as the months passed by he begged his uncle to allow him to try taking pictures. Brady agreed and discovered Levin had a knack for taking fine portraits.

He taught him all he knew and within two years—by the time Levin Handy was fifteen—he was one of the youngest photographers in America, taking pictures of the many notables who came to Brady's gallery.

THE CAMERA UNDER WESTERN SKIES

MATHEW B. BRADY missed one of the greatest epochs of American history—the opening of the western frontier—but cameramen to whom he had passed on some of his spirit were on hand to record the great events and to preserve pictorially the magnificent drama for unborn Americans.

The indomitable Tim O'Sullivan, who had learned photography under Brady in the daguerreotype era, and who had walked with him on the bloody fields of Gettysburg, was the official photographer of the United States Geological Exploration of the Fortieth Parallel under the leadership of Clarence King. In 1870 he brought his camera into the jungles of the Isthmus of Darien (Panama) for the exploration and survey for a ship canal by way of the Isthmus of Darien. In 1871, '73 and '75 he was in charge of photographic activities on the United States Geographic Survey West of the One Hundredth Meridian and his photographs became an official part of the record of these surveys. His courage and ingenuity were praised by Captain Wheeler, who headed the western explorations.[203]

Alexander Gardner closed his "Gardner's Art Gallery" at 511 Seventh Street, Washington, two years after Appomattox and left for the West to photograph the Union Pacific, Eastern Division. Other photographers would follow, such as W. H. Jackson, who was the photographer for the Hayden surveys of the West and whose beautiful photographs of Yellowstone helped persuade Congress to set aside the region as the country's first national park. In 1872 Jackson photographed the wilderness that is now Grand Teton National Park. In 1874 he had taken many views in the heart of the Colorado Rockies, and in 1875 he and Ernest Ingersoll photographed ruins of cliff dwellings in what is now Mesa Verde National Park.[204]

Jackson's place in the Western history of the United States is well known but it is Tim O'Sullivan who deserves just as much credit but who has been sadly neglected by historians.

Tim O'Sullivan, like his friend, instructor and employer, Mathew B. Brady, is a shadowy figure composed only of a name, dates, official reports and a self-portrait. A friend described him as an "educated gentleman of superior qualifications in his profession and in every way personally worthy and a Tip Top Republican in the bargain . . ."

He was born in New York City about 1840, and learned photography in one of Brady's galleries, probably at 359 Broadway, where Brady had the most operators. During the war he is said to have served as a First Lieutenant on the staff of General Vielie and was honorably discharged at Hilton Head, S. C., in May, 1862.[205]

He probably then returned to Brady's employ, although Alexander Gardner said after the war that O'Sullivan worked for him for seven years as superintendent of field or map work for the Army of the Potomac.

Although it is hard to trace the working records of the Civil War photographers, it is evident that O'Sullivan was employed by Brady and was with him at Gettysburg. The stirring pictures that O'Sullivan took were published under Brady's by-line in *Harper's* and obviously came from Brady's studios.

After Appomattox Brady broke up his famous photographic teams and the restless O'Sullivan joined the first of the government geological survey teams as official photographer. This expedition was the United States Geological Exploration of the Fortieth Parallel under the leadership of Clarence King. It began in western

HIGH WATER.

GOLD HILL AND SILVER CITY.

THE PHOTOGRAPHER'S OUTFIT.

SHIFTING SAND-MOUNDS.

THE NETTIE.

TRAVELING ABOVE THE SNOW-LINE.

Figs. 31-36. Woodcut reproductions of Tim O'Sullivan's photographs for the King Expedition, from *Harper's Weekly*, September, 1869.

Nevada on July 1, 1867, and continued through the years 1867, '68 and '69. [206]

The expedition consisted of forty "scientific gentlemen," including civilians such as cooks and packers, numbering seventeen and a small boat, the *Nettie*. Eight troopers from the Eighth United States Cavalry guarded the party from marauding Indians. Two mules and "an experienced packer" were assigned to O'Sullivan to carry his equipment.

The team set out from California, stopping at Nevada City long enough to let O'Sullivan make the first ground shots of a mine several hundred feet underground at the Comstock Lode. These he made with the aid of burning magnesium wire.

The expedition then moved northward to the Truckee River, which empties its alkaline waters into the southern portion of Pyramid Lake. O'Sullivan erected his homemade darkroom in the stern of the *Nettie* and the oarsmen cast off to survey the unknown.

It was the first time a boat had gone down the river. Unknown to the party a large stretch of rapids and high falls had to be encountered before the boat slid into Pyramid Lake.

The men bent to their oars as O'Sullivan went about preparing his equipment. Suddenly a needle-pointed rock loomed up ahead, with white water foaming about it. The boatmen stabbed their poles deep and fought the current, in an endeavor to swing the boat to shore. A trunk of a tree swept past and as the sweating men in the boat watched, it hit the rapids, leaped high into the air, only to be swallowed, as if by a hungry monster.

As the *Nettie* entered the rapids she was slammed between two rocks. The sudden jerk and the current swept away the oars of the crew, who were almost thrown overboard.

The shore lay forty yards across the bubbling, hissing water. O'Sullivan, later described as "a swimmer of no ordinary power," stripped to the skin and dived overboard. While his crew watched breathlessly he fought the current, sometimes disappearing from sight. At last, after being swept two hundred feet downstream, O'Sullivan staggered up the bank and after a rest, walked back to where the boat was snagged.

A member of the crew threw O'Sullivan a hawser, using his pocketbook, containing three hundred dollars in twenty-dollar goldpieces, as a weight. O'Sullivan caught the hawser but the wallet fell into the water. "That was rough," he recalled, "for I never found that wallet again, although I prospected a long time, barefooted, for it."

O'Sullivan tied the rope about a tree trunk and after the crew worked the boat loose, O'Sullivan pulled it ashore. The *Nettie* was badly damaged, half-full of water and the provisions waterlogged. Fortunately, O'Sullivan's camera and chemicals, in watertight sacks, were not damaged. [207]

In the morning they portaged about the rapids, and late in the afternoon entered Pyramid Lake, a strange, windy spot thirty miles long and twelve miles wide.

O'Sullivan spent the next few days taking a number of pictures of the pyramid-like rocks, some five hundred feet high, which gave the lake its name. Once, trying for an elevated shot, by climbing on one of the rocks, O'Sullivan found himself in a bevy of angry, hissing rattlesnakes.

"Snakes! Rattlers!" the photographer yelled and the rest of the party came on the run with clubs and rocks and six-shooters. The morning was devoted to killing rattlers but it was finally agreed the snake army was too large, so O'Sullivan and his men retreated. That evening supper was of baked "*couier*," a fighting game fish resembling the landlocked salmon and weighing, O'Sullivan reported, as much as twenty-five pounds.

O'Sullivan made the return trip overland, packing the camera and equipment on his back, to a point where horses and additional equipment waited, while the others went back up the river on the *Nettie*.

O'Sullivan's camera next caught the wild beauty of the Humboldt Valley and Sink, a favorite spot for raiding Piutes looking for horses and stock.

O'Sullivan's trip through the Sink, a section of land formed by the fierce convulsions of the earth during an earthquake, was an unforgettable journey. Before it was over the photographer, his packers, and his mules were ready to drop from exhaustion; hooves and feet had been badly lacerated by sharp stones and rocks. More than once O'Sullivan froze in his tracks, a prayer on his lips, as a rock he had dislodged bounced down the sides of the Sink. As he later recalled, one false move could have started a landslide and he and his mules and his packers would have vanished without a trace.

They climbed ten thousand feet until the mules, gasping for breath in the thin air, lay down and refused to budge. Then O'Sullivan and his men went on alone, lugging the equipment.

Fever, probably malaria, called the "mountain ail," was rampant and what with bouts of fever, the rough country and the lack of water and food, O'Sullivan was finally forced to abandon the Sink and join the rest of the party exploring the mountain divides. Most of the traveling had to be done at midnight when the snow crust was hard enough to hold the weight of the horses and mules.

In the Ruby Range, "the finest of the Rocky cordon," O'Sullivan took pictures of breathless beauty; of wild mountain lakes, canyons large enough to hold a town and towering peaks.

When King told O'Sullivan of a shifting desert, a hundred miles to the south of the Carson Sink, and asked if he wanted to take some pictures of it, he readily agreed. For this trip King ordered a wartime ambulance turned over to O'Sullivan, with a team of four mules and enough water casks for his plates.

It was a rough and dangerous journey, but finally O'Sullivan found himself driving the creaking old ambulance into a quiet world of shifting pure white dunes that sparkled in the fierce sunlight like mounds of diamond chips. A soft, whispering wind frolicked among the dunes, and O'Sullivan, who sat in the driver's seat shading his eyes from the fierce sun, later recalled he could see tiny whirlpools "carry the sparkling crystals up the side of a mound, in the form of a whirlwind."

After taking a series of pictures, O'Sullivan joined the main party advancing eastward toward the beautiful Shoshone Falls on the Snake River, in the vicinity of Salt Lake. He took many pictures in this beautiful land, known but to the mountain men and the Indians.

O'Sullivan returned, whether to Washington or New York we do not know. We like to think he went back for a brief visit with the old picture-maker who had taught him so much, Mathew B. Brady.

But O'Sullivan evidently did not care for cities. In 1870 he joined Captain (later Commander) T. O. Selfridge's expedition to the jungles of Darien (Panama).[208]

Secretary of the Navy George M. Robeson directed the expedition to explore three proposed routes across the Isthmus: the San Blas from the bay of that name on the Atlantic Ocean to the mouth of the Bayamo, or Chepo River, on the Pacific; the route which led across the jungles from the Caledonia Bay to the Gulf of San Miguel, and the third, the Tuyra Route, a jungle trail which crossed the mountains in the vicinity of the mouth of the Atrate River, following the floor of the valley of the Darien, or Tuyre River, to the Gulf of San Miguel.

It was an enormous task. The country was wild and largely unexplored—"rarely traversed by white men," as Selfridge described it—and inhabited by savage tribes, particularly the San Blas or Darien Indians, led by an evil old villain nicknamed "Shoemaker" because of his love of white men's shoes. Legends and the tales of trappers and clipper seamen who had touched Panama's seaport towns, painted the San Blas Indians as bristling with poison darts and arrows which supposedly killed a man within minutes.

The party left the Battery on New Year's Day, 1870, on the Navy schooner, *Nipaio,* loaded down with 7,000 pounds of bacon, 10,000 pounds of bread, 2,500 pounds of coffee and more than 600 pairs of shoes, some for walking, some for Chief "Shoemaker's" Indians.

The expedition consisted of two hundred and eighty men, including naval officers, surveyors, geologists, mapmakers, and experts in many other fields. Tim O'Sullivan was listed as official photographer. He took aboard several hundred wet plates, chemicals, cameras, a portable darkroom, such as he used on the King expedition in the West and also equipment to make a crude dark-

room aboard the smaller boats which the expedition would use on the winding rivers.

Several weeks later they disembarked at Porto Bello, where Selfridge tried to hire Palenque guides, a dark, handsome race "descended from the Spanish maroons." But when the navy commander told them he was planning to enter the interior, they threw up their hands and shook their heads. Selfridge wrote, "No inducement on my part could persuade them to go with the expedition; their fear of the Indians overpowered their love of gain."

Despite the dire predictions of the Palenques, Selfridge gave the order to march and the long column wove its way into the jungle, with Selfridge in the lead, followed by O'Sullivan leading his mules on which he had packed his cameras and equipment.

They followed the Diablo, a twisted river of boiling rapids and thunderous waterfalls. It wound through the rain forests, heavy with the stench of decaying vegetation, and alive with the calls of strange and beautiful birds.

The army and navy officers sent out after the Civil War on such explorations told their stories in official reports simply, without underscoring the drama of their accomplishments, and although Selfridge wrote knowingly of terrain, river routes, climate and animal habitation of the Isthmus of Darien, he spoke casually of the hardships he and his men endured for months in the terrible jungles. "Hardly a day passes without seeing a tiger and the growth is so thick, they (the members of the party) had to hack their way through with machetes, and wild pigs and peccaries are in abundance. . . ." his report reads.

Selfridge's official reports included colorful engravings based on the three hundred negatives which O'Sullivan took in that year; here are the almost unimpenetrable rain forests, the raging rapids they either portaged around or ran in the log boats supplied by the Indians; and here too are the exhausted members of the party, who, Selfridge later said, had been reduced to human skeletons by hardships and fatigue, sprawled about the small campfire on the bank of some lonely jungle river.

It was O'Sullivan's camera which captivated the San Blas Indians from the first time they saw the white men. "Shoemaker" was curious, but would not pose until he had been bribed with several pairs of shoes.

There is no official account of how the Indians, described by Selfridge as "squat and suspicious," treated O'Sullivan or his camera but if they behaved like the Indians of the Western plains, one can visualize them at first studying the camera, muttering and grunting to themselves, then, as they conquered their fear, crowding about, peering into the strange, upside-down world of the lens and poking O'Sullivan perhaps as if he were some unearthly spirit.

An Indian whom Selfridge named "Jim" guided them

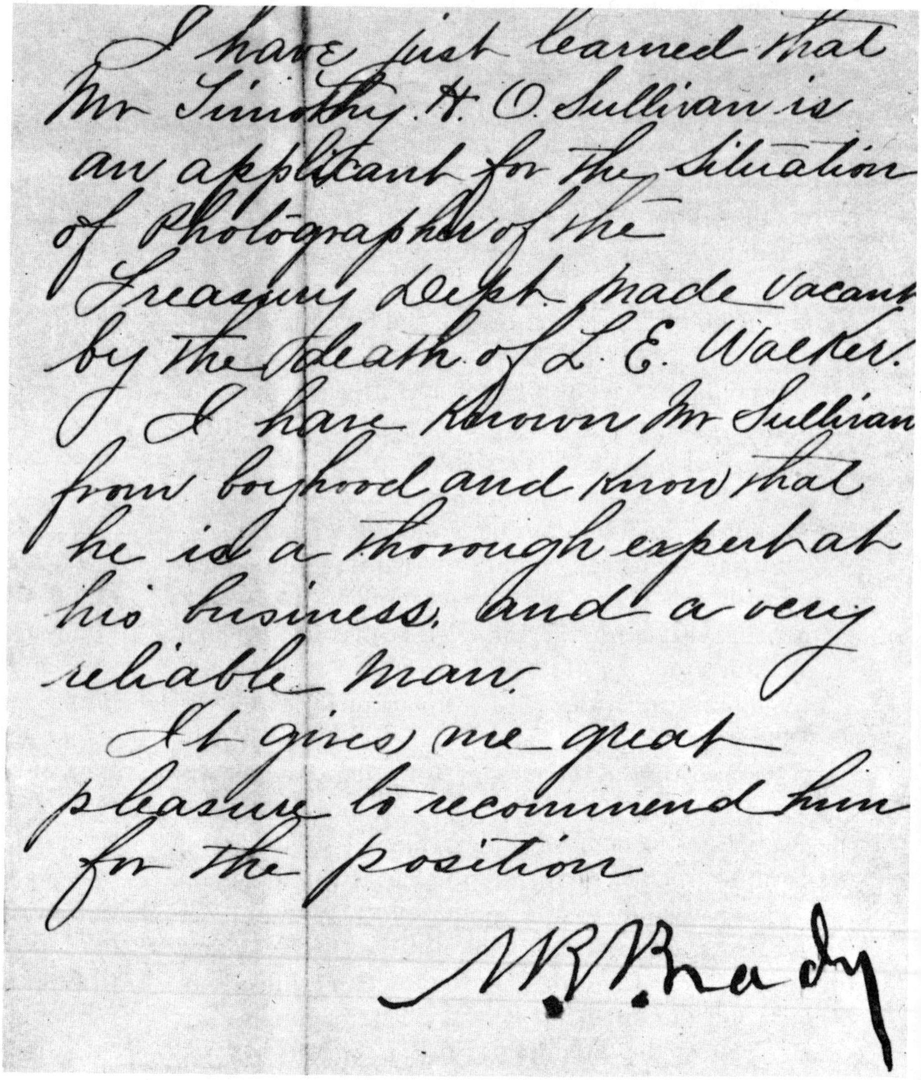

I have just learned that Mr Timothy H. O'Sullivan is an applicant for the situation of Photographer of the Treasury Dept. made vacant by the death of L. E. Walker.

I have known Mr Sullivan from boyhood and know that he is a thorough expert at his business, and a very reliable man.

It gives me great pleasure to recommend him for the position

M. B. Brady

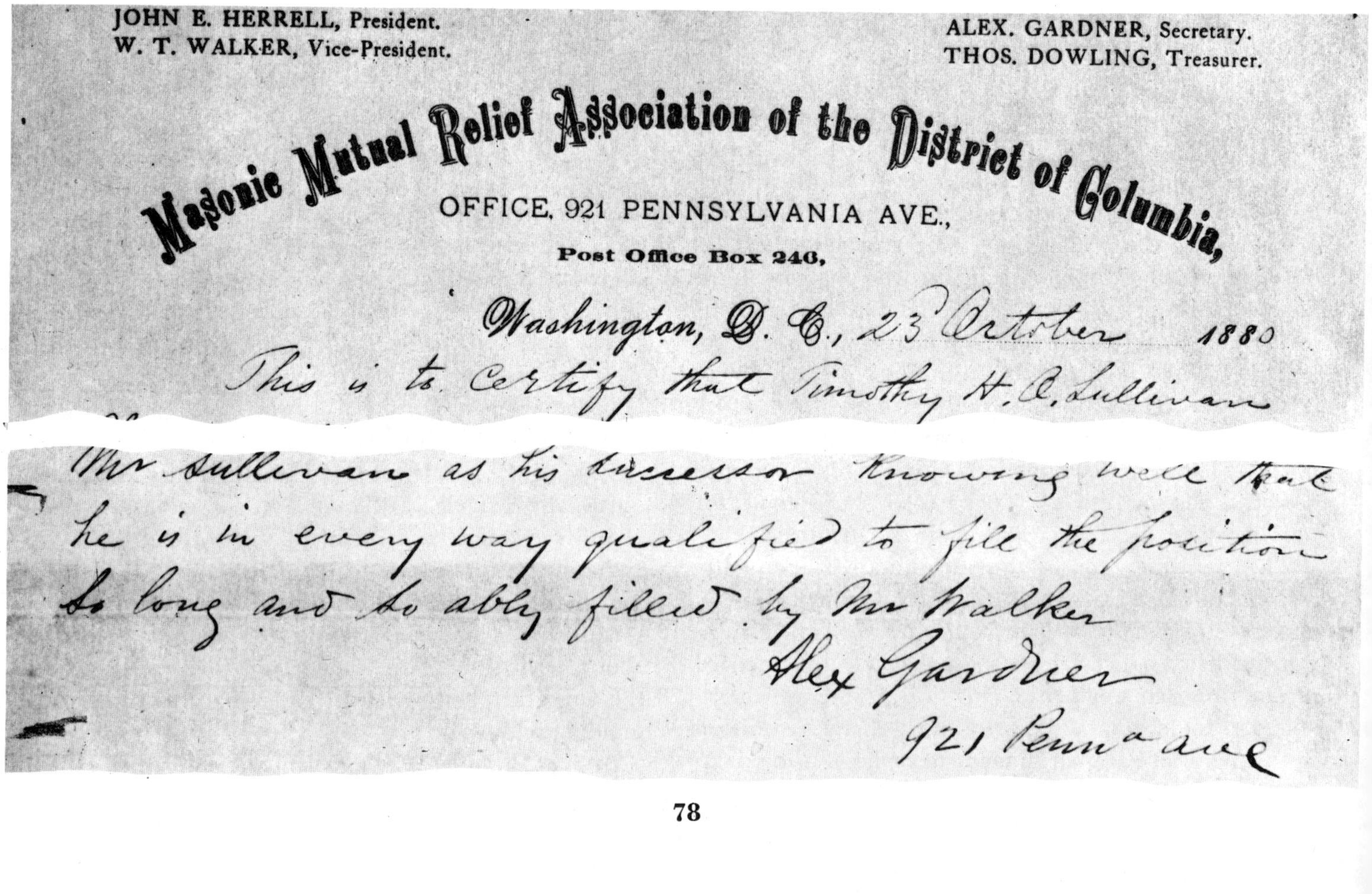

Figs. 37 and 38. Brady and Gardner letters of recommendation for O'Sullivan, *Treasury Department, National Archives.*

JOHN E. HERRELL, President.
W. T. WALKER, Vice-President.

ALEX. GARDNER, Secretary.
THOS. DOWLING, Treasurer.

Masonic Mutual Relief Association of the District of Columbia,

OFFICE, 921 PENNSYLVANIA AVE.,

Post Office Box 246,

Washington, D. C., 23 October 1880

This is to certify that Timothy H. O. Sullivan

Mr Sullivan as his successor knowing well that he is in every way qualified to fill the position so long and so ably filled by Mr Walker

Alex Gardner

921 Penn ave

78

along the San Blas River to the mouth of the Bayamo. When they were nearing the end of their surveys, it rained, as Selfridge wrote, "such a rain as may be called a deluge . . ."

The myth of the deadly poison of the Indians was exploded somewhere along the survey; how, Selfridge does not disclose. He says simply that the drug the Indians used was not fatal but "raised only a few minor blisters."

Jungle tribes are traditionally reluctant to divulge secrets of their weapons and it would be fascinating to know how he arrived at this conclusion.

The expedition returned in the winter of 1871. The health of the expedition was "a matter of surprise," as Selfridge noted, with many cases of malaria and minor infections and wounds. There was only one death, an accidental drowning.

However, despite the low mortality rate, O'Sullivan and the other members of the exploring parties, were reduced to bearded, emaciated skeletons, as Selfridge noted, "was due more to exhaustion than to climate . . . all were worn out and much in need of rest."

O'Sullivan returned to Washington, a sick and an exhausted man. In a few months he slipped from history's pages. We will not hear of him until 1880 when Brady and Alexander Gardner both sent letters recommending him for a job as a photographer in the Treasury Department.

Like O'Sullivan, Alexander Gardner was restless after the war and in 1867 he closed his Washington gallery and went west to photograph the Union Pacific, Eastern Division.

From September to October, 1867, he made one of the finest collections of scenes of the Western frontier. McCoy was moving his great herds up north along the Chisholm Trail to Abilene; Ellsworth was a town only three months old, Salina and Hays City had been born almost on the very day Gardner planted his camera on their Main Street. He took McCoy's stockyard only a short time after the great trail-blazer had established it as a railhead for Texas beef cattle driving north.

Gardner drove a small carriage, the back part of which was equipped as a crude darkroom. A dour-looking, taciturn man, the Lawrence *Daily Tribune* noted on September 15, 1867, as he rode unconcernedly down Massachusetts Avenue "to take a view." He was in town under the auspices of the Union Pacific "to make draughts of points along the road."

Gardner was an indefatigable worker; he took pictures not only of "gandy-dancers" laying track, but of anything else that seemed interesting. As a result, in the Kansas State Historical Society is a fine collection of early scenes of the West when the early wagon trains were beginning to move out.

Other great photographers, not all Brady-trained, of course, followed O'Sullivan and Gardner. And of course, there had been some who preceded them, such as the little known Oliver Jennings, who planned to take a series of pictures of the "Indians in their natural surroundings" in Oregon in 1851, but whose camera and chemicals were stolen by "thieving soldiers."

Joseph Buchtel, who placed one of the first photographic advertisements in the West in the Oregon City *Spectator* on January 30, 1851, was another. Buchtel, who has been called "the Brady of the Northwest," took excellent daguerreotypes of early leaders of the Northwest, Indians, captives, mountains and valleys.[209]

In September, 1853, the Baltimore daguerreotypist, S. N. Carvalho, had accompanied Colonel John C. Fremont's expedition and made a series of scenes under extreme difficulties. Carvalho's copper plates were brought back to New York in the winter of 1855 and Brady was employed to copy them by the wet plate process so that paper prints could be made.[210]

The daguerreotypes and the paper prints were believed to have been consumed in a fire in which Mrs. Fremont said many of their possessions were destroyed. However, in the Brady daguerreotype collection in the Library of Congress is a faded-copper plate of an Indian village. From the style of the tepee it would seem to be one of the western plains Indian villages. It may be one of the Carvalho daguerreotypes of the first Fremont expedition and one of the earliest pictures ever taken of the American West.[211]

THE LAST YEARS

IN 1869 there was a new regime. Ulysses S. Grant was now President and there was a new air in Washington. E. L. Godkin found it a gayer city, populated by people "who wanted to amuse themselves." The streets were paved, the hogs and chickens were gone and many great new mansions had been built. There was a new "smartness and enterprise about the place." Even the men in both Houses of Congress were wearing clean shirts "almost every day."

The horse-drawn streetcars were crowded to the very last step with government clerks who earned from $1,000 a year to $6,000. A young widow, a friend of a New York *World* reporter, received $1,200 a year as a clerk on which to raise six children, and her sister, a "copyist who was only twenty," earned $900.

This was the busy, lively city Brady knew and loved. It is well worth accompanying a New York *World* reporter who inspected it on a spring morning in 1871. Most of the people he met were friends of Brady; many his favorite subjects.[212]

The church bells were tolling eight as he joined the hundreds of government employees who walked rather than rode to work. As he passed the War Department he saw Secretary of War Belknap, with his golden brown beard and his startling blue eyes, tip his hat to a young secretary as he entered the building.

A block away from the White House he saw "the most talked about man in America" coming out of the Presidential mansion for his fifteen-minute morning stroll, an inevitable cigar clenched in one corner of his mouth and his gloved hands clasped behind him. Grant moved ponderously "poking along on a beeline," his chin on his vest, his eyes seemingly fixed on a spot several feet in front of him. His face was impassive and he did not seem to hear or see the people who made way for him. "Only the most audacious of officeholders"

dared to tip their hats and bid him good morning. A block or two later he met Vice President Colfax who, in contrast to the brooding Grant, walked at a brisk, fast pace, every few steps tipping his hat to a lady and inquiring as to her health, as if he were "running for office every morning."

The avenue was alive with vendors of milk, oysters and vegetables. An oysterman held up a dripping bit of oyster meat, swallowing it in one gulp and shouting, "Oyster! Oyster! Heah, I say! Try them fo' yoself, suh."

A few feet distant was a vegetable cart and a Negro who was juggling potatoes, his booming cries echoing over the avenue. "Tatoes! Tatoes! Get your tatoes here." From a suddenly opened window across the street a young Negro maid shrilled down at him, "What fo' you make all dat noise? You wake the dead, man."

At Fifteenth and Pennsylvania Avenue one of the streetcars stopped and a tall, robust man wearing an open gray shirt, black slouch hat and brown pants with one trouser leg rolled up, leapt off the platform with the ponderous grace of a huge bear. A young clerk pointed him out. "There goes Walt Whitman."

Another replied, "Is that the author of *Leaves of Grass?* I might have thought so."

A tall man, appearing much taller with his shiny black hat, hurried through the crowd, the warm spring breeze flirting with the tails of his black coat. After a quick puff he flipped his cigar butt into the gutter and with one last deep breath of the mild spring air, Secretary Boutwell entered the Treasury.

The morning mist had been burned away and about a mile down the avenue the gleaming dome of the Capitol was visible. At the south end of the Treasury, workmen were busy about the foundation which was to support a statue of Grant on a bronze horse. Lined up at the curb at Willard's. were more than twenty-five hacks, their Negro drivers, dressed in ragged coats and broken boots, shouting at prospective customers as they passed. Opposite Willard's, on "Newspaper Row," young Hogjaw, a familiar Negro bootblack, ran up. His mouth, they said, was so big that the pitcher of the Atlantic Club "could easily pocket his ball in Hogjaw's mouth at thirty yards."

After a five-cent shine Hogjaw turned around and whacked one of his enormous bare feet with a brush, "Lie still, lie still, you foot! Stirring up all dat dust dat way to make the gentleman dirty." For ten extra pennies Hogjaw danced a Virginia Juba, whirling about and jigging up and down, his feet making loud slapping sounds on the pavement. When a crowd collected he opened his mouth wide and pointed to it, the signal for the spectators to throw in nickels and pennies until Hogjaw's cheeks ballooned. With a last glimpse of the Capitol, gleaming bravely in the morning sun, the reporter turned to the business of the day.

The society of this bustling city was ruled for a time by proud Kate Chase Sprague, whose imperial sway was reminiscent of the power Aaron Burr's daughter Theodosia held over men's imaginations. Kate, one of the most astute politicians in Ohio when she was still in her teens, was the daughter of Chief Justice Chase.[213] At a time when most young girls were occupied with dolls, she was running her father's household—at five she was soothing her father's tired brain by reading him the Book of Job and reciting poetry as he relaxed before retiring.

When her father entered the Cabinet as Lincoln's Secretary of the Treasury she was twenty. Her poise, intellect and beauty captured Washington and her suitors were legion. Always ambitious, she visualized her father as President and herself as the mistress of the White House. At twenty-four, when she had overshadowed Dolley Madison's reputation as a hostess, she married the handsome and wealthy Senator Sprague of Rhode Island. Her wedding was one of the most famous of its time, her guest list the most fabulous in the land, her trousseau that of a princess. By the end of the war she was the unchallenged arbiter of Washington's society, a position strongly resented by Mary Todd Lincoln, who preferred to reign unrivaled as "First Lady of the Land."

A few years after her marriage the first hint of the dark shadows that were to cloud her life edged across her heart. Sprague was an alcoholic and although his intoxication publicly humiliated her, she was always a poised beauty who could parry the compliments of diplomats with brilliant repartee.

The birth of Kate's first child was hailed as a great national event. The details of her baby's layette were reported fully in the large newspapers and when her child began to talk, its babyish sayings were passed from person to person.

Brady took several poses of her when she was at the height of her social power. Whether he personally took the pictures we do not know. Young Handy might have snapped the shutter, but Brady was there to direct the lighting and the poses.

In contrast to her studied elegance was the raffish charm of a white-haired old lady who visited Brady's gallery one day. She was Peggy O'Neal Eaton, who at seventy could entice a young musician many years her junior into a brief but hilarious marriage.[214]

When she tottered into Brady's Washington gallery sometime during Grant's first administration, it was one of her rare excursions from her home on I Street. It wasn't every day that Peggy became flesh and blood instead of the glamorous legend who had danced and loved her way through the most stirring times of American history.

The daughter of a tavern-keeper, her name became a *cause célèbre* when Andrew Jackson insisted that as the wife of one of his Cabinet members she be accepted by diplomatic Washington society. The scandal concerned her relationship with Mr. Eaton while she was married to a Mr. Timberlake.

One wishes that Brady had been able to take a picture of Kate Chase in her last years after the disintegration of her marriage and her affair with Roscoe Conkling when she was reduced to selling milk and eggs from a farm near Washington. But Kate, unlike Peggy, would never let the camera capture her image on the wet plate in those tragic days when she was a living ghost, wearing old-fashioned gowns and hats and torn gloves which failed to hide her rough, red hands, once kissed by presidents.

Another romantic visitor to Brady's was Senator Isaac Christiancy of Michigan, whose love story had the society ladies of Washington whispering over their teacups. The senator had the audacity to marry a young German girl, described by the *World* as "a pretty but obscure government clerk."[216]

The day after the news broke of the quiet wedding, the wives of the senators met and found the young girl "guilty of trying to force her way into their exclusive society." Over their teacups they voted the verdict—ostracism. The newly married couple found all doors closed to them.

Mrs. John A. Logan, wife of the Civil War general, who told about it in her memoirs of Washington society, met with Mrs. Hamilton Fish and together these ladies decided the Senator and his lady must have "vindication."[217]

Dressed in their best, they visited the young girl and had tea. Before they left Mrs. Fish invited the couple to a dinner at her home to be held in their honor. As Mrs.

Logan wrote with satisfaction, "No further adverse comments were heard."

Brady's gallery never lacked the presence of beautiful women. One of the most striking portraits he, or one of his assistants, took in those days was that of Madame Catacazy, wife of the Russian minister. Though past her bloom when she sat for him, the statuesque woman with the thick golden hair was still enchanting. Society reporters still talked of her "complexion delicately tinted as the heart of a seashell, of her gorgeous hair with massive braids shot through with a dead gold arrow."[218]

At the time she posed for Brady or one of his assistants, her mansion on I Street near Fourteenth, with its beautiful Paris furniture, was one of the showplaces of the city.

Her "consort" accompanied her to Brady's gallery. Their romantic story was one the society matrons in Brady's time liked to tell their daughters. Madame Catacazy had been married as a young girl to a man old enough to be her grandfather, and she went as his wife to Dom Pedro's court. There she met and fell in love with young Catacazy, then Secretary of the Russian Legation.

One day they disappeared and later were found living together in a small house. When her lover was recalled to Russia she followed him, risking death or imprisonment. A year later they were married and Catacazy was named Russian Ambassador to the United States.

There were many other Brady sitters who had played their part in History's drama and then were forgotten. But some—like Robert E. Lee— had not been forgotten.[219]

Perhaps Lee wanted to see the man who had photographed him in his battle gray after Appomattox, or Lee may have gone to Brady's studio because it was the thing to do, the accepted custom of men in the public eye.

The years must have passed swiftly across their minds as they met; Lee in the chair and Brady standing near the camera while one of his assistants took the picture. Or perhaps on this great occasion Brady once again peered into the lens.

The years show in Brady's picture of Lee; the short beard and hair were now snow-white, the ravages of war and defeat quite marked.

Surely they talked of the war . . . of men they had both known who were now dead, and of the great days. But the words and memories they recalled that quiet afternoon were lost. Brady had no Boswell.

They were all conscious of History, these men who had worn the blue and gray. The Negro helpers had only begun to gather up the bones on the Cold Harbor battlefield when they began to write and publish their memoirs. When they came to Washington as Congressmen or Senators they seldom missed the opportunity to have their pictures taken at Brady's studio. To them Brady was the historic photographer and they knew full well the part both had played in one of the great dramas of the world.

Fitzhugh Lee, Thomas L. Rossner, Beverly Robinson, William Paine, Pierce Young, all Confederate generals, met in Washington and after a few drinks drove to Brady's to pose for a picture. The print disappeared and was only recently discovered in the Brady-Handy Collection. Senator William Mahone, of Petersburg fame, still wearing the beard which gave him a photographic kinship to some of John Brown's late portraits, walked in one day dressed in a conservative tweed suit

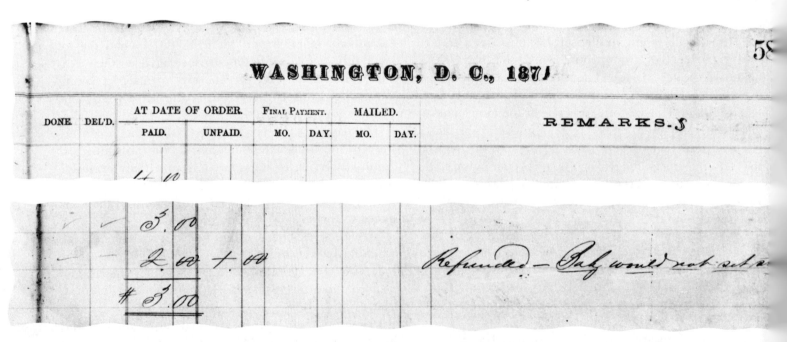

Fig. 39. From Brady's Washington *Register*, 1871. *Brady-Handy Collection, Library of Congress.*

to pose for several fine portraits. The drummer boy, John Clem, whose exploits with Rosecrans' army in Tennessee were still occasionally mentioned in the newspapers, came to Brady. Indians who came to Washington to see the Great White Father; General Custer, Ben Butler who remembered Brady when others had forgotten him; General Garfield, to become a President; General Crook, who fought the Indians of the Western plains; generals, admirals, heroes, villains, scoundrels, Presidents, emperors, society belles, actors, actresses—the list is endless—found their way to Brady's studio.

But the debts Brady had acquired during the war were too much; the money he made never seemed to be enough to pay for rent and supplies.

Brady tried several times by exhibitions to interest the government in buying his collection but was unsuccessful. On March 3, 1871, the Joint Committee on the Library recommended to Congress the purchase of the collection which they called "A National Collection of Portraits of Eminent Americans."[220] Congress had little time to consider the purchase of photographic negatives and ignored the Joint Committee's message.

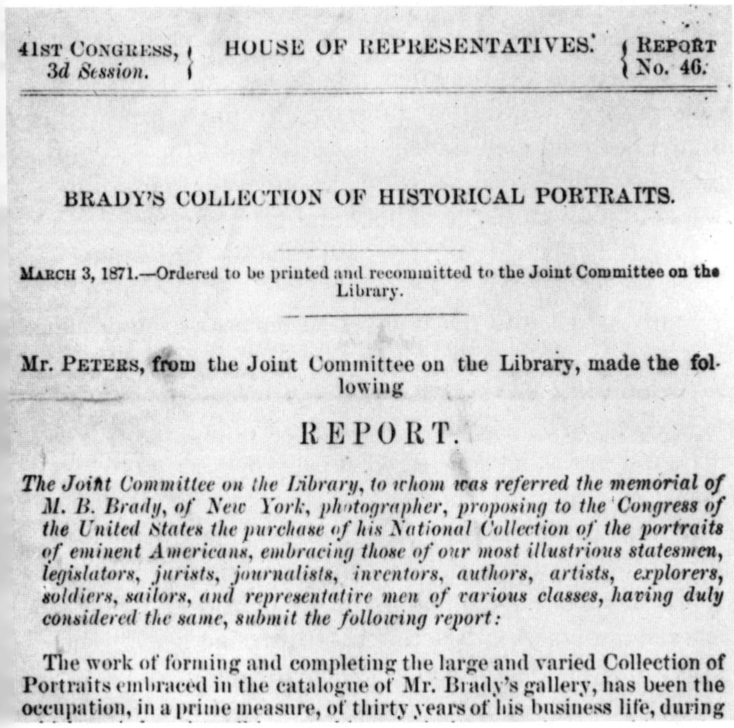

41st Congress, 3d Session.	HOUSE OF REPRESENTATIVES.	Report No. 46.

BRADY'S COLLECTION OF HISTORICAL PORTRAITS.

March 3, 1871.—Ordered to be printed and recommitted to the Joint Committee on the Library.

Mr. Peters, from the Joint Committee on the Library, made the following

REPORT.

The Joint Committee on the Library, to whom was referred the memorial of M. B. Brady, of New York, photographer, proposing to the Congress of the United States the purchase of his National Collection of the portraits of eminent Americans, embracing those of our most illustrious statesmen, legislators, jurists, journalists, inventors, authors, artists, explorers, soldiers, sailors, and representative men of various classes, having duly considered the same, submit the following report:

The work of forming and completing the large and varied Collection of Portraits embraced in the catalogue of Mr. Brady's gallery, has been the occupation, in a prime measure, of thirty years of his business life, during

Fig. 40. From the *Congressional Record*, 1871.

In the winter of 1871 there was added sadness. There was one last legal recourse: bankruptcy. The official records, cannot reveal his despair, but surely the end of the road must have seemed perilously near.

Three years later, in the spring of 1874, Brady was notified by the owners of the warehouse where he kept a great number of wartime plates that he owed $2,840 and that unless the fee were paid his property would be put up for auction.

Brady was unable to pay and the auction took place. Ironically, the buyer was the United States Government.

Secretary of War Belknap put in a bid and the plates were transferred to a government warehouse where indifference and carelessness destroyed many of them. Belknap later said the amount paid by the government was from money accumulated by provost marshals during the war and which had been turned over to the Adjutant General after hostilities had ended.

A year passed and Brady's financial reverses grew more critical. In 1875 Butler and General Garfield stood up for him in Congress and demanded that he be paid for his devotion to his country's history.[221]

It was during the close of the 43rd session of Congress, when Butler and Garfield tried to force through an amendment to the Sundry Civil Appropriation Act to pay Brady $25,000 for the full title to the Brady Collection of Civil War Plates. Butler argued that the government did not have clear title to Brady's plates, even though Secretary of War Belknap had paid the storage fees.

The businessmen in Congress were not interested in a man who had used up his own fortune to preserve his country's heritage and as one Congressman pointed out to Butler and Garfield, why spend money for pictures "when every town and hamlet in America preserves and perpetuates whatever is valuable and glorious in the late struggle?"

Garfield, who knew Brady quite well, then stood up and in a ringing speech denounced the government for abandoning a man who had risked his life and fortune to preserve for unborn Americans the darkest and the brightest hours of their country's history.

His voice echoing about the stilled House, Garfield said, "Here is a man, who for twenty-five years has fought to preserve our National Monuments. Some of his men were starved, some wounded in the struggle. Then his government got three-quarters of his collection of these wonderful pictures in lieu of a storage bill. The government should not take advantage of a man's distress."

He made his final appeal to the House to pass the necessary appropriation, "as an act of great mercy to a suffering and worthy man."

A Representative wanted to know the value of the plates and both Garfield and Butler said $150,000. The amendment giving Brady $25,000 was finally passed, but one wonders whether Congress was more impressed with Garfield's and Butler's estimation of the price of the plates, than their evaluation of Brady as a fine American whose worthy efforts should be finally rewarded.

On April 15, 1875, the money was turned over to Brady. Again it was too late. The negatives stored in the New York warehouse had been turned over to the Anthonys for payment of Brady's debts and they had obtained a clear title in the courts. It is not to their credit that the Brady stereoscopic views they issued bore their name and not the name of the man who had sacrificed so much to take them.

There was poverty, failure, sadness and death in Brady's life in those years—and there were also the inevitable "honors." In 1877 Brady received the Certificate of Award, a bronze Centennial Medal, for his "display of best photographs, crayons, portraits and photographic views" at the Centennial which was held in Philadelphia during 1876.

Surely this sad and embittered man must have realized by this time that honors, like the laurels of spring, soon wither and die. The walls of his gallery had held many "honors" but the great wartime views for which he had sacrificed so much were gathering dust.

Hunger and Dispossess were grim specters stalking his footsteps day and night, but Brady, with his nephew Levin Handy doing most of the actual photography, struggled on, though the flame, once taut with ambition, idealism and energy, now wavered. Brady spent only a few hours a day at his gallery, unless some special portrait was to be made, then walked down Pennsylvania Avenue, his weak eyes peering through the thick blue lenses at the hurrying, bustling world which no longer wanted him, returning to the one person who did—Julia.

These were sad days. Julia was obviously dying of a heart condition. There was nothing Brady could do but be with her. What did they talk about in the hotel bedroom which had been their only home? Their hours of hardships had been flecked with joy. Their memories spanned the pioneer Republic and the harried postwar years; they had been young and in love in one of the most romantic periods of their country's history; they had known the joys of courtship and married love, the strain of conflict when Brady gave all for his ideal; long days of separation and the balm of return. There was one blight: there had been no children. Yet a strong sense that they were devoted to each other comes across the years. "My beloved wife," Brady would say softly many years later.[222]

One of their friends was the dying Alexander Stephens, the onetime Vice President of the Confederacy, who also lived at the National Hotel. In February, 1869, Stephens had been severely injured at his estate, Liberty Hall, when a gate had fallen on him. He spent a long time on crutches and was never able to walk without assistance. In 1866 he was elected a U. S. Senator but was refused a seat. In 1873 Georgia sent him to Congress; three other candidates immediately withdrew from the field when he announced his candidacy. With his faithful Negro servant who had been taking care of him for many years, he left for Washington and lived at the National from 1873 to 1882.

He was the strangest figure Congress had seen since the days of John Randolph. A newspaper reporter described him as he appeared in these days: "A little way up the aisle sits a queer-looking bundle. An immense cloak, high hat and, peering somewhere out of the middle, a thin, pale little face. This brain and eyes enrolled in countless thicknesses of flannel and broadcloth wrappings belong to Hon. Alexander H. Stephens of Georgia. How anything so small, sick and sorrowful could get there all the way from Georgia is a wonder . . . if he were laid out in his coffin he would not look any different . . ."[224]

Brady had taken many earlier pictures of Stephens. One, the best known, has Brady's clock (Brady's name was on the face) at Stephens' elbow. But in the late years when he was unable to walk, Stephens had his servant wheel him up to Brady's in his "roller chair" for one last portrait. Brady's camera captured the frail body, the wisps of white hair and the thin, pale face and sad eyes which had seen so much violence and tragedy. In the spring of 1882 Stephens said goodbye as he was returning to Georgia to serve as governor. He died soon after.

In 1881 Brady's portraits of Webster, Calhoun and Clay (paintings which had been made from his daguerreotypes and which had long hung in his galleries) were sold to the government. They hang today in the main corridor of the Senate.

It was about this time that Johann Olsen, an old-time photographer visiting Washington, dropped in to see Brady. Both old men traded memories until the twilight crept into the room and young Handy said gently that it was time to close the gallery and go home.

"What happened to your war plates, Mr. Brady?" Olsen asked.

Brady stared into space. Then, after a long pause he said sadly, shaking his head.

"I don't know."[225]

The year 1882 closed. The world of photography was changing fast. The Scoville Company had acquired the American Optical Company and the famous Harrison Lens Company. Edward Muybridge had gained fame by photographing animal locomotion and W. J. Jennings made his first photograph of lightning, using a Scoville camera. A satisfactory substitute had been found at last for wet collodion as a vehicle for the haloid salts: gelatin. Now the wheel had made a full cycle; collodion had killed the age of the daguerreotype and now gelatin had doomed the wet plate and was producing a whole new line of cameras and apparatus.

Death, too, was claiming the pioneers. In the spring of 1882, Alexander Gardner, although a robust man, fell sick of "a wasting disease." During the summer he grew very weak and by November he could not get out of bed. Several specialists were called in and vaguely diagnosed his ailment as "an obscure disease." In December he was dead. A few months later the Anthonys produced their famous "detective" camera (hand cameras were often disguised as common objects such as opera glasses and canes, so that informal pictures could be taken without attracting attention'), and Henry Anthony died suddenly.[226]

On May 20, 1887, a large part of Brady died; his beloved Julia passed away. Now the sad old man gave up his apartment at the National and went to live with Handy, no longer "young" Handy. He was content with reading the newspapers with the aid of a thick magnifying glass and taking walks, tapping the sidewalk with the ivory-handled cane given to him by the Prince of Wales in remembrance of that great day in 1860 when he had become the "royal photographer."[227]

In 1882, someone in the War Department had raised the question of Brady's plates and an Albert Bierstadt was called in to examine the collection. He informed the government "the breakableness (sic) of the glass and the fugitive character of photographic chemicals will in a short time obliterate all traces of the scenes they represent. Unless they are reproduced in some permanent form they will soon be lost.[228] The government sent Bierstadt fifty-two negatives and he reproduced six "by a photographic process."

The government was again financially cautious, deciding that the expense of making the prints at seventy dollars a thousand was prohibitive.

John C. Taylor of Hartford, Conn., Secretary of the Connecticut Prison Association and Commander of Post 50, Grand Army of the Republic, began a search for the "lost Brady plates" which the Anthonys had acquired. As he recalled years later he found the invaluable collection "in an old garret."[229]

Edward Anthony told Taylor he had drawn prints from some wet plates, but that on the whole the great photographic essay, for which Brady had given so much to produce, had remained undisturbed since 1866. Taylor purchased the prints the Anthonys had made "and made a deal with him to allow me to use the prints exclusively."[230]

Taylor continued to use the prints, but General Albert Ordway of Washington and Hartford, together with Colonel Arnold A. Rand of Boston, later purchased the entire collection from Anthony as well as the legal title to them which the Anthonys had obtained in the courts.

Taylor in turn bought the collection from Ordway and Rand "with the intention of bringing them before the eyes of the soldiers that they might see that the lens had forever perpetuated their struggle for the Union."

In continuing his work of trying to assemble the entire Brady collection, Taylor made a survey of the collection owned by the government. He found, to his dismay, that "nearly" three hundred of the precious plates had been smashed or so badly chipped by careless clerks they were unprintable.

He notified the curiously lax Department of War, who, in turn, asked Taylor to supply his own collection on loan so that prints could be made of the damaged plates or duplicates of those plates their collection lacked.

Taylor sent his 7,000 negatives to Washington in care of the Navy Department—probably a wise selection in view of the carelessness of the War Department—and they were placed in a fireproof warehouse at 920 E. Street, northwest.

Taylor recalled, "I did all that was possible to facilitate the important work."[231]

Taylor, while in Washington, paid Brady a visit. Years later he recalled how the old man sat by the window, watching the ebb and flow of the busy street, as he recalled the great days.

When Taylor told him he had acquired 7,000 of his best pictures "Brady seemed pleased."

Recalling the hardships during the war, Brady said, "No one will ever know what I went through in securing the negatives. The whole world can never appreciate it. It changed the whole course of my life. By persistence and all the political influence I could control I finally secured permission from Stanton, Secretary of War, to go into the battlefield with my camera. Some of these negatives nearly cost me my life."[232]

Taylor next interested Secretary of War Daniel Lamont and several other prominent statesmen in purchasing his collection but the question of money again stalled the project and it was forgotten. Then Brigadier General A. W. Greeley, in charge of the government's collection, issued a curious statement, praising the great historical value of the plates but regretting that the collection could not be shown to the American public: "The government has stated positively that their negatives must not be exploited for commercial purposes. They are the historical treasures of a whole people and the government has justly refused to establish a dangerous system of 'special privilege' by granting permission for publication to individuals. As the property of the people, the government negatives are held in sacred trust . . ."[233]

The great Brady collection was owned by the people but the people could not see it.

Later, army officers who recognized the value of the plates urged the Secretary of War and the War Department to publish "a sort of official photographic history of the war."

Again the War Department issued a strange statement hinting that perhaps there might be individuals who would not want to have the Brady Collection published.

"The photographic views of the War showing the battlefields, military divisions, fortifications, etc., are among the most authentic and valuable records of the Rebellion. The preservation of the interesting records of the war is too important to be entrusted in glass plates so easily destroyed by accident or by design, and no more effective means than printing can be devised to save them from destruction."[234]

A few proofs were taken from the plates and inserted in one of the national histories, but that was the extent of the idea to draw prints from the plates before they were destroyed. In 1894, *The Memorial War Book* by George Forrester Williams, with engravings reproduced largely from photographs taken by Brady and Gardner, was published by the Lovell Bros. Company in New York.

The peculiar course of the War Department may have been to cover its astounding negligence. Francis Trevelyan Miller, the historian, quotes "one who is acquainted with the condition of the plates," and from different sources, official and unofficial, that "a number of negatives were broken by careless handling by employees of the War Department."[235]

After this brief flurry of interest the plates were turned over to the War Records Office and placed under the supervision of Colonel R. N. Scott.

While the controversy flared up and quickly subsided, Brady, alone, sick and penniless, remained silent as the clouds of obscurity closed in on him. A few years later veterans, stirring up their memories over old Brady stereoscopic war views they had treasured, would wonder "how many years has the picture-maker been dead?"

One spring day in 1891 "Gath" Townsend, the swashbuckling reporter of the New York *World,* stopped short when he saw Brady's name on a sign over the Pennsylvania Railroad ticket office, near the Treasury Department. Brady! The Civil War photographer still alive? He went upstairs and found an American legend. He had a white mustache and goatee, his hair frosted with gray, and blue spectacles.[236]

Townsend found Brady at sixty-seven a "trim, wiry, square-shouldered figure with the light of an Irish shower-sun in his smile." He found himself almost asking Brady about Willy Custis and Lord Cornbury and Captain John Smith.

Mark Twain had visited Brady only a few days before.

"What said he?" Townsend asked.

Brady replied, "He looked over everything visible but of course not at the unframed copies of my works, and he said, 'Brady, if I was not tied up in my enterprises I would join you upon this material in which there is a fortune. A glorious gallery to follow that engraved by Sartain and cover the expiring mighty period of American men can be had out of these large, expressive photographs. It would make the noblest subscription book of the age.'"

"From the first," Brady said, "I regarded myself as under obligation to my country to preserve the faces of its historical men and women. Better for me, perhaps, if I had left out the ornamental and been an ideal craftsman."

Fig. 41. The Townsend interview in the New York *World,* April 12, 1891.

As Townsend wrote after leaving Brady, he felt like Leigh Hunt "taking the hand of the old Poet-Banker Rogers who had once been touched for the king's evil by Queen Anne." When he had asked Brady how old he was, the photographer had chuckled and reminded him that "Never ask that question of a lady or a photographer; they are sensitive."

We don't know exactly how long Townsend spent with Brady, but it must have been a considerable length of time judging from Townsend's two-column interview. When it was over Brady thanked Townsend as only he could. He took his portrait. Townsend, however, tripped when he wrote his story. He spelled Brady's first name "Matthew" instead of "Mathew."

Misfortune continued to stalk Brady. On April 16, 1895, the evening of Emancipation Day, he was struck by a horsecar as he was crossing the street in front of the Riggs House, and his leg was broken. It took him a long time to recover. The following spring, one of the photographic journals noted that Brady was again seen on Broadway, "hobbling with the aid of his cane and wearing thick glasses with blue lens."

In the few last years left to him Brady continued to fight adversity. He now had a plan to give an "exhibition" of his war scenes on slides. He approached his nephew, Levin Handy, who agreed to make one hundred and twenty-eight slides. Brady, full of enthusiasm, set the date for the exhibition on January 30, 1896. Despite the protests of Handy and his wife, he moved to a New York City rooming house at 127 East 10th Street, not far from the home of an old friend, William M. Riley, at 119 East 15th Street. Now he could confer on plans for his exhibition with the officers of the Seventh Regiment who had made him an honorary member, and members of the Artists' Club which he had helped to found.[237]

In the winter of 1895 Brady was seized with a kidney ailment and a doctor ordered him to bed. He was in great pain and so weak he could not lift his head from his pillow.

The exhibition was still on his mind. Perhaps he felt the end was near and was determined to strike one last blow for recognition of his work.

On December 1, Levin Handy and his wife sent him a Christmas package. It warmed the old man's heart and at his request his friend Riley thanked the Handys for the gift. From his office in the Bogota and Magdalena Railway Company at 155 Broadway, Riley wrote: "Your letter of yesterday is at hand, also the box which is apparently in good condition. A letter from Mrs. Handy is also received. A former one from her containing a Christmas remembrance to Brady with which he was much pleased and for which he thanks her very kindly.

"Brady is very weak and does not sit up at all, but I think is slowly mending. Will advise you from time to time of his condition and also as to the progress of the proposed Exhibition. It is, as I last wrote you, under the management of Mr. Lincoln, an experienced and active worker in such affairs . . ."[238]

Riley dated the letter December 4, 1896, a mistake in the year, as Brady's death certificate shows.

Brady kept sinking during the next few weeks. But even in his weakened condition he continued to outline to Riley, who came to sit with him every night, the plans for his last big showing. Carnegie Hall was finally selected after the loyal Riley had arranged to get a long list of prominent New York residents, many former Union generals, as "sponsors."

The opening night of the exhibition was to be January 30, 1896, and General Horace Porter of Grant's staff was to make the opening address.[239]

The winter days passed. Brady remained in bed, tended during the day by friendly neighbors and at night by Riley, who tried to bring a smile to the old man's face with more news of the great night-to-be at Carnegie Hall.

Just before Christmas Brady's condition worsened. On December 16, Riley brought him to the Presbyterian Hospital, and as one account has it, he was placed in the "alms ward." It was a lonely Christmas and a dismal New Year's Day for the feeble old man who had once been the prince of photographers.

Riley saw him every day but it was evident that Brady was dying. He last saw him on the night of January 14. In the morning Brady was in a semi-coma. At about five o'clock on January 15, 1896, Mathew B. Brady, historian with a camera, died—alone and forgotten.[240]

Riley was notified and hurried to the hospital. But it was too late. He sadly went about writing to Handy, notifying him of his uncle's death and visiting Brady's East 10th Street room to gather his effects.[241]

As Riley wrote to Handy, these were pitifully few; two threadbare frock coats, a broken satchel, a few worn shirts, the beautiful ivory-handled cane and a ring which Brady had received from the Prince of Wales when he was the "royal photographer."

Riley sent Brady's body to Washington (cost $27.10) and he was buried in Arlington in the gallant company of the great generals and heroes whose portraits he had taken for posterity.

As newspaper reporters often tripped over the spelling of his first name, so did the chisel of the tombstone maker, who placed his death in 1895 instead of 1896.

The Washington and New York newspapers carried long obituaries of Brady, and as the Washington *Evening Star* said: "News of his passing will be received with sincere sorrow by hundreds and hundreds who knew this gentle photographer, whose name is today a household word all over the United States . . ."

But the New York *Globe* said it best: "After life's fitful fever he sleeps well . . ."

Mathew B. Brady had come home.

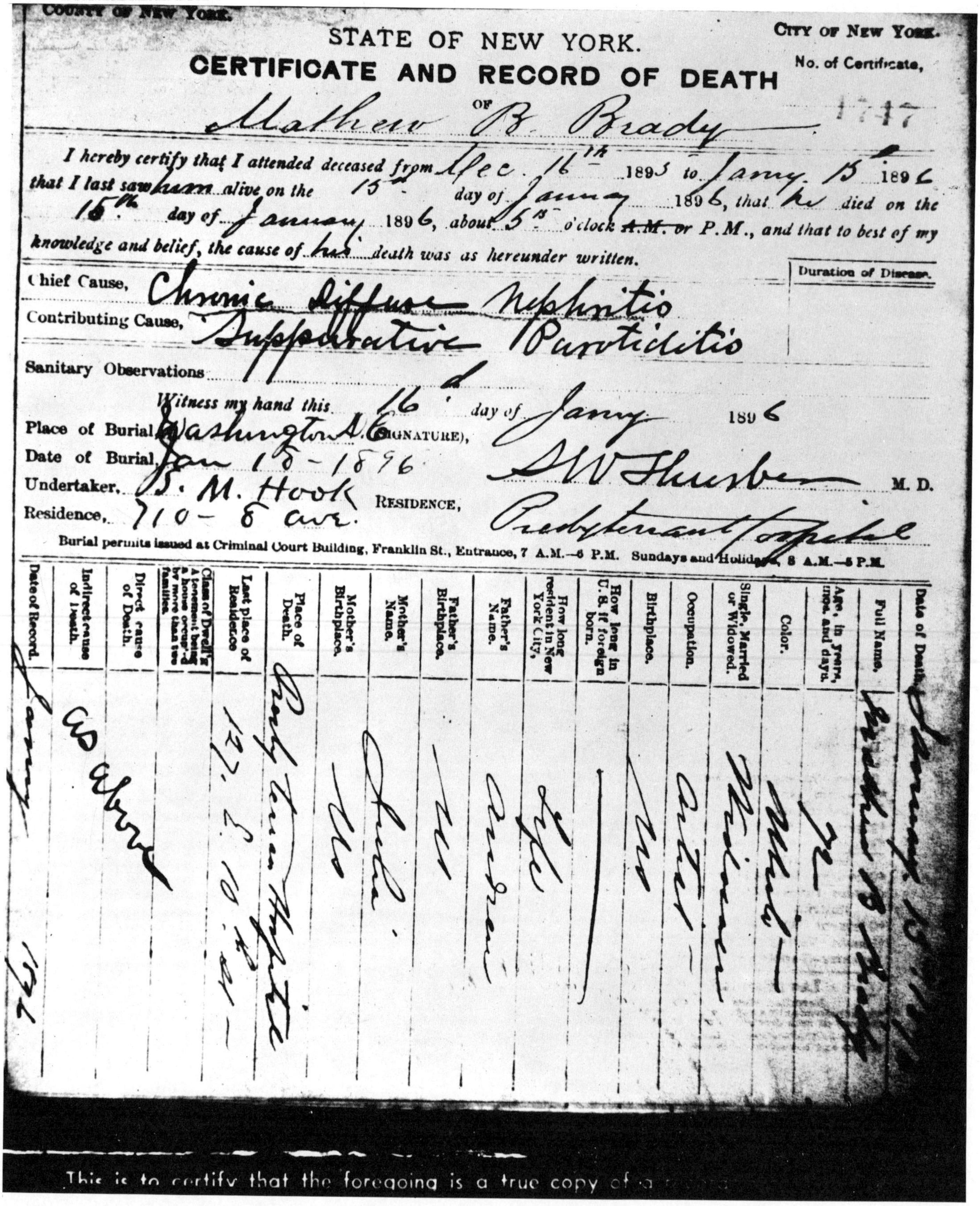

STATE OF NEW YORK.
CERTIFICATE AND RECORD OF DEATH

No. of Certificate, **1747**

OF *Mathew B. Brady*

I hereby certify that I attended deceased from *Dec. 16th* 189*5* to *Jany. 15* 189*6* that I last saw *him* alive on the *15th* day of *Jany* 189*6*, that *he* died on the *15th* day of *January* 189*6*, about *5* o'clock A.M. or P.M., and that to best of my knowledge and belief, the cause of *his* death was as hereunder written.

Duration of Disease.

Chief Cause, *Chronic Diffuse Nephritis*

Contributing Cause, *Suppurative Parotiditis*

Sanitary Observations

Witness my hand this *16* day of *Jany* 189*6*

Place of Burial *Washington D.C.* (SIGNATURE),

Date of Burial *Jan 18 - 1896* *S W Thurber* M.D.

Undertaker, *J. M. Hook* RESIDENCE,

Residence, *710 - 8 ave.* *Presbyterian Hospital*

Burial permits issued at Criminal Court Building, Franklin St., Entrance, 7 A.M.—6 P.M. Sundays and Holidays, 8 A.M.—5 P.M.

Date of Record.	Indirect cause of Death.	Direct cause of Death.	Class of Dwell'g A tenement being occup'd by more than two families.	Last place of Residence	Place of Death.	Mother's Birthplace.	Mother's Name.	Father's Birthplace.	Father's Name.	How long resident in New York City.	How long in U. S. if foreign born.	Birthplace.	Occupation.	Single, Married or Widowed.	Color.	Age, in years, mos. and days.	Full Name.	Date of Death
January 1896	*W Ebers*		*Presbyterian Hospital*	*710 8 ave*	*New York*	*Ire*	*Julia No*	*Ire*	*Andrew*	*Life*	*No*	*Ire*	*Artist*	*Widower*	*White*	*72*	*Mathew B. Brady*	*January 15 1896*

This is to certify that the foregoing is a true copy of a record

Fig. 42. Brady's death certificate, which this author discovered in the New York City Department of Health, Bureau of Vital Statistics. Published here for the first time.

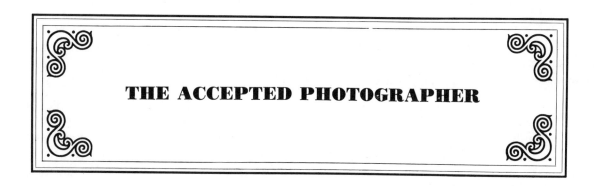

THE ACCEPTED PHOTOGRAPHER

AFTER Brady's death Levin Handy took over custody of Brady's last great collection of thousands of his precious wet plates and daguerreotypes. The famous Brady National Photographic Gallery at 627 Pennsylvania Avenue, N.W., had been closed and Handy had gone into business for himself at 494 Maryland Avenue, S.W., which was to become the famous L. C. Handy Studios, known to thousands of historians, authors and publishers.[242]

The building, built by Amos Kendall, Postmaster-General under Jackson and Van Buren, has changed very little. It is an old-fashioned red brick building just a few blocks from the Capitol and was the scene of many famous pictures.

Handy, long overshadowed by his famous uncle, soon emerged as a photographer of extraordinary talents. Robert Lincoln, Grant, and the great and near great found their way to the tiny studio, and Brady's cameras again began to capture history.

Handy started to make pictures and copies of famous historic documents for the government, and can be described as the government's first unofficial photographer. As his card read—"the Accepted Photographer." He made pictures for the State Department, Library of Congress, the Department of Agriculture, and numerous other Federal agencies. One of his darkrooms was in the Library of Congress, the forerunner of the Library's present extensive photoduplication service.

Handy was a quiet, undemonstrative man, who loved photography as deeply as Brady had.

In 1903 the original copy of the Declaration of Independence, the Constitution, Washington's Farewell Address, Lincoln's Gettysburg Address, the Madison Papers and several hundred other important historical papers were on exhibition at the Jamestown Exposition, when several of the buildings caught fire. The fire was checked as it was scorching the sides of the wooden building housing America's most important historical papers.[243]

When the Secretary of State heard the news he promptly issued an order that the priceless papers "should never under any circumstances leave the archives of the State Department again." When an undersecretary pointed out that the State Department structures themselves were not "the most fireproof in the world," Hay decided to have the documents photographed "as a safeguard against possible loss."

At a meeting in Hay's office Handy was unanimously selected as the photographer to do the job. Hay summoned him to the State Department and gave him the assignment which was to last three years. At weekly intervals Handy carefully photographed thousands of historic documents which were delivered to the Maryland Avenue studio under heavy guard.

When the assignment had been completed, Hay inspected the finished product and, according to the Washington *Times,* "was delighted with the results."

One of Handy's most famous pictures is Theodore Roosevelt "at repose" which the late President said was his favorite picture.

One spring day during Roosevelt's first administration, the President summoned Handy to the White House.

Handy was ushered into the President's office to find him surrounded by several Cabinet members.

The President waved his hand. "Never mind us, Mr. Handy," he called out, "just go right ahead and focus your camera."

Handy set up his camera and peered through the lens under the black cloth. The image was clear but the President's thick lenses were reflecting the light, as Handy had expected. He had studied other pictures of the President after he had received the Presidential order and he had come prepared.

He dropped the cloth and walked over to Roosevelt, who looked up in surprise.

"Mr. President," said Handy, "will you please wear these for a moment?"

Handy held out a pair of empty frames. Roosevelt studied them for a moment, then looked about at his Cabinet members and chuckled.

"I'm clay in the molder's hands, Mr. Handy. Do with me what you like."

Roosevelt put on the empty frames and Handy posed him against his office door and took several photographs to carry on the Presidential tradition of Brady photographs.[244]

For years Congressmen, Senators and members of the diplomatic corps, foreign visitors, actors, writers, editors and military leaders continued to find their way to 494 Maryland Avenue.

The great collection of Brady's and Handy's work, meanwhile, was carefully guarded from outsiders. Requests for individual prints, however, were granted to historians and publishers.

The century turned with the other Brady plates still the center of controversy. Edward B. Eaton, first president of the *Connecticut Magazine,* a leading historical magazine of its day, tried to persuade the War Department to publish the Brady collection while men who had fought in the Civil War were still alive. The War Department refused. Eaton then proposed that the publication of the plates be sponsored by a "responsible group." Again he was turned down. He was told the only way the Brady plates could be published was by "private publications."

Eaton located Taylor's collection in Washington and after a survey found that it duplicated the government's collection and also contained a thousand other negatives.

Johann Olsen of Hartford, the old-time photographer who had visited Brady in the eighties, also examined the plates in the Taylor collection which had been stored in the government warehouse for many years. He urged immediate action "because many of the plates are undergoing chemical action which will soon destroy them. Others are in a remarkable state of preservation. The modern development of the art is at a disadvantge when compared with some of Brady's negatives. I do not believe that Garfield (in his speech to the 43rd Congress) overestimated their value at $150,000. I was personally acquainted with some of Brady's men at the time and I know something of the tremendous difficulties in securing them . . ."[245]

In 1907 Eaton finally secured a clear title to the collection owned by Taylor, "with a full understanding that he would immediately place the scenes before the public."

The plates were then removed from the Navy-owned warehouse in Washington and stored in another fire-proof warehouse in Hartford, Conn.

Evidently Eaton rushed into print immediately after securing the collection. In 1907, the same year he had gained title to the plates, he published privately a huge, 126-page book, *Original Photographs Taken on the Battlefields during the Civil War by Mathew B. Brady and Alexander Gardner,* with a brief foreword by Francis Trevelyan Miller, the historian. The photographs were called "rare reproductions selected from 7,000 original negatives." The book sold for three dollars a copy and today usually brings ten dollars or more in Americana bookshops. A "partial" catalogue of the Brady plates in the Eaton Collection was also included in the book.[246]

Eaton did his best to bring the great scenes before the eyes of the American public. Not only did he publish the book but also he arranged for Grand Army posts or Civil War veterans to come to Hartford to see the collection on exhibit, or to write for free copies of their favorite pictures.

Eaton's book had only a fair sale. Miller's ten-volume *Photographic History of the Civil War,* published in 1911 by the Review of Reviews Company, contained the pictures of all other war photographers besides Brady. While that publication renewed interest in Brady's pictures, the revival was temporary. In 1912 two other volumes were published, *The Civil War Through the Camera* by Henry W. Elson, and *A History of the Civil War and the Causes That Led Up to the Great Conflict* by Benson John Loessing, both illustrated with Brady pictures.

The Brady Collection which the government purchased was finally transferred from the Records to the National Archives, where the wet plates are now carefully protected and catalogued. In 1944 the Library of Congress purchased Eaton's Brady Collection from the Phelps Publishing Company of Springfield, Mass. This too was carefully catalogued.

In the fall of 1954 the great Brady-Handy Collection was acquired by the Library of Congress for $25,000 from Mrs. Alice Cox and Mrs. Mary Evans, grandnieces of Brady and his only heirs. Mrs. Cox and Mrs. Evans recalled Brady in his last years, peering at a newspaper through a thick magnifying glass or enjoying a stroll down Maryland Avenue, tapping the sidewalk with the rosewood cane the Prince of Wales had given him.

Mrs. Cox and Mrs. Evans, only young girls when Brady lived with their father, Levin Handy, remember him as a quiet old man, always neat about his personal appearance, gentle in his manner and soft-spoken. On rare occasions he would speak wistfully of Lincoln, Grant, Sherman and Sheridan and the long-dead days.[247]

Once, in discussing photography, he said, "The camera is the eye of history . . . you must never make bad pictures. . . ."

History's cameraman had spoken.

A Picture Album

THE BIRTH OF PHOTOGRAPHY

1. Louis Jacques Mandé Daguerre, inventor of the daguerreotype. This is a photographic copy made by Brady from an original daguerreotype taken by Charles R. Meade of New York City in 1848 at Brie-Sur-Maine, Daguerre's chateau. Ironically, Daguerre had an aversion to having his picture taken. Meade, president of Meade Brothers in New York City, was refused, along with two other American photographers, but the enterprising New Yorker returned to the Chateau later in the day and persuaded Daguerre's niece and wife to intercede for him.

2a. A painting of Mathew Brady made in 1857.
By Charles Loring Elliott

2. Probably the earliest picture of Mathew B. Brady. The available information indicates that the daguerreotype from which it was made was taken in 1845, less than two years after he had opened his first studio in New York. This lithograph accompanied an article on Brady's work written by C. Edwards Lester, leading art critic of his day, in the first issue of the *Photographic Art Journal*, January, 1851. The lithograph was made by F. D'Avignon.

3. William Page, the well-known American portrait artist, who befriended Mathew Brady. Taken probably in the late eighteen-forties. *By Brady*

4. Samuel F. B. Morse, father of American photography and Brady's first instructor in the art of daguerreotypy. From a wet plate taken when Morse was 75. *By Brady or assistant*

6. The first patented camera. The patent was issued May 8, 1840, to Alexander S. Wolcott.

5. John Plumbe, early New York photographer, Iowa pioneer and originator of the first plan for a transcontinental railroad.

7. Downtown New York showing Brady's first gallery at Fulton Street and Broadway in the late eighteen-forties. Note Barnum's Museum, at left.

8. An unpublished daguerreotype of John M. Clayton, Secretary of State under President Zachary Taylor.
By Brady

9. An unpublished portrait of William C. Bouch, governor of New York, 1843-44.
By Brady

10. Andrew Jackson, seventh President. From a
India ink copy of an original daguerreotype made a
the Hermitage in 1845 just before his death. This
in the Brady-Handy Collection and it is probably
Brady picture. Almost half a century later Brady hin
self recalled, in an interview, that he had "sent" t
have the picture taken for posterity. Marquis Jame
says in his *Andrew Jackson* that Brady transported th
equipment and made the picture on April 15, 184
By Brady or assistar

11. Thomas J. Jackson, a rare photograph of the
great Confederate commander who won the name of
"Stonewall" at the first battle of Bull Run. This portrait was believed to have been taken in Mexico City,
in August, 1847. Brady also made small photocopies of
this picture which he sold during the Civil War. Either
Brady or someone on his staff faked stars on the neck
of the uniform of an 1851 portrait of Jackson, making
a clean-shaven Jackson a Civil War general. The writing scratched into the plate reads "from India Ink made
from original daguerreotype."   *By Brady*

12. John Tyler, tenth President. A daguerreotype taken probably in 1845. *By Brady*

13. John Quincy Adams, sixth President. A rare daguerreotype taken in the mid-forties not long before he died of a paralytic stroke. *By Brady*

14. James Knox Polk, eleventh President. A rare daguerreotype taken in the White House shortly before his death on June 15, 1849. Polk mentions this portrait in his diary.

15. A rare copy of a daguerreotype of Washington, D. C. in 1843. Someone in Brady's studio wrote the identifications on the original plate. This picture was taken before Brady had opened his branch gallery in the capital. *Probably by Brady*

16. This is believed to be the earliest photograph of the White House ever taken, but there is no year indicated on the jacket of the plate. It is a view from the north front. *By Brady*

17. A daguerreotype taken about the time of Brady's marriage to Julia Handy. Julia is on the left, seated next to a Mrs. Haggarty, believed to be a relative, with Brady standing behind them.

18. The Reverend George Whitefield Samson, minister (1843-59) of the old E Street Baptist Church in Washington, who married Julia and Mathew Brady. The wet plate carries the notation "married mother of L. C. Handy and Samuel Handy." He was a prolific author, prominent educator and one of the early sponsors of Liberia. *By Brady or assistant*

19. A rare and unpublished daguerreotype of Dolly Madison in the eighteen-forties. She died, at 81, in 1849. *By Brady*

18a. Unpublished early daguerreotype of Senator John J. Crittenden of Kentucky, author of the unsuccessful Crittenden Compromise, which was designed to keep the Southern states in the Union (1860). *By Brady*

20. An unpublished daguerreotype of Cyrus West Field. It was through his suggestion and financial aid that the first Atlantic cable was laid. He later became a prominent promoter of New York's elevated railroad and owner of two newspapers. *By Brady*

21. An unpublished daguerreotype of Cornelius Vanderbilt, who founded the famous Vanderbilt clan and fortune. *By Brady*

22. An unpublished daguerreotype of the great American actor, Edwin Forrest. *By Brady*

23. Phineas T. Barnum, a daguerreotype of the famous showman. *By Brady*

24. A rare and probably unpublished daguerreotype of Jenny Lind, Barnum's "Swedish Nightingale," taken about 1850, when her concerts made history.

By Brady

25. In Brady's first year as a professional daguerreotypist, 1844, he won the top award of the American Institute and won the same first prize for the next five years. As can be seen from this curious advertisement, Brady was quick to publicize this award, as later, he advertised the award of the gold medal in the London Exhibition of 1851.

26. A daguerreotype of editor James Gordon Bennett, with whom Brady traveled to England in 1851.
By Brady

27. M. M. Lawrence, who also won a medal at the London Exhibition in 1851. The portrait of Lawrence, a New York photographer, is from the *Photographic Art Journal*, February, 1851.

THE PRIZE MEDAL

Was awarded, at the Great Exhibition of the Industry of All Nations, in London, 1851,

TO M. B. BRADY,

FOR THE BEST DAGUERREOTYPES.

28. The medal won by Brady at the 1851 Exhibition.

THE GREAT INDUSTRIAL EXHIBITION OF 1851.

29. The first world's fair, the Industrial Exhibition at the Crystal Palace in London, 1851, where Brady gained international fame when his daguerreotypes won a prize medal. The awards committee declared, "All are so good that selection is almost impossible."

"I took many a great man and fine lady . . ."

30. A rare and unpublished daguerreotype of Cardinal Nicholas Patrick Stephen Wiseman of England. Brady undoubtedly took this picture of Cardinal Wiseman in 1851 when he was in England and Wiseman had just been named a Cardinal and Archbishop of Westminster by the Vatican. *By Brady*

31. This rare and unpublished daguerreotype bears the inscription, "Believed to be Joseph Bonaparte." It could not have been Joseph, who died at the age of 76 in 1844. Probably it is Prince Joseph Charles Paul Bonaparte (1822-91), known as "The First Prince of the Blood" and also as "Plon-Plon."
By Brady

32. A rare and unpublished daguerreotype, one of the few remaining here and abroad of General Giuseppe Garibaldi, liberator of Italy. Garibaldi was in Staten Island, New York, in 1850-51. *By Brady*

These are copies made from the original daguerreotypes. Lithographs were made by D'Avignon for inclusion in Brady's volume, *The Gallery of Illustrious Americans*, published in 1850. There were twelve lithographs in the book, the others being John James Audubon, Winfield Scott, Millard Fillmore, William Ellery Channing, Lewis Cass, Zachary Taylor, John Charles Fremont and Silas Wright.

33. Henry Clay.   *By Brady*

34. John C. Calhoun.   *By Brady*

35. Daniel Webster.   *By Brady*

36. William H. Prescott, historian.   *By Brady*

37. Sam Houston. A rare daguerreotype. *By Brady*

38. An unpublished daguerreotype of August Belmont. *By Brady*

39. Senator Thomas Hart Benton of Missouri, a copy negative of a daguerreotype. *By Brady*

40. William Cullen Bryant. A copy of the original daguerreotype from Brady's collection which won the prize in London, 1851. *By Brady*

41. A daguerreotype of Brigham Young. *By Brady*

42. Caleb Cushing, an early daguerreotype. He was Attorney-General in Pierce's Cabinet, negotiated the treaty opening five Chinese ports and acted as U. S. counsel in the *Alabama* claims case. *By Brady*

43. A copy of a rare daguerreotype of the great English tragedian Junius Brutus Booth, probably unpublished. He was the father of Edwin and John Wilkes Booth. *By Brady*

44. A rare daguerreotype of Nathaniel Hawthorne. *By Brady*

45. A daguerreotype of Washington Irving in the eighteen-fifties. *By Brady*

46. A daguerreotype of Edgar Allan Poe. *By Brady*

47. A rare daguerreotype of Stephen A. Douglas, the "Little Giant." *By Brady*

48. A daguerreotype of Mrs. Stephen A. Douglas. *By Brady*

49. A rare daguerreotype of Sam Houston, probably taken in the early fifties. *By Brady*

50. Unpublished daguerreotype of Phoebe Cary, poetess. *Probably by Brady*

51. A rare and unpublished daguerreotype of Niagara Falls about 1854. The Falls were a popular subject for photographers. The sixth man from the left may be Mathew Brady, who customarily wore a short, squat straw hat "like those the French artists wear."

52. A rare and unpublished daguerreotype of Franklin Pierce, fourteenth President. *By Brady*

A NEW ERA IN PHOTOGRAPHY

53. A rare and unpublished wet plate photograph of Rembrandt Peale, son of the famous artist Charles Willson Peale. Born in 1778, young Peale studied under his father, then under Benjamin West in London in 1802. In 1795 he began his portrait of George Washington, from which he made many replicas, the last in 1823, later bought by the government in 1832. Peale also painted Thomas Jefferson, Dolly Madison, Commodore Perry, Decatur, Houdon and an equestrian portrait of Washington now in Independence Hall. In 1825 he succeeded John Trumbull as president of the American Academy of Fine Arts. When Brady took this picture Peale was the only painter alive in America who had painted Washington from life.   *By Brady*

54. A rare and unpublished wet plate photograph of Nicholas Philip Trist, who had been one of Thomas Jefferson's private secretaries. An example of how Brady's camera linked the early American republic and the early nineties.   *By Brady or assistant*

55. Martin Van Buren, eighth President. *By Brady*

56. John C. Fremont, the "pathfinder of the Rockies." *By Brady or assistant*

57. Alexander T. Stewart, the merchant prince who gave Brady a job as a clerk when he first came to New York. This wet plate was made about 1856.
By Brady or assistant

58. Original wet plate of Horace Greeley.
By Brady or assistant

59. An unpublished early portrait of Judah P. Benjamin when he was a Senator from Louisiana.
By Brady

60. Sir Francis Napier, Envoy to the United States 1857-58, then minister to the Netherlands, later governor of Madras. *By Brady or assistant*

61. A rare wet plate of the Capitol without its dome, taken from the rear of the building, about 1858. Note old canal and greenhouse in the foreground.
By Brady or assistant

62. A copy of Brady's daguerreotype of President Buchanan and his Cabinet. Seated, left to right: Jacob Thompson, Secretary of the Interior; John B. Floyd, Secretary of War; Isaac Toucey, Secretary of the Navy; Jeremiah Black, Attorney-General. Standing, left to right: Lewis Cass, Secretary of State; President Buchanan; Howell Cobb, Secretary of the Treasury; Joseph Holt, Postmaster General. This picture was taken probably in 1859 when Holt became a member of the Cabinet. *By Brady*

63. A rare portrait of James Buchanan, fifteenth President. *By Brady*

64. Harriet Lane, President Buchanan's niece, who served as his hostess in the White House. *By Brady*

65. A rare daguerreotype, at first believed to be Edwin Booth, but Paris readers of this book have identified it as that of Louis Blanc, the famous French politician and historian. *By Brady*

66. Adelina Patti, world-famous opera and concert star. A copy of a daguerreotype. *By Brady*

67. Edwin Forrest in costume. *By Brady*

68. Charlotte Cushman as "Meg Merriles." *By Brady or assistant*

69. Maggie Mitchell, actress. *By Brady or assistant*

70. Dion Boucicault, actor and playwright.
By Brady or assistant

71. F. C. Bangs, actor. *By Brady or assistant* **72.** E. Lamb, actor. *By Brady or assistant* **73.** Ole Bull, violinist. *By Brady or assistant*

74. Agnes Robertson, actress, wife of Dion Boucicault. *By Brady or assistant*

75. Ellen Tree (Mrs. Charles Kean), actress. *By Brady or assistant*

76. Clara L. Kellogg, opera star. *By Brady or assistant*

77. Laura Le Claire and Lottie Forbes, dancers. *By Brady or assistant*

78. Mrs. George H. Gilbert, actress. *By Brady or assistant*

79. Lucille Western, actress. *By Brady or assistant*

80. The Board of New York Police Commissioners, taken in the spring of 1860 when they were engaged in a controversy over the resignation of Police Superintendent Amos Pilsbury, who "refused to toady to the Board of Commissioners." *By Brady or assistant*

81. The first aerial picture taken in America. The wet plate was made in 1861 by Professor Samuel A. King and J. W. Black. Oliver Wendell Holmes described it as "Boston as the eagle and the wild goose see it."

82. The reception room of Brady's Broadway and Tenth Street gallery, from *Frank Leslie's Illustrated Newspaper,* January 5, 1861.

83. The Prince of Wales, later Edward VII, and his royal entourage when he visited Brady's new gallery in 1860. The prince is in the center. The man second from his left is Lord Lyons, who was the British minister in Washington from 1858 to 1865.

By Brady

THE ROYAL PHOTOGRAPHER

84. The Prince of Wales.   *By Brady*

85. A few years ago forty-four Brady plates were found in an upstate New York barn and were later acquired by Ansco. This unidentified wet plate may be a portrait of the Prince of Wales.   *By Brady*

Note: Since this book went to press this wet plate has been identified by Buckingham Palace as a picture of the Duke of Connaught, younger brother of the Prince of Wales.   *By Brady*

THE FIRST WAR PHOTOGRAPHERS

Brady was not the first to bring a camera to the battlefield. An unknown daguerreotypist took several battlefield pictures, the first in the history of the world, during the Mexican War. They are owned by H. Armour Smith and are still in perfect condition. They have been exhibited many times in museums and art galleries. Mr. Smith found them in a wooden case in the attic of an old mansion in Yonkers, N. Y.

86a. General Woll and his staff entering Calle Real.

86b. The Virginia regiment entering Calle Real.

86c. Webster's battery at Minon's Pass.

87. Roger Fenton, the world's second war photographer. Fenton was studying art in Paris when he became interested in photography. In 1853 he became the first secretary of the Photographic Society of London. In the spring and summer of 1855 Agnew and Sons of London sent him to cover the war in the Crimea. He returned with 350 negatives of French and British soldiers and campsites in Balaklava Bay.

88. Roger Fenton on the Crimean battlefield in his version of what later was called Brady's "What-is-it" wagon.

89. Balaklava, looking seaward, with the commandant's house in the foreground.   *By Roger Fenton*

A CRITICAL ELECTION

Rumblings of War

90. An unpublished wet plate showing one of the wings of the Capitol near completion in the early sixties. *By Brady or assistant*

91. A probably unpublished portrait of John Bell of Tennessee, who ran for President against Lincoln in 1860. *By Brady*

92. A portrait of J. C. Breckenridge of Kentucky, who also ran against Lincoln for the presidency in 1860. *By Brady*

93. Brady's first portrait of Abraham Lincoln, taken on February 27, 1860, at the time of his famous Cooper Institute speech. This print was distributed by the thousands, numerous lithographs were made of it by Currier & Ives and of it Lincoln said, "Brady and the Cooper Institute made me President."

By Brady

94. John Brown's fort.   *By Brady or assistant*

95. An early portrait of John Brown.

To Dr Thomas Featherstonhaugh.
with Compliments
James E Taylor

John Brown arraigned before the
court at Charlestown.

96. Published here for the first time, this sketch is not in the Featherstonhaugh Collection of the Library of Congress.   *By James E. Taylor*

WAR!

97. Henry A. Wise, governor of Virginia, who made a martyr of John Brown by allowing his death sentence to be carried out. Wise later became a Confederate general. *By Brady or assistant*

98. Edmund Ruffin, "Father of Secession in Virginia," who supposedly fired the first shot of the Civil War by pulling the lanyard of a cannon which sent the first shell against the ramparts of Fort Sumter. *By George S. Cook*

99. Interior of Fort Sumter. *By S. R. Seibert*

102. Lincoln's Secretary of State, William H. Seward. A close examination of the print with a magnifying glass shows that Seward's head and top hat have been superimposed on the body. Note the Brady clock.
By Brady

100. Lincoln's Secretary of War, Edwin McMasters Stanton. This is one of the Brady plates found in the upstate New York barn. *By Brady or assistant*

101. A rare portrait of Stanton without his familiar glasses. *By Brady*

103. Salmon P. Chase when he was Secretary of the Treasury. *By Brady or assistant*

104. Lincoln's Secretary of the Treasury (1864-65), William Pitt Fessenden. One of the plates discovered in the New York state barn. *By Brady or assistant*

105. Gideon Welles, Secretary of the Navy during the Civil War. *By Brady or assistant*

106. Montgomery Blair, Postmaster General in Lincoln's Cabinet. *By Brady or assistant*

107. Cassius M. Clay of Kentucky, who served as minister to Russia in the eighteen-sixties. *By Brady or assistant*

108. Hannibal Hamlin, Lincoln's first Vice-President. *By Brady or assistant*

109. James Henry Lane, the "grim chieftain of Kansas" during the terrible "border wars." He was the Federal parallel of Quantrill of Missouri, who once vowed to skin Lane alive. *By Brady or assistant*

110. A rare wet plate portrait of Simon Cameron. Lincoln's first Secretary of War. *By Brady or assistant*

111. Unpublished daguerreotype of Francis B. Cutting, prominent attorney who was an important figure in Lincoln's second campaign for the presidency. *By Brady*

114. A strange portrait of Jefferson Davis in a Federal uniform. Copyrighted in 1861 by C. D. Fredericks and Company, the New York photographers.

112. Jefferson Davis.   *By Brady*

113. Jefferson Davis and his second wife, Varina Howell Davis. A copy of an early daguerreotype.

115. This is believed to be a wet plate portrait of Judah P. Benjamin, Secretary of State of the Confederacy. *By Brady*

116. Stephen Mallory of Florida, the Confederate Secretary of the Navy.

117. Alexander H. Stephens, the "little human steam engine" who became the Confederacy's first Vice-President. Note the clock with Brady's name on the face, a traditional trademark in Brady pictures. *By Brady or assistant*

118. A wet plate portrait of Alexander H. Stephens, former Vice-President of the Confederacy, Congressman and later governor of Georgia, with his faithful Negro servant. Stephens, an invalid from a fall, was a neighbor of Brady's at the National Hotel in Washington. *By Brady*

119. R. M. T. Hunter of Virginia, Confederate Secretary of State.

120. C. G. Memminger, Confederate Secretary of Treasury.

121. John Slidell, from a daguerreotype made when he was a Senator from Louisiana. When he and James Mason, were taken from a British ship on the high seas by a Federal captain there was an international "incident." *By Brady*

General Emeritus

122. General Winfield Scott, the first Lieutenant-General of the army after Washington and the hero of the Mexican War, is shown here with his staff in Washington in 1861. In active service for half a century, he never lost a battle. He was in his 75th year and so swollen with dropsy that he could not mount a horse when this picture was taken. On his left is Colonel E. D. Townsend, on his right, Henry Van Rensselaer. *By Brady or assistant*

123. Colonel Elmer E. Ellsworth, "the first man killed in the Civil War."   *By Brady*

124. The Marshall house, Alexandria, Va., where Colonel Ellsworth was shot down by the caretaker when he tried to lower the Confederate flag.
By William R. Pywell

125. A typical Brady What-is-it wagon.
By Brady or assistant

126. Mathew B. Brady after his return from the battle of Bull Run. If you look closely you can see the outline, under the linen duster, of the sword given him by the New York Zouaves.   *By a Brady assistant*

127. Bull Run with its destroyed bridge, 1861. *By Brady*

128. Confederate dead on Matthews Hill after the first battle of Bull Run. *By Brady*

129. Congressman Alfred Ely of New York, who went to see the battle of Bull Run and was taken prisoner by the Confederates and imprisoned in Richmond for six months. *By Brady or assistant*

130. The Antietam bridge and wagon trains, September, 1862. *By Alexander Gardner*

131. Sharpsburg road, Sharpsburg, Md., 1862. *By Gardner*

132. Dunker church and the dead, September, 1862.
By James Gardner

133. General Kearney's wounded soldiers at Fredericksburg. *By Brady or assistant*

134. Only a few Federal officers knew that the man with the cigar in his hand was Allan Pinkerton, founder of the famous detective agency. Pinkerton, who organized McClellan's Secret Service, was known only as "Major Allen." Directly behind him is John C. Babcock, who worked under Pinkerton and later Burnside. Next to him is George H. Bangs, later a famous Pinkerton superintendent. Another Pinkerton operative, Augustus K. Littlefield, is at the left and the other seated man is William Moore, Secretary of War Stanton's private secretary. This picture was taken at McClellan's headquarters near Antietam.

By Brady or assistant

135. Fredericksburg in ruins, 1862, "utterly desolate . . . the solid shot plunged through the masonry as though it were pasteboard; other buildings afire, and before sundown a score of houses are in ashes."

By Brady or assistant

136. The aftermath of Sedgwick's assault, May 3, 1863, on Marye's Heights. Pictured are Confederate caisson wagons and horses, destroyed by a shot from the Second Massachusetts siege-gun battery planted across the river at Falmouth to support the Federal assault. Leaning against the stump is General Herman Haupt, chief of the Bureau of Military Railroads, and next to him is W. W. Wright, superintendent of the Military Railroad.

By Brady or assistant

137. A wheat field at Gettysburg, scene of General John F. Reynolds' death, July 1, 1863. Brady is standing in the righthand corner.   *By Tim O'Sullivan*

138. Scene of Pickett's charge at Gettysburg.   *By Brady, Tim O'Sullivan or Alexander Gardner*

139. A Gettysburg battle scene.
By Brady or assistant

140. Three Confederate soldiers captured at Gettysburg. *By Brady or assistant*

141. Dead of the 24th Michigan Infantry, Gettysburg. *By Tim O'Sullivan*

142. Pulpit Rock, the summit of Lookout Mountain, 1863. *By George N. Barnard*

143. This is the most famous Brady picture of Lincoln, although there is evidence that it may have been taken actually by A. Burgess. It was taken in Brady's Washington gallery on February 9, 1864, and it is the picture of Lincoln which appears on our five-dollar bill and which also appeared on the 1923 issue of the three-cent stamp. *By Brady or A. Burgess*

144. The earliest known portrait of Abraham Lincoln, made in 1846 in Springfield, Ill. This is a Brady wet plate copy of the daguerreotype.

By N. H. Shepherd

145. A Brady wet plate copy of an early daguerreotype of Mrs. Abraham Lincoln. Robert Todd Lincoln recalled that these two portraits hung on a wall of a room in the Lincoln home. *By N. H. Shepherd*

146. Abraham Lincoln, taken in 1862 in Brady's Washington gallery. *By Brady or assistant*

147. Abraham Lincoln taken in Brady's studio in 1862. The anxieties and the responsibilities of the first year of the war were already leaving their mark on his face. *By Brady or assistant*

148. Abraham Lincoln, believed to have been taken in 1863 on the November Sunday before he made his famous Gettysburg address. Noah Brooks wrote in his *Washington in Lincoln's Time* that on the way to Gardner's studio Lincoln suddenly remembered he needed a paper and hurried back to his office. He returned to join Brooks in Gardner's studio carrying a long envelope which he told the journalist was an advance copy of Edward Everett's address, to be delivered at the Gettysburg cemetery dedication ceremonies. *By Alexander Gardner*

149. Abraham Lincoln in Brady's studio sometime in 1863. This may have been the "full-length landscape" taken at the time of Lieutenant Cunningham's visit to Brady's Washington gallery. *By Brady or assistant*

150. Lincoln and his beloved son Tad with a screen showing the unfinished Washington monument and the Potomac River used as a background. The photograph was taken on Monday, April 10, 1865, the day after Lincoln returned to Washington from City Point. *By Alexander Gardner*

151. Abraham Lincoln, taken August 9, 1863. This was shortly after Gardner had left Brady's employ. *By Alexander Gardner*

152. Abraham Lincoln in 1864, the picture mentioned in the unpublished diary of Francis B. Carpenter, the painter. *By Brady or A. Burgess*

154. A portrait of Lincoln taken on February 23, 1861, the day the President-elect arrived in Washington for his inauguration. *By Brady*

153. Lincoln and Tad. This picture has appeared many times as a portrait taken by Brady in the White House. The artist Francis B. Carpenter wrote in his diary that A. Berger—he probably meant Andrew Burgess—made this picture on February 9, 1864, the date of the famous Brady portrait of Lincoln (No. 143) taken in Brady's gallery.

By Brady or Andrew Burgess

155. John Nicolay, one of Lincoln's secretaries, author with John Hay of the famous ten-volume biography *Abraham Lincoln, A History.*

156. John Milton Hay, one of Lincoln's secretaries, later ambassador to Great Britain, Secretary of State 1898-1905. *By Brady or assistant*

157. Ruth P. Randall in her *Mary Lincoln* quotes Mrs. Lincoln: "There is an excellent painted likeness of me at Brady's in New York taken in 1861 . . . in a black velvet." This is probably the wet plate portrait from which the painted likeness was made.

158. A photograph of Mrs. Lincoln wearing her 1861 inaugural ball gown. She said of her photographs, "My hands are always made in them very large and I look too stern." *By Brady or assistant*

159. This photograph of Mrs. Lincoln was made just before the 1861 inauguration, the same day as No. 158. *By Brady or assistant*

160. Another "gown" photograph of Mary Lincoln. This may possibly be her second inaugural gown. *By Brady or assistant*

161. Admiral David Glasgow Farragut.
By Brady or assistant

162. Admiral David Dixon Porter, a rare portrait.
By Brady or assistant

163. Admiral John Lorimer Worden.

164. Lieutenant Commander William B. Cushing, naval hero noted chiefly for torpedoing the *Albemarle*.
By Brady or assistant

165. John Ericsson, Swedish-born invent of the *Monitor*. *By Bra*

166. The *Monongahela* (photographed in 1873). Farragut ("Damn the torpedoes") sent the *Monongahela,* "my heart of oak," to ram the Confederate ironclad *Tennessee.* She struck the *Tennessee* fair amidships, wrenching off her iron prow and shattering the butt ends of her bow planks.

By Brady or assistant

167. The U. S. S. *Galena,* one of the early Federal ironclads. The sides of the *Galena,* a small corvette, were plated with three-inch iron.

168. The double-turreted Federal ironclad *Onondaga.* *By Brady or assistant*

169. Farragut's flagship, the *Hartford*, and others at Baton Rouge, La.

170. The Federal transport *Chickamauga*.
By Brady or assistant

171. A Hoboken-New York ferry-boat converted to the gunboat *Commodore Perry*. The *Perry* was equipped with cannon and her pilot-house armored. A casemate of iron plates was provided for the guns.
By Brady or assistant

172. McClellan and staff at Upton Hill.
By Brady or assistant

173. General George Brinton McClellan, who succeeded McDowell six days after the battle of Bull Run. *By Brady or assistant*

174. Allan Pinkerton (smoking pipe) and three of his scouts in 1862 near Cumberland Landing, where all was ready for McClellan's advance to the Chickahominy—and Richmond. *By Brady or assistant*

175. General Philip Henry Sheridan, commander of the Army of the Shenandoah in 1864. This is one of the plates discovered in an upstate New York barn.
By Brady or assistant

176. General Phil Sheridan with hat. The identification on the yellowed slip of paper attached to the wet plate was written by someone in Brady's studio.
By Brady or assistant

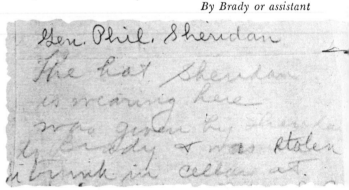

177. A rare ambrotype of the one-armed General Phil Kearney. *By Brady or assistant*

178. General Lew Wallace.
By Brady or assistant

179. General Samuel P. Heintzelman and staff, taken on the steps of Arlington, Va.   *By Brady or assistant*

180. General Judson ("Kill Cavalry") Kilpatrick.   *By Brady or assistant*

181. General George H. Thomas, the "Rock of Chickamauga."   *By Brady or assistant*

182. General James H. Wilson, a cavalry leader.   *By Brady or assistant*

183. General Winfield Scott Hancock. This is one of the wet plates found in an upstate New York barn. *By Brady or assistant*

184. Colonel John B. Astor.
By Brady or assistant

185. General Emerson Opdyke.
By Brady or assistant

186. Believed to be General Orville E. Babcock, aide-de-camp to Grant, 1864-65.
By Brady or assistant

187. General Benjamin F. Butler.
By Brady or assistant

188. Butler after the war.
By Brady or assistant

189. General John A. Dix after whom Fort Dix, N. J., is named. He was noted for his famous order, "If any man dare pull down the American flag, shoot him on the spot." *By Brady or assistant*

190. General William T. Sherman, taken on the same day he posed with his generals.

By Brady or assistant

191. Sherman and his generals, 1865. Left to right, seated: J. A. Logan, W. T. Sherman, H. W. Slocum and F. Blair. Left to right, standing: O. O. Howard, W. B. Hazen, Jefferson C. Davis and J. A. Mower.

By Brady or assistant

192. Captain George A. Custer of the Fifth U. S. Cavalry, then an aide on McClellan's staff, with one of his first prisoners, Lieutenant J. B. Washington, C. S. A. Custer and Washington were classmates at West Point. The boy is believed to be Washington's young slave, who followed him onto the battlefield.
By Brady or assistant

193. A portrait of General Custer.
By Brady or assistant

194. General Custer, his brother Thomas, and probably their sister. *By Brady or assistant*

195. A portrait of Custer, with gauntlets and spurs, as a major general in the Civil War. After the war, Custer was a brevet major general and a lieutenant colonel of the 7th Regiment, but in full command.
By Brady or assistant

BRADY'S GALLERY OF CONFEDERATE OFFICERS

The following is a gallery of Confederate officers, many published for the first time. They were not taken by Brady, but probably by Julian Vannerson, George Cook and other Confederate photographers.

How they came into Brady's possession is not known. Possibly after the war the Southern photographers loaned or sold their plates to Brady.

196. General James Longstreet.

197. General Albert Sidney Johnston.

198. Colonel John Singleton Mosby.

199. General J. E. B. Stuart.

200. General Braxton Bragg.

201. General Jubal A. Early.

202. General George Pickett.

203. General Turner Ashby.

204. General Wade Hampton.

205. General Simon B. Buckner.

206. Brigadier General G. J. Rains.

207. General John H. Winder.

208. General William J. Hardee.

209. General Milledge L. Bonham.

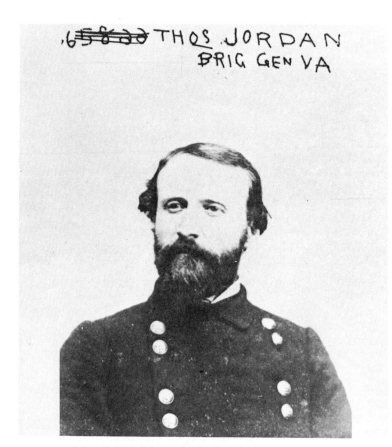

212. Brigadier General Thomas Jordan.

210. Brigadier General Henry A. Wise.

213. Confederate generals photographed in Mexico on October 9, 1865. A probably unpublished print.

211. Brigadier General Martin E. Green.

214. Derailed train, Manassas, Va.
By Brady or assistant

215. Camp kitchen.
By Brady or assistant

216. Building a stockade, Alexandria, Va.   *By Brady or assistant*

217. Winter quarters at Centerville, Va., built by the Confederate army and abandoned a few days later. *By Brady or assistant*

218. A future historian takes part in history in the making. In the center of this group, taken before the fall of Petersburg, 1864, is Captain Charles Francis Adams, Jr., then an officer of the First Massachusetts Cavalry. On his left is Lieutenant G. H. Teague and on his right, Captain E. A. Flint.

By Brady or Tim O'Sullivan

219. A stereoscopic view of Park Row, looking south, with City Hall on the right and the *New York Times* building at left. St. Paul's steeple can be seen above the trees. *By Brady or assistant*

220. A stereoscopic view, looking north, of Broadway and Fifth Avenue, 1862, showing the Mexican War monument, the spire of the Marble Collegiate Church and the clock (left center), still standing. *By Brady or assistant*

221. A stereoscopic view of Broadway from Barnum's Museum, showing barracks. *By Brady or assistant*

222. Barnum's Museum, 1862.
By Brady or assistant

223. Broadway and Spring Street, 1867.   *By Brady or assistant*

CARTES DE VISITE

Samples of typical *carte de visite* photos which Brady or his assistants produced by the hundreds of thousands in the New York and Washington galleries, particularly during the war, for soldiers.

224. General Kimball.
By Brady or assistant

225. General Joseph Kiernan.
By Brady or assistant

226. Judge Clifford.
By Brady or assistant

227. Brownell.
By Brady or assistant

228. Union private.
By Brady or assistant

229. Lt. Col. N. L. Farnham.
By Brady or assistant

230. Confederate cavalrymen.
By Brady or assistant

231. Confederate private.
By Brady or assistant

232. Clara Barton in Brady's Pennsylvania Avenue studio. *By Brady or assistant*

233. Kit Carson, famous Rocky Mountain scout. *By Brady or assistant*

234. Joe Coburn, a well-known pugilist of the period. In one of his bouts with Jem Mace, neither man struck a blow during the hour and seventeen minutes of the fight. *By Brady or assistant*

235. The Reverend Eleazar Williams, who claimed that he was the lost Dauphin, son of Louis XVI and Marie Antoinette. Though he died in 1858, he was a legend for many years after. *By Brady or assistant*

236. John Clem with his brother. John, who first served as a drummer boy at the age of 12, was probably the youngest person who ever bore arms in the Civil War. *By Brady or assistant*

237. Seth Kinman, who posed for Brady before he went to the White House to present Abraham Lincoln with a chair made of elkhorn.

By Brady or assistant

238. George Augustus Sala, the London *Daily Telegraph's* correspondent during the Civil War. *By Brady or assistant*

239. Julia Jackson, daughter of "Stonewall" Jackson. *By Brady or assistant*

240. Mrs. George B. McClellan, wife of the general. *By Brady or assistant*

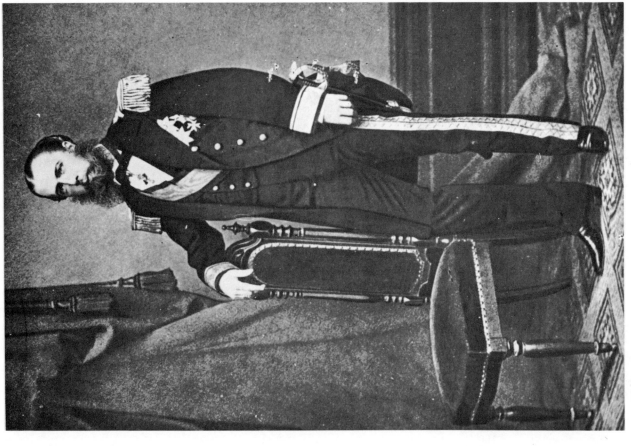

242. Maximilian, Emperor of Mexico. This was probably taken by Andrew Burgess, Brady's partner after the Civil War, who went to Mexico at the request of the State Department to gather "evidence" that French troops were there.

241. The famous publishing firm of Harper & Brothers, James, John, Joseph Wesley and Fletcher, in 1863. Brady's portrait symbolizes the unity of the four brothers, who liked to refer to themselves as the Cheeryble Brothers; after Nicholas Nickleby.

By Brady or assistant

243. Miss Lavinia Warren, Barnum's Giant, and Commodore Nutt. *By Brady or assistant*

244. Tom Thumb. From the picture album of Mrs. Tom Thumb. *By Brady or assistant*

246. General Tom Thumb, his wife and a baby (not theirs), one of Barnum's hoaxes. From the Mrs. Tom Thumb Collection. *By Brady or assistant*

245. The wedding of Tom Thumb and Miss Lavinia Warren in a posed studio shot either before or after the wedding. The background is a single painted curtain. *By Brady or assistant*

247. The earliest photograph taken of the interior of the Capitol building, showing the old House of Representatives chamber as it appeared about 1861.
By Brady

248. A section of the famous frescoes executed by Constantino Brumidi, which can be seen today in the "eye of the dome" of the Capitol. This picture was taken while the paintings were still on an enormous easel.
By Brady or assistant

249. One of the first views ever taken of the State Department at 14th and S Street N.W.   *By Brady*

251. Interior of the Treasury building during Lincoln's first administration. This is the "cash room," looking out from behind the counter.

By Brady or assistant

250. A wet plate of the old Navy Department before the Civil War.   *By Brady or assistant*

252. Pennsylvania Avenue from 15th Street toward the Capitol, probably Lincoln's second inaugural parade. This early street scene is probably unpublished.   *By Brady or assistant*

253. A Civil War parade scene on Pennsylvania Avenue between 7th and 9th Streets.

By Brady or assistant

254. Alexander Gardner's photographic gallery at 7th and D Streets, N.W.   *By Brady or assistant*

255. Richard Bickerton Pemell, first Earl Lyons, British minister in Washington 1858-65.
By Brady or assistant

256. Emma, queen of the Sandwich Islands (Hawaii) on her visit to America. The widow of King Kamehameha IV, she was given a reception by President Johnson in 1865. *By Brady or assistant*

257. Admiral Lisovski, commander of the Russian Atlantic Squadron which visited New York in 1863.
By Brady or assistant

257a. Members of the crew of the Russian Atlantic squadron commanded by Admiral Lisovski.
By Brady or assistant

258. General Ulysses S. Grant when he came to Washington to receive his third star from Lincoln. Brady's camera caught the fatigue, the anxiety and the terrible responsibility that lay upon his shoulders during the Vicksburg campaign. These three wet plates of Grant were among those found in the up-state New York barn. *By Brady or assistant*

259, 260. Two portraits of Grant taken after he had received his third star. *By Brady or assistant*

Momentous Decision

A series of three pictures taken from the steeple of Bethesda Church, Va. by Tim O'Sullivan showing General Grant discussing and making the decision "to fight it out" at Cold Harbor (June 3, 1864).

261. In this picture General Horace Porter, at Grant's right, is reading a newspaper; on his left is General Rawlins, his chief of staff, next to Colonel Ely S. Parker. Grant is listening to a report that Colonel Bowers, his adjutant-general, is reading as he stands inside the circle to the far right in the picture. Evidently Bowers moved slightly as O'Sullivan took this picture.   *By Tim O'Sullivan*

262. In this picture Grant has risen and has walked about the circle of church pews to where Meade is sitting and is now leaning over Meade's shoulder, consulting his map. A newly arrived officer is bending forward, either giving or receiving a front-line report. Colonel Parker has passed his newspaper to another officer. Soldiers from the Third Division of the Fifth Army Corps, whose wagons were passing, stopped and looked on curiously. This is the wet plate in the series which was believed to have been lost through the years. *By Tim O'Sullivan*

263. In this picture Grant has made up his mind and is back at his original seat, writing out his orders for the battle of Cold Harbor the next day. *By Tim O'Sullivan*

264. Confederate defenses before Atlanta, Ga., 1864.   *By Brady*

265. The Last Train from Atlanta, 1864.   *By George N. Barnard*

266. Father Mooney saying mass for the 69th New York State Militia in Virginia, 1861.

By Brady or assistant

268. The notorious Federal siege-gun, the "Swamp Angel," which bombarded Charleston in 1863.

269. Kate Chase, the daughter of Salmon P. Chase and a reigning belle of Washington society, visiting General John J. Abercrombie at his headquarters.
By Brady

270. Major General Ambrose Powell Hill, C.S.A.
By Julian Vannerson

271. City Point, Va., Grant's supply depot, June, 1865.
By Brady or assistant

272. Troops of the 21st Michigan Infantry, part of Sherman's army.

By Brady or assistant

273. The Telegraph Corps, Brandy Station, Va., April, 1864.

By Brady or assistant

274. Brady under fire at Petersburg.   *By a Brady assistant, probably Tim O'Sullivan*

275. Brady under fire before Petersburg, 1864. He has his hands in his pockets and is standing behind the first gun of Battery B, First Pennsylvania Light Artillery.   *By Tim O'Sullivan*

276. Photographic headquarters at Petersburg. Believed to be Alexander Gardner's staff or Army photographers who were employed to take photographs and copy maps.   *Probably by Alexander Gardner*

277. Bomb-proof quarters of Fort Sedgwick. *By Alexander Gardner*

278. Confederate soldier of Ewell's corps killed in the attack of May 19, 1864. *By Tim O'Sullivan*

279. A dead Confederate soldier, April, 1865.   *By Thomas C. Roche*

280. Belle Boyd, one of the romantic spies of the Civil War. A graceful horsewoman at twelve, she began her career as "Stonewall" Jackson's courier at seventeen. *By Brady or assistant*

281. Rose O'Neal Greenhow with her daughter in the courtyard of the Old Capitol Prison. She was the "queen bee" of the Confederate spy ring in Washington. *By Brady or assistant*

282. Pauline Cushman, "Scout of the Cumberland" and later a frontier woman in Arizona. This picture was taken after she had been sentenced to death by the Confederates and was rescued by the Federals just before the execution. *By Brady or assistant*

283. John Bigelow, whose brilliant diplomacy and personal secret service group helped to prevent the Confederacy from getting its British-built iron rams released from shipyards in England and France. *By Brady or assistant*

285. Fernando Wood, ex-mayor of New York City, who was said to be a leader of its Copperhead element at the time Confederate terrorists burned a number of hotels there in 1864.

By Brady or assistant

286. Clement Vallandigham of Ohio and a group of associates. He was the leader of the treasonable Knights of the Golden Circle, a secret organization which attempted to disrupt the northwestern states during the Civil War. Vallandigham is seated in the center; the others are unidentified.

By Brady or assistant

287. Railroad trestle in wartime. It is believed that the man with a top hat is a Pinkerton man detailed to watch military railroads and vital points.

By Brady or assistant

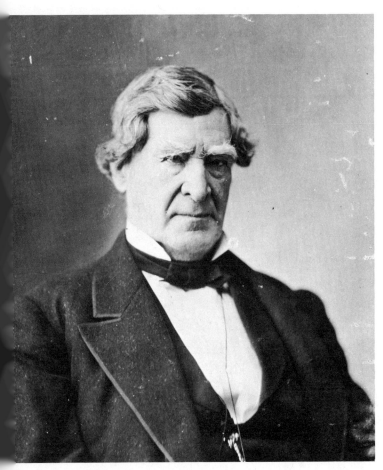

288. Judge Jeremiah Black. He was sent secretly to Canada by the Federal government to negotiate unofficially for a peace with the Confederates.

By Brady or assistant

289. General William Starke Rosecrans, commander during the Cumberland campaign, who saved Pauline Cushman from hanging as a spy.

By Brady or assistant

290. The ruins of Richmond, 1865, from across the James River.   *By Brady or Alexander Gardner*

291. Ruins of the state arsenal, Richmond, 1865.   *By Brady*

292. Veterans of the Sixth Army Corps in the Grand Review, the parade that was reviewed by President Johnson, his Cabinet and General Grant in May, 1865. The Sixth was the Corps that saved Washington from capture. *By Brady or assistant*

BRADY'S LANTERN VIEWS

A few of the views Brady intended to use in his last photographic exhibition of Civil War scenes. This was just before he died. Levin Handy, his nephew, had prepared these transparencies for him. The identifications were written by Handy or his daughter.

293. Inauguration of President Lincoln.
By Brady or assistant

294. New York *Herald* headquarters.
By Brady or assistant

295. Fort Sumter after bombardment, 1865
By Brady or assistan

296. Contrabands.
By Brady or assistant

297. Pontoon on wheels.
By Brady or assistant

298. Cooking beans.
By Brady or assistan

299. Welcome visitor.
By Brady or assistant

300. Mail wagon.
By Brady or assistant

301. Camp of 80th N. Y., City Point, Apri 1865.
By Brady or assistar

302. General Robert E. Lee after Appomattox, and **303.** Lee seated between his son, G. W. C. Lee, on his right and Lieutenant Colonel Walter H. Taylor of his staff. These are two of a series taken by Brady in 1865 in the basement below the back porch of Lee's Franklin Street home in Richmond and are from the original wet plates in the Brady-Handy Collection.

By Brady

General Robert E. Lee

304. General Robert E. Lee, C.S.A.

By Julian Vannerson

305. Lee on "Traveler," 1866.   *By Michael Miley*

306. Abraham Lincoln's second inauguration, 1865. This is one of the wet plates from which Handy made transparencies (No. 293) for Brady's last exhibition. Note that though the small segment showing Lincoln was considerably enlarged for the transparency, the clarity is excellent. *By Brady or assistant*

"NOW HE BELONGS TO THE AGES"

307. Lincoln's funeral procession on Pennsylvania Avenue on the way to the Baltimore & Ohio station. *By Alexander Gardner*

308. Ford's Theater. *By Brady*

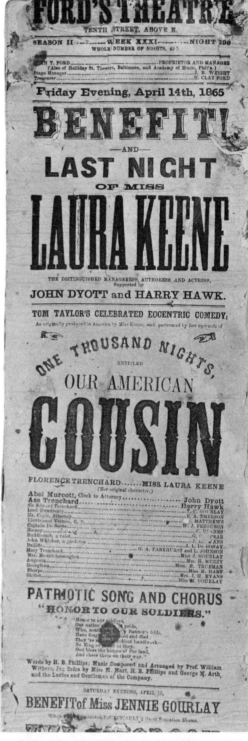

310. Major Henry Rathbone, whom John Wilkes Booth stabbed after the major lunged at him just before he jumped over the railing of the box to the stage eleven feet below.
By Brady or assistant

311. Laura Keene.
By Brady or assistant

309. The playbill, April 4, 1865.

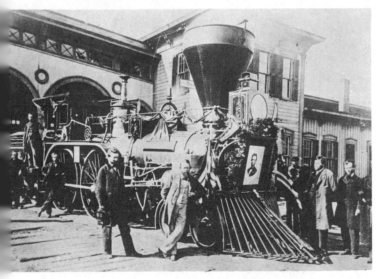

312. Locomotive of Lincoln's funeral train, leaving the Baltimore & Ohio station for Springfield, Ill.
Probably by Alexander Gardner

313. Dr. Charles A. Leale, who climbed to the box from the stage to attend the dying President.
By Brady or assistant

314. Clara Harris, who, with her fiancé, Major Rathbone, was in the box with Lincoln when he was assassinated. *By Brady or assistant*

THE PLOTTERS

Conspirators and accessories in the Lincoln assassination plot. All the men (except Booth and John Surratt) shown on these two pages were photographed immediately after their arrest, probably in the Washington Penitentiary. Booth was shot resisting arrest; Payne, Herold (not shown) and Atzerodt were hanged with Mrs. Surratt (not shown); Spangler, Arnold, O'Laughlin and Mudd were imprisoned. John Surratt remained in hiding in Canada for a while, then escaped to Europe. He was arrested and brought back to the United States for trial but later released.

315. John Wilkes Booth as Mark Antony, 1864.

316. Lewis Payne.   *By Alexander Gardner*

317. George Atzerodt.   *By Alexander Gardner*

318. Edward Spangler.   *By Alexander Gardner*

319. Samuel Arnold. *By Alexander Gardner*

320. John Surratt in Zouave uniform. *By Brady or assistant*

321. For years this was believed to be **Dr. Samuel Mudd**, taken on board one of the monitors in the Navy Yard. Most of the prisoners were held on the ships between April 18 and April 29, 1865. However, a recent comparison by experts in the Library of Congress, of pictures of Mudd, reveal that this could not be the unfortunate physician. It probably was someone confined on the monitors but never brought to trial, like Hartman Richter. *By Alexander Gardner*

322. Michael O'Laughlin. *By Alexander Gardner*

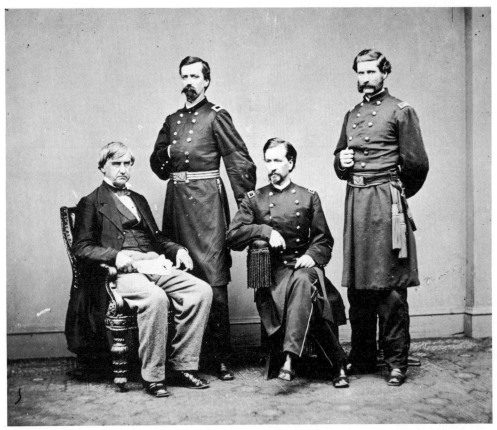

323. Some of the members and staff of the military commission which tried the Lincoln conspirators in the Old Capitol Prison in June, 1865. Shown here, left to right, are Judge Advocate General Joseph Holt, General Robert S. Foster, Colonel H. L. Burnett and Colonel C. R. Clendenin. The generals shown below are, left to right: Thomas M. Harris, David Hunter, August Kautz, Joseph H. Elkins, Lew Wallace and John A. Bingham. Bingham and Burnett were not members but assistants to the Judge Advocate General. *By Brady or assistant*

324. Benn Pitman, the courtroom reporter who took the testimony in the Lincoln conspiracy trial. He had introduced to the United States the shorthand system invented by his brother Isaac. *By Brady or assistant*

325. Some of the members of the military commission. See also No. 323 above. *By Brady or assistant*

ANDERSONVILLE

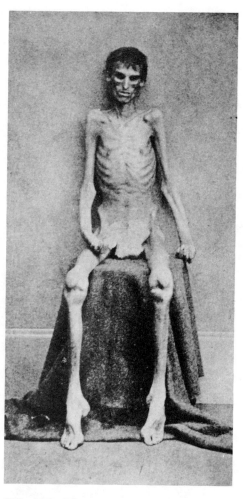

326. Andersonville prison. In the foreground is the open latrine. Note the stream running through it. During the trial of Henri Wirz, the commandant, witnesses brought out that this stream was the only source of water supply for the camp.
Probably by George S. Cook

328, 329. These two living dead men are Union soldiers after their release from Andersonville in 1865.

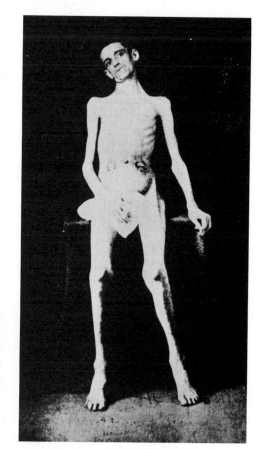

327. Another view of Andersonville showing the famous dead-line fence. Sharp-shooters on the walls had orders to shoot any prisoner passing the fence or even putting his hand or foot through it.

"WIRZ, REMEMBER ANDERSONVILLE"

This series showing the hanging of Henri Wirz is published complete here for the first time.

330. The newspaper correspondents, November 10, 1865, outside the Washington Penitentiary.
By Alexander Gardner

331. Major Russell reading the death warrant.
By Alexander Gardner

332. Adjusting the rope. The Catholic priest is asking Wirz if he wishes to make a confession and Wirz, protesting his innocence, refuses. The soldiers, forming a square at the base of the gallows, are chanting, "Wirz, remember Andersonville . . ." while the crowd hoots and jeers.
By Alexander Gardner

333. The trap is sprung.   *By Alexander Gardner*

334. The drop failed to break Wirz's neck and he twisted for a few minutes in his death agony while the soldiers and spectators kept up their ghastly shouting and jeering. The taut rope may be seen and possibly also, in the foreground between the upper two planks of the scaffold, Wirz's head.

By Alexander Gardner

A Famous Family

335. The Beecher family. Lyman Beecher seated, Henry Ward Beecher standing at extreme right and Harriet Beecher Stowe, seated second from the right.

By Brady or assistant

A Successful Commission

336. The Joint High Commissioners who finally in 1871 settled the differences between the United States and Great Britain arising out of the war, such as the *Alabama* claims.

By Brady

337. Thaddeus Stevens, who brought about the impeachment of President Andrew Johnson. He was Majority Leader of the House of Representatives during the Lincoln and Johnson administrations.

338. Charles Sumner, Congressman from Massachusetts. He was a violent abolitionist and one of the early builders of the Republican Party.

By Brady or assistant

339. The body of Thaddeus Stevens lying in state in the rotunda of the Capitol in 1868, with a company of the Butler Zouaves standing honor guard. This scene has been incorrectly identified many times as the picture of the body of Lincoln lying in state.

340. Henry Jarvis Raymond, founder of the *New York Times*.

By Brady or assistant

341. Editor John Forney, a good friend of Thaddeus Stevens. It was at Forney's Washington apartment that Brady met many leaders of politics, diplomacy, literature and science.   *By Brady or assistant*

342. Carl Schurz, exiled from Prussia after the 1848 revolution, was influential in the Republican Party and an effective writer and orator against slavery. He was a major-general in the Union Army and Secretary of the Interior, 1877-81.   *By Brady or assistant*

343. Preston King of New York, one of President Johnson's advisers. He was said to have prevented Mrs. Surratt's daughter from seeing Johnson to plead for her mother's life on the eve of her execution.
By Brady or assistant

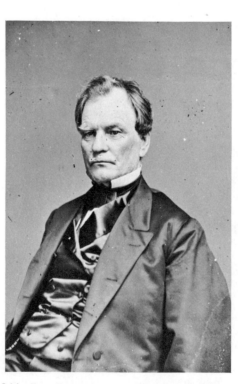

344. Ben F. Wade, co-author of the Wade-Davis Manifesto, a denunciation of Lincoln's plan for reconstruction.
By Brady or assistant

345. Senator Theodore Frelinghuysen of New Jersey, who later became Secretary of State in the Garfield-Arthur administration.
By Brady or assistant

346. Andrew Johnson, seventeenth President.
By Brady

347. The Andrew Johnson impeachment committee. A rare and unpublished photograph taken by Brady before one of the meetings of the House managers, or impeachment committee. Thaddeus Stevens, second from left, with cane, seated next to Benjamin Butler, was already a dying man when this picture was taken. George W. Julian, in his unpublished diary, which Claude G. Bowers used in his *The Tragic Era,* published in 1929, wrote that he believed Stevens tried but was too ill to get out of his sickbed to join the committee at Brady's gallery. But the grim old warrior did succeed and hobbled into Brady's Pennsylvania Avenue studio with the spark of life flickering low in his breast. Seated, left to right, Butler, Stevens, T. Williams, J. A. Bingham. Standing, left to right, J. F. Wilson, G. S. Boutwell, J. A. Logan. *By Brady*

348. Robert E. Lee taken in Brady's Washington gallery in 1869 when he was President of Washington College at Lexington, Va., later Washington and Lee University.
By Brady or assistant

349. Frederick Douglass, runaway mulatto slave who became famous as an orator, lecturer and writer.
By Brady or assistant

350. Hamilton Fish of New York, Secretary of State, 1869-77.   *By Brady or assistant*

351. Ulysses S. Grant, eighteenth President, about 1869. One of the plates found in a New York State barn several years ago.

By Brady or assistant

352. Mrs. U. S. Grant with her father Mr. Dent, her daughter Nellie and her son Jesse.

By Brady or assistant

353. President Grant about 1869. Note the large reflector to one side.   *By Brady*

354. General Grant, his wife and twelve-year-old son Frederick Dent Grant at City Point, Va., toward the end of the war.   *By Brady or assistant*

355. Nellie and Jesse Grant. One of the plates found in an upstate New York barn.   *By Brady or assistant*

356. A rare portrait of Jesse Grant, the general's father.   *By Brady or assistant*

357. A stereo of Grant's first inauguration, March 4, 1869.   *By Brady*

358. Senator Oliver P. Morton, former Governor of Indiana. *By Brady or assistant*

359. Roscoe Conkling, Senator from New York, 1867-81.   *By Brady or assistant*

360. Senator Zachariah Chandler of Michigan, later U. S. Secretary of Interior.
By Brady or assistant

POSTWAR FIGURES

361. General John A. Rawlins, U. S. Secretary of War (1869). He had been Grant's close friend and adviser, U. S. Army chief of staff. *By Brady or assistant*

362. Marshall Jewell, Grant's Postmaster General. *By Brady or assistant*

363. George Sewall Boutwell, Secretary of the Treasury, 1869-73. This is one of the plates found in a New York barn. *By Brady or assistant*

364. Adolph Sutro, "the millionaire miner," who planned the tunnel to reach the Comstock Lode, 1869-78. *By Brady or assistant*

365. Vinnie Ream, a sculptress and government clerk who had a studio in the basement of the Capitol. *By Brady or assistant*

366. Dr. Willard Parker, the first in America to operate successfully on an abscessed appendix (1867). *By Brady or assistant*

367. Senator George Hunt Pendleton of Ohio. *By Brady or assistant*

368. Richard Jordan Gatling, inventor of the Gatling gun, patented 1862. *By Brady or assistant*

369. James G. Blaine of Maine, who was five times a candidate for the Presidency. This is one of the plates discovered in an upstate New York barn.
By Brady or assistant

370. Robert Todd Lincoln, Secretary of War from 1881- 85. *By Brady or assistant*

371. Senator, formerly General, Ambrose Everett Burnside of Rhode Island, famous for his side-whiskers. *By Brady or assistant*

372. Horatio Seymour, defeated Democratic candidate for the Presidency, 1868.
By Brady or assistant

373. Whitelaw Reid, Civil War correspondent, editor of New York *Tribune,* notable diplomat. *By Brady or assistant*

374. Former General John B. Gordon, Senator from Georgia, 1873. *By Brady or assistant*

375. Former General Wade Hampton, Senator from South Carolina. *By Brady or assistant*

376. Former Brigadier General William Mahone, Senator from Virginia, 1881-87. *By Brady or assistant*

377. Senator Benjamin H. Hill of Georgia, 1877-82. *By Brady or assistant*

378. General Fitzhugh Lee, center, and his fellow generals T. L. Rosser, Beverly Robertson, William Paine and Pierce Young, as they appeared in 1877.
By Brady or assistant

379. Senator David L. Yulee of Florida.
By Brady or assistant

380. Senator Zebulon B. Vance of North Carolina, one of the early leaders of the Klan.
By Brady or assistant

381. Lucius Quintus Cincinnatus Lamar of Mississippi, Secretary of the Interior in Cleveland's Cabinet, Supreme Court judge.
By Brady or assistant

382. A rare and unpublished view of the White House, 1865. *By Brady*

383. East Capitol Street from the Capitol steps in the seventies. Carroll Row to right. Site of Library of Congress and the United States Supreme Court. *By Brady or assistant*

384. Ninth and F Streets, N.W., in the eighties. *By Brady or assistant*

385. A picture taken from Brady's studio looking toward Center Market, Pennsylvania Avenue and 7th Street, N.W., in the early eighties. *By Brady*

A series of wet plates showing various stages in the building of the Washington Monument. The cornerstone was laid on July 4, 1848, but not until December, 1884, was the monument completed. The aluminum capstone was put in place on December 6, 1884.

386. Halfway up. About 150 feet of stone have been laid.
By Brady or assistant

387. At the top.
Probably by Levin Handy

388. Putting the capstone in place. It weighed 3,300 pounds. *Probably by Levin Handy*

389. Dedication of the Washington Monument, February 21, 1885. An account of the ceremony states that it was a bitter cold day and a high wind was blowing.
By Brady or assistant

390. Office of the Chief Clerk, Department of State, in the eighties. *Probably by Levin Handy*

Belles and Beaux

392. A copy of a rare print of Peggy O'Neil Eaton, whose romantic exploits shocked the capital when Andrew Jackson was President.

393. Peggy Eaton in her last years. She died in 1879.
By Brady or assistant

394. Kate Chase Sprague, wife of Senator Sprague.
By Brady or assistant

395. Senator William Sprague of Rhode Island.
By Brady or assistant

396. Senator Isaac P. Christiancy from Michigan. *By Brady or assistant*

397, 398. The Catacazys. *By Brady or assistant*

399. Salmon P. Chase, Chief Justice, 1864-73. *By Brady or assistant*

400. Alphonso Taft, statesman, father of President William Howard Taft. *By Brady or assistant*

401. Susan B. Anthony, campaigner for woman suffrage. *By Brady or assistant*

402. Charles A. Dana, an editor of the New York *Tribune* and editor and founder of the New York *Sun,* 1868-97. *By Brady or assistant*

403. Robert G. Ingersoll in the seventies. *By Brady or assistant*

404. Mark Twain, seated between George Alfred Townsend, who later interviewed Brady for the New York *World* and David Gray of Buffalo. This picture was taken February 7, 1871. *By Brady*

406. Rutherford B. Hayes, nineteenth President. *By Brady*

407. Charles Stewart Parnell, the Irish leader, believed to have been taken on his visit to the United States. *By Brady or assistant*

408. Mrs. James A. Garfield. *By Brady or assistant*

409. James A. Garfield, twentieth President. *By Brady*

410. Garfield and his daughter. *By Brady or assistant*

411. Chester A. Arthur, twenty-first President, on a fishing trip. *By Brady or assistant*

412. Thomas A. Edison, who demonstrated his phonograph for President Hayes. *By Levin Handy*

413. Mark Twain in his later years. *Probably by Brady*

414. Walt Whitman. *By Brady or assistant*

415. Grover Cleveland, twenty-second and twenty-fourth President. *By Brady or assistant*

416. William McKinley, twenty-fifth President. *By Brady, Levin Handy or assistant*

417. National Council of Women Conference, 1888. The woman seated second from the right is probably Susan B. Anthony, the "woman's rights" leader.

By Brady or assistant

419. McKinley's inaugural parade nearing 15th Street on the way to the White House. In the distance at the far right, the building with the sign "Bradbury Pianos" was Brady's original Pennsylvania Avenue gallery.

Probably by Levin Handy

420. Mathew B. Brady in the seventies.
By Levin Handy

421. Levin Handy, at right, when he first came to work for Mathew Brady. The other boy is believed to be Levin's brother. *By Brady*

422. Levin Handy standing in the doorway of the Handy Studios at 494 Maryland Avenue, S.W., in Washington. Alice Handy Cox and her son Frederick are in the foreground. Brady spent most of his last years in this house.

423. Mathew B. Brady in 1889, taken in Brady's Washington studio. *By Levin Handy*

424. Alice Handy Cox, Levin Handy, Jr. and Mary Handy Evans, taken in the Handy Studios on Mary land Avenue. *By Levin Handy*

425. When the famous Indian chiefs came to see the Great White Father, Brady, Handy or an assistant was on hand with his camera to record the event. This picture of Ute chief Ouray and his squaw Chipela was made in the late seventies.

By Brady, Handy or assistant

426. Theodore Roosevelt, twenty-sixth President. This portrait was taken by Levin Handy in Roosevelt's private office in 1901. To avoid the reflection from his eyeglasses Handy asked the President to wear empty frames. *By Levin Handy*

427. Tim O'Sullivan, who took many photographs of Civil War scenes when he was in Brady's employ. This is a copy of a stereoscopic print made in an Indian village on the Isthmus of Darien. O'Sullivan was the official photographer for the Selfridge expedition to Panama in 1870.

428. Tim O'Sullivan's boat, in which he descended the Colorado River. Note the small dark tent for developing in the bow. Black Canyon, site of Hoover Dam, is in the background. *By Tim O'Sullivan*

429. Shoshone Falls, Snake River, Idaho. *By Tim O'Sullivan*

430. Camp Beauty, Cañon de Chelly. *By Tim O'Sullivan*

431. Lost Lakes, head of the Conejos Cañon, Calif. *By Tim O'Sullivan*

433. The steamer *Mary McDonald* at Wyandotte, Kans.

432. Here is a selection of pictures from the more than one hundred and fifty that Alexander Gardner took of the early West after the Civil War when the Union Pacific was spanning the continent. All the pictures, except 432, showing the bearded Gardner and his photographic wagon, are by Gardner.

434. Kansas City.

435. Fifth Street, Leavenworth, Kans.

436. Section men at Salina, Kans. The extreme distance is five miles off.

437. Bull train crossing the Smoky Hill River at Ellsworth, Kans.

438. Ellsworth, Kans.

439. Loading cattle at MacCoy's stockyard, Abilene, Kans.

440. Cattle fording the Smoky Hill River at the old Santa Fe crossing, Ellsworth, Kans.

441. Fort Riley, Kans.

442. Fort Harker, Kans.

443. Packing house, Junction City, Kans.

444. Construction train west of Fort Hays, Kans.

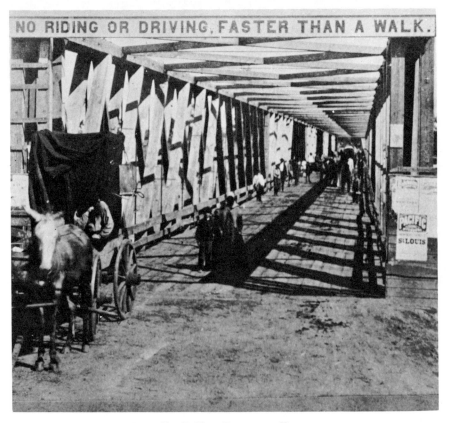

445. View across Turnpike Bridge, Lawrence, Kans.

446. The "Mayor" of Prairie Dog Town, Abilene.

447. Walnut Street, Ellsworth, Kans.

448. Group with tame elk on ranch at Clear Creek, Kans.

450. The Big Blue.

449. Ferry across the Kaw at Lecompton, Kans.

451. Laying track 600 miles west of St. Louis.

452. Mathew B. Brady's tombstone. The year of his death is wrong. Brady died in 1896.

April 17, 1953. Bunting and flags on the speaker's stand at the Carswell Air Base near Fort Worth, rippled in the spring breeze. The great words had died away. A young WAC leaned over and smashed a photographer's bulb filled with "hypo" across the nose of the giant ship.

The doors were closed and the ground chief gave the traditional "thumbs up" signal to take off.

The RB-36, the largest photo-reconnaissance plane in the world, roared across the field and rose, like a great silver eagle, into the sky. The name in big black letters stood out: MATHEW B. BRADY.

The wheel had made a complete turn: the man whose camera had linked the early Republic with the brink of the twentieth century was now a part of the atomic age.

453. A photo-montage made at the time of the christening of the *Mathew B. Brady,* RB-36 photo-reconnaissance plane of the Army Air Force Photographic Division, April 30, 1953.

SOURCE NOTES

1. From the foreword to *A Diary of a President,* Allan Nevins, Longmans, Green & Company, N. Y., 1929. Excerpt from Polk's diary, Library of Congress.
2. An article on Brady by C. Edwards Lester, *Photographic Art Journal,* January, 1851.
3. The exact date and place of Brady's birth is not known. He told George Alfred ("Gath" Townsend, the New York *World* correspondent, in 1891 "I go back to near 1823-24." Although Brady also told him that he was born in Warren County, N. Y., "in the woods about Lake George," a search of the county records failed to produce a birth certificate. Henry Wysham Lanier, art editor and publisher, claimed in Miller's *Photographic History of the Civil War,* Vol. I, which was published in 1912, that Brady was born in Cork, Ireland. Brady's death certificate, obtained by the author, indicates that Brady was born of native American parents in the United States in 1823. Brady was conscious when he entered the Presbyterian Hospital in New York and it can be assumed that he supplied the hospital with his own vital statistics, which were later incorporated in the certificate.
4. As late as 1865 there were survivors in the Mohawk Valley of the bloody guerrilla fighting. Eighty-four years after the Revolutionary battles Nicholas Veeder was ready to "shoulder arms" against the Confederacy. In an interview published in the March 30, 1861 issue of *Leslie's Illustrated Newspaper* he recalled how he marched with General Herkimer at the famous battle of Oriskany and Burgoyne's surrender of his sword to Gates at Saratoga. Like many of the Mohawk veterans he was still bitter against the Butlers and their Indian Tories.
5. George Alfred ("Gath") Townsend's interview with Mathew B. Brady in the New York *World,* April 12, 1891, p. 23. (Hereafter cited as Townsend interview.)
6. The New York *Sun,* in a special anniversay edition August 24, 1935, included the Morse letter to the New York *Observer.* The *Journal* of the Franklin Institute, Vol. XXVIII, 1839, p. 209, revealed that a letter had been written by a reader to the editor of the *United States Gazette* to the effect that a "scientific friend" in Paris had sent him an authorized version of Daguerre's process, which was to be given to the public.
7. *Samuel F. B. Morse, His Letters and Journals,* Vol. II, E. L. Morse, Houghton Mifflin Company, New York, 1914, p. 129.
9. *American Journal of Sciences and Arts,* Vol. XXXVII, p. 375. Also *Niles Register,* September 21, 1839, p. 64.
10. Norwich, Conn. *Courier,* May 9, 1826.
11. *Diary in America* by Frederick Marryat, American edition, pp. 258–60.
12. "Mathew Brady, Photographer," the Sunday *Star,* Washington, D. C. (date missing from clipping)
13. Townsend interview.
14. *Photographic Art Journal,* Vol. II, p. 280.
15. Morse Papers, Library of Congress, and miscellaneous Morse Papers, Manuscript Division, New York Public Library, show that Morse was, as he said in a letter to a relative February 14, 1841, "endeavoring to realize something from the daguerreotype portraits."
16. Doggett's *New York City Directory,* 1843–44 and

1844-45, tell something of Brady's early activities. The 1843–44 directory listed Brady as a "jewel case man," 164 Fulton Street, with his residence at 27 John Street. The following year he had moved his "surgical case and miniature business" to 187 John Street but had opened his daguerreotype parlor at Fulton Street, making another entrance at 207 Broadway. Brady had also moved to 62 Barclay Street. In 1846–47 the directory had the same listing for both his business and his home. Other city directories, such as *Trow's New York City Directory,* reveal that Brady lived on Ashland Place in the late forties and at one time resided on Staten Island.

17. "Annals of Iowa," Series 3, edited by John King from a series in the Dubuque, Iowa *Times,* January, 1869. (Hereafter cited as King.)
18. *Memoirs of John William Draper,* 1811–82, by George F. Barker, read before the National Academy of Sciences April 21, 1888.
19. Draper's *Textbook of Chemistry,* p. 93, Harper & Brothers, 1846. Also *Photography and the American Scene* by Taft, p. 29, The Macmillan Company, New York, 1938. (Hereafter cited as Taft.)
20. King.
21. King.
22. New York *Morning Herald,* September 30, 1839.
23. Townsend interview.
24. *Photographic Art Journal,* Vol. II, p. 280.
25. Henry Papprill's aquatint of a drawing by J. W. Hill, "New York from the Steeple of St. Paul's Church, looking East, South and West," shows Brady's early gallery at Fulton Street with skylights in the roof. The New York City building plans, 1844, for the Fulton Street building also indicate skylights.
26. For a sketch of Jeremiah Gurney's life see the New York *Star,* November 6, 1887. The *Daguerrean Journal,* Vol. II, 1851, p. 340, and the *Photographic Art Journal,* Vol. VI, 1853, p. 383, give accounts of Gurney also.
27. The Washington *Times,* May 28, 1922, p. 7.
28. When all of the Brady-Handy Collection has been catalogued it will be seen that few great Americans of Brady's time escaped his camera.
29. Townsend interview.
30. *McClure's Magazine,* Vol. IX, 1897, p. 795.
31. Townsend interview.
32. Townsend interview.
33. Townsend interview.
34. Brady submitted this statement to the Joint Committee on the Library on February 23, 1881, when he sold the three portraits for $4,000. They hang today in the main corridor of the Senate. The price paid for the Webster portrait was $1,900; the total price for those of Calhoun and Clay was $2,100.
35. Townsend interview.
36. Townsend interview, also Rose O'Neal Greenhow letters in the Captured Confederate Correspondence, State Department files, National Archives.
37. This story of Brady's first meeting and courtship of Julia Handy was told to me by Mrs. Mary H. Evans and Mrs. Alice H. Cox, who recall hearing it from their father, Levin C. Handy. As they pointed out, this is only a family legend.

38. Edgar C. Cox made an extensive survey of the marriage records of the E Street Baptist Church. There were several Bradys but not Mathew B. The Washington newspapers also failed to produce an exact date of their marriage.

39. See A Pictorial Bibliography of Brady Pictures, listing Brady pictures used by *Harper's Weekly* and *Leslie's Illustrated Newspaper*.

40. A copy of *The Gallery of Illustrious Americans* is in the Art and Architecture Division, New York Public Library.

41. *The Gallery of Illustrious Americans*, containing the portraits and biographical sketches of twenty-four of our most eminent citizens of the American Republic since the death of Washington. From daguerreotypes by Brady, engraved by F. D'Avignon. Editor, C. Edwards Lester. Published January 1, 1850, by the D'Avignon Press, 323 Broadway, N. Y.

42. Townsend interview.

43. *Edward Anthony*, published by the American Museum of Photography, 338 South 15th St., Philadelphia, Pa.

44. Taft, p. 54.

45. *U. S. Decennial Census Reports*, 1840–1870.

46. *Humphrey's Journal*, Vol. I, 1852.

47. *Memoirs of John Quincy Adams*, Vol. II, p. 401, p. 430, J. B. Lippincott and Company, Philadelphia, 1876.

48. *The Daguerrean Journal*, Devoted to the Daguerrean and Photogenic Art, Also Embracing the Sciences, Arts and Literature, November 1, 1850; S. D. Humphrey, editor and publisher, 335 Broadway, New York. The *Photographic Art Journal*, Vol. I, 1851; H. H. Snelling, editor, W. B. Smith, publisher, 61 Ann Street, New York.

49. The *Illustrated London News*, Vol. XVIII, 1851, p. 425.

50. *Humphrey's Journal*, 1851, p. 292.

51. *Photographic Art Journal*, Vol. I, 1851, p. 136.

52. *Photographic Art Journal*, Vol. III, p. 320. Also Townsend interview.

53. *Exhibitions of the Works of Industry of All Nations*, 1851. *Reports by the Juries*, 1852. Printed for the Royal Commission. Also official description and illustrated catalogue, London, 1852, 3 vv., Vol. III, p. 1464.

54. *Illustrated London News*, Vol. XVIII, 1851, p. 425.

55. *Exhibition of the Works of Industry of All Nations*, 1851, pp. 63–64. *Reports by the Juries*, London, 1852.

56. *Exhibition of the Works of Industry of All Nations*, 1851, pp. 63–64. *Reports by the Juries*, London, 1852.

57. *Photographic Art Journal*, Vol. III, February, 1852, p. 130.

58. *Daguerrean Journal*, Vol. II, 1851, p. 114. *Photographic Art Journal*, Vol. III, 1852, p. 271. *Photographic Art Journal*, Vol. II, 1851, p. 94. *The Camera and the Pencil*, p. 364.

59. *The Chemist*, March, 1851, London.

60. *Photographic Art Journal*, Vol. III, 1852, p. 230.

61. New York City map, 1852, The New York Historical Society.

62. Daguerrean Artists' Registry, *Humphrey's Journal*, 1852.

63. A small clipping from an unidentified newspaper or trade journal in the possession of Mrs. Evans and Mrs. Cox.

64. A small clipping from an unidentified newspaper or trade journal in the possession of Mrs. Evans and Mrs. Cox.

65. *American Journal of Photography*, Vol. I, 1858–59, p. 112.

66. *Photographic Art Journal*, frontispiece, April, 1853.

67. *Harper's Weekly*, October 17, 1859, p. 659.

68. *Photographic Art Journal*, Vol. VII, 1854, p. 96.

69. *Humphrey's Journal*, Vol. XIII, 1861–62, p. 292.

70. *The Story of Agfa Ansco*, 1939, published by Agfa Ansco Corporation, Binghamton, N. Y.

71. *Humphrey's Journal*, Vol. V, 1853.

72. Clipping owned by Mrs. Cox and Mrs. Evans.

73. *Humphrey's Journal*, Vol. V, 1853, p. 1.

75. Family Bible owned by Mrs. Cox and Mrs. Evans.

77. Obituary of Alexander Gardner, *Photographic Journal of America*, Vol. XX, 1883, p. 92.

78. *Anthony's Photographic Bulletin*, December, 1882, p. 408.

79. *American Journal of Photography*, Vol. II, August 1, 1859, p. 75.

80. New York *Herald*, March 14, 1860, p. 2.

81. *Leslie's Illustrated Newspaper*, January, 1861.

82. Boston *Herald*, October 15, 1860, reprinted in *Photo Miniature*, Vol. V, p. 145, 1903. Also King's version in *American Journal of Photography*, Vol. III, 1860–61, p. 188.

83. *Atlantic Monthly*, Vol. XII, 1863, pp. 11–12.

84. "Aerial Photography," *Photo Miniature*, 1903, p. 145.

85. *Six Months in the White House*, Francis B. Carpenter, 1866, New York, p. 46.

86. *Six Months in the White House*, Francis B. Carpenter, and *The Life of Lincoln*, Ida M. Tarbell, Vol. II, New York, p. 158.

87. *Leslie's Illustrated Newspaper*, January, 1861.

89. Townsend interview.

90. *American Journal of Photography*, Vol. IV, 1861, p. 67, p. 213.

91. Townsend interview.

92. Recollections of George Story, curator emeritus of the Metropolitan Museum of Art, in an undated clipping from the New York *World*, owned by Mrs. Cox and Mrs. Evans, probably published in the eighties.

93. *Anthony's Photographic Bulletin*, No. 2, 1882.

94. "Brady's portrait of Hon. John Tyler, ex-President of the United States and President of the Peace Convention, sitting in Washington," *Leslie's Illustrated Newspaper*, February 16, 1861, p. 204.

95. *Battles and Leaders*, Vol. I, p. 7. (Hereafter cited as *Battles and Leaders*.)

96. *Battles and Leaders*.

97. *Battles and Leaders*.

98. *Reveille in Washington*, 1860–65, Margaret Leech, Harper & Brothers, New York, 1941, p. 57–58. (Hereafter cited as Leech.)

99. *Anthony's Photographic Bulletin*, No. 2.

100. *Abraham Lincoln* (*The Prairie Years* and *The War Years*, one-volume edition), Carl Sandburg, Harcourt, Brace and Co., New York, 1954, p. 596.

101. "The Wild Rose," *Desperate Women*, James D. Horan, G. P. Putnam's Sons, New York, 1950. (Hereafterward cited as *Desperate Women*.)

104. Leech, p. 89, p. 96.

105. Townsend interview.

106. Leech, p. 99.

107. *Battles and Leaders*.

108. *Battles and Leaders*.

109. At least one historian recalled that he had once seen a Brady photograph of a frightened mob of retreating soldiers and civilians at Bull Run. Efforts to locate this

photograph, however, have been unsuccessful.

110. Brady's portrait taken after his return from Bull Run. The tip of the sword given him by the Zouaves can be seen below the edge of his duster.

111. *Humphrey's Journal,* Vol. XII, 1861–62, p. 133.

112. *American Journal of Photography,* August 1, 1861.

113. *Sketchbook of the Civil War,* by Alexander Gardner, published by Philip and Solomon, Washington, 1865.

114. *Photographic History of the Civil War* (ten volumes), Francis Trevelyan Miller, Editor-in-chief, Review of Reviews Co., 1912, New York, P. 31. (Hereafter cited as Miller.)

115. Miller.

116. Miller.

117. "Reminiscences of War-time Photographers," *Anthony's Photographic Bulletin,* No. 2. Also Miller, pp. 30–54.

118. *Anthony's Photographic Bulletin,* No. 2. Also Miller.

119. *Anthony's Photographic Bulletin,* No. 2. Also Miller.

120. Miller, Vol. II, pp. 55–78.

121. Miller, Vol. II, pp. 55–78.

122. "Doings of the Sunbeam," *Atlantic Monthly,* Vol. XII, pp. 11–12.

123. *Leslie's Illustrated Newspaper,* April 5, 1862, p. 334.

124. *Leslie's Illustrated Newspaper,* April 5, 1862, p. 334.

126. Leech.

127. Miller, Vol. II, p. 83.

128. Miller, Vol. II, p. 93.

129. Miller, Vol. II, p. 102.

130. Brady has been credited with taking this picture but Gardner was the photographer. He was still in Brady's employ at the time.

131. *The Pinkerton Story,* James D. Horan and Howard Swiggett, G. P. Putnam's, New York, 1951; *Desperate Women,* by James D. Horan, G. P. Putnam's Sons, New York, 1950.

132. *Three Years With the Adirondack Regiment, 118th New York Volunteers, Infantry.* From the diaries and other memoranda of John L. Cunningham, privately printed, Norwood, Mass., 1920, New York Historical Society. Also Carl Haverlin's article, "Lincoln at Brady's Gallery," spring 1955 issue, the *Journal of the Illinois State Historical Society.*

133. Gardner issued some of these stereoscopic views after the war under his name.

134. Leech, pp. 204-205.

135. Miller, Vol. II, pp. 107, 108, 109, 113.

136. Miller, Vol. II, pp. 106–128.

137. Miller, Vol. II, p. 125.

138. Brady's New York *Register,* Manuscript Division, New York Public Library.

139. Brady-Handy Collection, Library of Congress.

140. *Lincoln and the Russians,* Albert A. Woldman, World Publishing Company, New York, 1952, p. 141. (Hereafter cited as *Lincoln and the Russians.*)

141. *Diary of Gideon Welles,* Vol. I, 1911, p. 443.

142. *Harper's Weekly,* Vol. VII, November 21, 1863, p. 746.

143. *Harper's Weekly,* Vol. VII, November 21, 1863, p. 746.

144. *Lincoln and the Russians,* pp. 156-166.

145. Brady's New York *Register.* There are notations in the handwriting of various clerks or operators with many references to send bills, or charge advertising, or to contact Brady in Washington.

146. Brady's New York *Register.*

147. Miller, Vol. III, p. 264.

148. *Harper's Weekly,* August 22, 1863.

149. Miller, Vol. III, p. 257.

150. *Confederate Agent,* James D. Horan, Crown, New York, 1954, a biography of Captain Thomas H. Hines, C. S. A.

151. Leech, p. 231.

152. Carpenter's unpublished diary, owned by his grandson, Emerson Ives, Pawling, N. Y.

153. Carpenter's caption on the back of the damaged Brady plate of Lincoln. Burgess, whose name also appears in some early sources as A. Berger, was Brady's Sunday shooting partner. Burgess and his brother Willard worked for Brady both before and during the Civil War. Sometime in 1863 or early 1864, Brady made Andrew a partner in his Washington studio. At the end of the war, Brady, at the request of the State Department, sent Burgess to Mexico. The object of the mission was to obtain "evidence" of French troops in Mexico. This may explain the Maximilian plate in the Brady collection. Andrew returned to the states in 1868 and two years later was sent by the U. S. government to Italy as a member of the 1870 Eclipse Expedition. In 1874 he bought out Brady, but when his fire alarm invention became successful, he sold the business back to Brady.

154. Carpenter's caption on the back of the plate.

155. *Washington in Lincoln's Time,* Noah Brooks, p. 285.

156. An entry in Carpenter's diary, April 26, 1864.

158. *The Web of Victory,* Earl Schenck Miers, Knopf, New York, 1955, an excellent portrait of Grant at Vicksburg.

159. Chicago *Evening Post,* February 11, 1893.

160. *The Tragic Era,* Claude G. Bowers, 1929, p. 160. (Hereafter cited as Bowers.)

161. Chicago *Evening Post,* February 11, 1893.

162. The excellent stories of Grant portraits by Brady, discovered in an upstate New York barn a few years ago, graphically show this to be true.

163. "Photographic Reminiscences of the Late War," J. F. Coonley, *Anthony's Photographic Bulletin,* No. 2, p. 311.

164. *Anthony's Photographic Bulletin,* No. 2, p. 311.

165. *Anthony's Photographic Bulletin,* No. 2, p. 311.

166. *Recollections of the Art Exhibit, Metropolitan Fair, New York City, April, 1864.* Photographed and published by Brady in aid of the U. S. Sanitary Commission. John F. Trow, Book & Job Printers, 50 Greene Street, New York City, Art and Architecture Division, New York Public Library.

167. Miller, Vol. I, pp. 22–23. Lieutenant Gardner's reminiscences of the day Brady took the pictures before Petersburg, p. 32.

168. Miller, Vol. I, pp. 22–23.

169. Tim O'Sullivan, one of Brady's best photographers who has not received the credit he so richly deserves, took most of the pictures for Brady at Petersburg. Brady was there, probably in a supervisory capacity.

170. The series of pictures, "The Siege and Fall of Petersburg," show the scope of the photographic coverage of the battle. Miller, Vol. III.

171. "Photographic Reminiscences of the Late War," Captain A. J. Russell, *Anthony's Photographic Bulletin,* No. 1.

172. McLean mansion by Tim O'Sullivan. Miller, Vol. III, p. 315.

173. Chicago *Evening Post,* February 11, 1893.

174. Chicago *Evening Post,* February 11, 1893. Also Townsend interview.

175. The story of Sherman and his generals at Brady's gallery is in the Chicago *Evening Post* article on Brady, February 11, 1893.

176. Townsend interview.
177. The Wirz trial was covered in various issues of *Harper's Weekly* from April to November, 1865. (Hereafter cited as Wirz.)
178. Andrew Johnson's portrait, credited to Gardner, appeared in *Harper's Weekly*, May 13, 1865.
179. The series of photographs of the Lincoln conspirators taken by Gardner appeared as engravings in *Harper's Weekly*, May 27, 1865. The original plates are now in the possession of the Library of Congress.
180. Neither *Harper's Weekly* nor *Leslie's* has anything by Brady on the burning of Barnum's Museum during July, 1866.
181. The series of prints of Union prisoners from Andersonville, which were obtained by Chaplain J. J. Geer, appeared in *Harper's Weekly* June 27, 1865, labeled exact facsimile of photographs." There is no evidence that they were taken by Brady.
182. *Harper's Weekly*, June 27, 1865.
183. *The Assassination of President Lincoln and the Trial of the Conspirators*, 1866. Benn Pitman, editor. Facsimile edition, 1954.
184. Wirz. Also *The Horrors of Andersonville Rebel Prison and the Trial of Henry Wirz*, a pamphlet by General N. P. Chipman, Judge Advocate of the Wirz Military Commission, published by the Bancroft Company, San Francisco, 1891. The account of the Union soldiers chanting "Wirz, remember Andersonville," is in the *Harper's Weekly* account of the execution of Wirz.
185. New York *Herald*, July 8, 1865.
186. *Life of Dickens*, John Forster, Vol. III, Philadelphia, 1874, p. 423.
187. *Thaddeus Stevens*, E. B. Callender, Boston, 1882, p. 143.
188. *Thaddeus Stevens*, E. B. Callender, Boston, 1882, p. 143.
189. Bowers, p. 76.
190. *Reminiscences*, Carl Schurz, Vol. I, New York, 1908, p. 214.
191. *Anecdotes of Public Men*, John Forney, Vol. I, New York, 1873, p. 75.
192. *Life of Schuyler Colfax*, C. J. Hollister, New York, 1886, p. 372.
193. *Life of Schuyler Colfax*, C. J. Hollister, New York, 1886, p. 273.
194. *Diary of Gideon Welles*, Vol. II, Boston, 1911, p. 392.
195. Bowers, p. 162.
196. New York *World*, June 20, 1867.
197. *History of the American Reconstruction*, Letters to *Le Temps* by Georges Clemenceau, New York, 1926, p. 176.
200. Miller, Vol. I, p. 7.
201. Miller, Vol. I, p. 7.
203. *American Journal of Photography*, Vol. I, 1858–59, p. 112. Also *Exploration and Surveys for a Ship Canal by Way of Isthmus of Darien*, T. O. Selfridge, Washington, 1876. (Hereafter cited as Selfridge.)
204. An excellent account of Jackson's work can be found in *Pioneer Photographer*, Charles Scribner's Sons, New York, 1952.
205. "Tim O'Sullivan," Hermine M. Baumhofer, *Image*, April, 1953. In his letter recommending O'Sullivan for a government position, Brady declared he had known O'Sullivan since boyhood. This letter is in the O'Sullivan file, Treasury Department, National Archives.
206. *Report of the Secretary of War, Chief of Engineers Report*, 2nd Session, 42nd Congress, Vol. II. Also *Systematic Geology, United States Geological Exploration of Fortieth Parallel*, Clarence King, 1878.
207. "Photographs from the High Rockies," *Harper's Weekly*, Vol. XXXIX, 1869, p. 465.
208. Selfridge.
209. *Oregon Historical Quarterly*, March, 1948, p. 30–49.
210. *Incidents of Travel and Adventure*, S. N. Carvalho, New York, 1859.
211. It is not known what became of Carvalho's plates after they were turned over to Brady for reproduction. One of the plates in the Brady Daguerreotype Collection in the Library of Congress may well be the only remaining Carvalho daguerreotype which was not destroyed in the fire which Mrs. Fremont said swept their home.
212. New York *World*, January 21, 1870.
213. "Daguerreotype of a Blue Reception," New York *World*, April 28, 1872.
214. New York *World*, September 20, 1868.
216. *Reminiscences of a Soldier's Wife*, Mrs. John A. Logan, New York, 1913, p. 269.
217. *Reminiscences of a Soldier's Wife*, Mrs. John A. Logan, New York, 1913, p. 269.
218. New York *Herald*, February 21, 1870.
219. Brady's stereos of Lee taken when he returned to Washington, clearly show how much he had aged since Appomattox. Brady-Handy Collection.
220. *Original Photographs taken on the Battlefields during the Civil War of the United States*, from the Private Collection of Edward Bailey Eaton. Privately printed. Hartford, 1907. (Hereafter cited as Eaton.)
221. *Congressional Record*, 43rd Congress, p. 2250.
222. Reminiscences of Mrs. Cox and Mrs. Evans.
224. *Alexander H. Stephens*, Louis Pendleton, Philadelphia, 1907, p. 386–87.
225. Eaton, p. 9.
226. *Photographic Journal of America*, Vol. XX, 1883, p. 92.
227. The cane is still in the possession of the Brady heirs.
228. Eaton, p. 9.
229. Eaton, p. 9.
230. Eaton, p. 9.
231. Eaton, p. 9.
232. Eaton, p. 11.
233. Eaton, p. 9.
234. Eaton, p. 9.
235. Eaton, p. 9.
236. Townsend interview.
237. Letters of Riley to Levin Handy, owned by Mrs. Cox and Mrs. Evans. (Hereafter cited as Riley Letters.)
238. Riley letters.
239. Reminiscences of Mrs. Cox and Mrs. Evans.
240. Death certificate, Mathew B. Brady, Department of Health, New York City.
241. Riley letters.
242. Washington *Times*, May 28, 1922.
243. Washington *Times*, May 28, 1922.
244. Washington *Times*, May 28, 1922.
245. Eaton, p. 13.
246. Eaton, pp. 116–126.
247. Reminiscences of Mrs. Cox and Mrs. Evans.
248. United States Army Air Force, Department of Information, Washington, D. C., 1955.

BIBLIOGRAPHY

As I have mentioned in my foreword, there are no "Brady Papers" and this absolute drought of personal correspondence has plagued me since I began gathering material for this biography. We are conscious of Brady's presence but the man is never really there.

Because of this lack of material I felt that a Brady bibliography would be valuable. In my research I examined countless issues of pioneer photographic trade journals and obviously I could not include every mention of "Mr. B." I have included only those books, magazines, newspapers, etc., which contain articles on Brady.

Heading the list must be Professor Robert Taft's *Photography and The American Scene, A Social History, 1839-1889,"* published by the Macmillan Company, New York, 1938, now unfortunately out of print. Though I disagree with his opinion of other authors who have written about Brady's work and am puzzled as to why he spelled his first name "Matthew," Taft's book must be consulted by any student of Brady or American photography.

Although I am sure there are no Brady letters in existence, I hope that some reader may be led to examine an old trunk in an attic or barn and come up with something more on Mathew B. Brady. This is not impossible when one recalls how forty-four precious Brady wet plates were discovered only a few years ago in an upstate New York barn.

J.D.H.

MANUSCRIPT COLLECTIONS

Mathew Brady letter, New York Historical Society.
Manuscript Division, New York Public Library.
Johnson Papers, Library of Congress.

NEWSPAPER CLIPPING COLLECTIONS

M. B. Brady clippings; William and Alfred Wauld clippings, Art Room, New York Public Library.

UNPUBLISHED MANUSCRIPTS

Francis B. Carpenter's diary, owned by Emerson C. Ives.

BRADY'S REGISTERS

January 2, 1863, to December 30, 1865, Manuscript Division, New York Public Library.
January 1871, to April, 1875, Brady-Handy Collection, Library of Congress.

LETTERS

Letters from William M. Riley to Levin C. Handy, owned by Mrs. Alice Cox, Washington, D. C.

OFFICIAL RECORDS

Brady's death certificate, Department of Health, Bureau of Vital Statistics, New York, N. Y.
(The Presbyterian Hospital informed me that the volume containing the record of Brady's illness is missing.)
Record of the sale of the Bradys' New York property in 1869, Archives, Hall of Records, County of New York, New York City.
Brady's bankruptcy proceedings, files of the Justice Department, Southern District of New York, January, 1873, National Archives. (unavailable)
Joint Committee on the Library, March 3, 1871, recommending that Brady's collection be purchased, *Congressional Record.*
Brady's statement of how and when he took the portraits of Clay, Calhoun and Webster, *Senate Document No. 95,* 69th Congress, 1st Session, Serial 8547.
Butler's and Garfield's speeches urging Congress to buy Brady's

collections and praising the photographer as a great American, *Congressional Record,* 43rd Congress, p. 2250.
Official Records of the New York State Daguerrean Association, Vol. II, p. 298.

BOOKS

Arts and Sciences, Vol. V, 1941, Arts and Sciences Society, Philadelphia, 1941. Louis W. Sipley, editor-in-chief; Margaret L. Brady, editor.
Brady's Portraits, no author, no publisher and no year. This book, virtually crumbling with age is owned by H. Armour Smith, Yonkers, New York and contains prints of daguerreotypes of famous Americans. Mr. Smith, a well-known collector and former director of the Hudson Valley Museum, believes the book was published long before the Civil War.
The Camera And The Pencil, by Marcus A. Root, New York, 1864.
Divided We Fought, A Pictorial History of the War, 1861-1865. By Hirst Milhollen, Milton Kaplan and Hulen Stuart, Editor: David Donald, The Macmillan Company, New York, 1952.
The Gallery of Illustrious Americans, C. Edwards Lester, editor; daguerreotypes by M. B. Brady, engraved by F. D'Avignon, C. Edwards Lester, Published by the D'Avignon Press, New York, 1850.
The History of Photography, by Beaumont Newhall, The Museum of Modern Art, distributed by Simon and Schuster, New York, 1949.
A History of the Civil War, by Benson J. Lossing, LLD. Compiled from the Official Records of the War Department. Illustrated with Fac-Simile Photographic Reproductions of the Official War Photographs Taken at the Time by Mathew B. Brady, New York. The War Memorial Association, 1912. (The first edition of this book contains color reproductions by H. A. Ogden.)
Lincoln: A Picture Story of His Life, by Stefan Lorant, Harper & Brothers, New York, 1952.
Lincoln: His Life in Photographs, by Stefan Lorant, Duell, Sloan & Pearce, New York, 1941.
Mr. Lincoln's Camera Man, by Roy Meredith, Charles Scribner's Sons, New York, 1946.
Mr. Lincoln's Contemporaries, by Roy Meredith, Charles Scribner's Sons, New York, 1951.
Original Photographs Taken on the Battlefields During the Civil War of the United States, Hartford, Connecticut, 1907. "Martyrs on the Altars of Civilization," by Francis Trevelyan Miller, editor of the *Journal of American History,* the foreword.
Photographic History of the Civil War, (in ten volumes), by Francis Trevelyan Miller, Editor-in-Chief, New York, Review of Reviews Co., 1912.
Photography and the American Scene, A Social History, by Robert Taft, 1839-1889, The Macmillan Company, 1938, New York.
Three Years with the Adirondack Regiment, 118th New York Volunteers, Infantry, from the diaries of John Cunningham, Norwood, Mass., 1920..

PAMPHLETS, MAGAZINES, ETC.

American Manual of Photography, 1937, Chapter 13, "Civil War Photography."
Art Digest, October 15, 1920, "Mathew B. Brady" by R. D. Turnbull.
American Photography, Vol. XXIX, "M. B. Brady and the Daguerreotype Era," by Robert Taft, pp. 486, 1935.
American Repertory of Arts, Sciences and Manufacturers, March, 1840, Vol. I.
Ansco, A Brief History, published by Agfa Ansco, Binghamton, N. Y.

Centennial of Photography, Pennsylvania Arts and Sciences, Philadelphia, 1939.

Doggett's New York City Directory, 1843-44, and 1844-45.

Edward Anthony: Pioneer American, Louis Sipley, curator, American Museum of Photography, Philadelphia, 1942.

Hound and Horn, Vol. VII, 1933, "M. B. Brady and His Photos" by Charles Flato, pp. 35-41.

Information Bulletin. Vol. XIII, "Historic Collection of Photographs Is Acquired by Library of Congress." Description of Brady-Handy Collection by Hirst Milhollen, No. 41 and No. 55-20.

Leslie's Illustrated Newspaper, Vol. XI, January, 1861, "Brady's Tenth Street Gallery," p. 106.

Photographic Art Journal, Vol. I, January, 1851, "M. B. Brady and the Photographic Art," pp. 36-40.

Photographic Art Journal, February, 1851. A discussion of Brady's and Lawrence's photographs.

Photographic Times, September 15, 1862.

Photography, 1839-1937, "Photography in the Civil War." Museum of Modern Art, New York, 1937.

Saturday Evening Post, January 7, 1939, "Photo By Brady."

Wilson's Photographic Magazine, Vol. XXXIII, 1896. "M. B. Brady," p. 121.

NEWSPAPERS

Chicago *Evening Post,* February 11, 1893. "Mathew B. Brady, The Great Civil War Photographer."

New York *Globe,* August 6, 1904. "Mathew B. Brady and the War."

New York *Herald Tribune,* April 25, 1953, "The Air Force Honors Brady."

New York *Journal-American,* March 26, 1953, "A Tribute to a Photo Pioneer," by Bob Considine.

New York Times Magazine, February 13, 1949, "His Photographs Conceal the Real Lincoln," by Stefan Lorant.

New York Times, October 26-27, 1953, Bess Furman's accounts of the sale of the Brady-Handy Collection to the Library of Congress.

New York *World,* April 12, 1891, "Still Taking Pictures."

New York *World Telegram,* February 10, 1955, "Brady, Photographer of Lincoln."

Washington *Evening Star,* January 18, 1896, "Matthew (sic) Brady, Photographer Dies."

Washington *Post,* January 18, 1896, Brady's obituary.

Washington *Post, "Camera Angles"* by Arthur Ellis, September, 4, 1938.

Note: Mrs. Cox, co-owner of the Brady-Handy Collection has several clippings relating to Brady which I examined. Many are so old they crumbled at my touch and in some instances it required many patient hours to paste them together. They are mostly undated and with the paper's name missing.

SPECIAL NOTICE

Guide to the Special Collections of Prints and Photographs (list of the Brady Collections) by Paul Vanderbilt, Library of Congress. It was Mr. Vanderbilt who discovered the Brady daguerreotypes in a storeroom in the Library and identified them after extensive research.

A PICTORIAL BIBLIOGRAPHY OF BRADY PICTURES

Harper's Weekly, 1861-65
and
Frank Leslie's Illustrated Newspaper, 1860-65

A few years after the birth of photography the first illustrated journals—forerunners of our pictorial magazines, tabloids and rotogravure sections—made their appearance. The earliest and most successful was Herbert Ingram's *Illustrated London News*, first published on December 15, 1842. The *News* produced Frank Leslie, a wood engraver, who started *Frank Leslie's Illustrated Newspaper*, first published on December 15, 1855. Leslie declared his to be "the most comprehensive and interesting pictorial record of events to be found in either hemisphere." *Leslie's* was followed by *Harper's Weekly*, founded in 1857 by Fletcher Harper.

Drawings were used at first to record passing events, but gradually photography came into use. Before the halftone process in 1880, only woodcuts and engravings could be used. The portrait or scene was sketched in reverse upon the wood and then engravers cut away the wood in the spaces between the lines, leaving the portrait or scene design in relief. The design could then be inked and an impression made. A design could be pressed into wax or clay beds, then into metal, when a large number of copies was needed.

Both *Harper's* and *Leslie's* used many of Brady's prints during the Civil War, and the credit line "Photograph by Brady" became commonplace in both the North and the South.

Here for the first time is a bibliography of Brady prints used by both periodicals from 1861 to 1865. Many of the original wet plates are now in the Brady-Handy Collection.

This list was prepared by Miss Patricia Horan. She was assisted in examining the last volumes of *Leslie's* by Brian Boru Horan.

HARPER'S WEEKLY, 1861

"The Georgia Delegation in Congress," Jan. 5, 1861, p. 1.
"The Seceding Mississippi Delegation in Congress," Feb. 2, 1861, p. 65.
"The Seceding Alabama Delegation in Congress," Feb. 9, 1861, p. 81.
"Hon. Joseph Holt, Secretary of War," Feb. 16, 1861, p. 109.
"Davis and Stephens, President and Vice-President of the Southern Confederacy," Feb. 23, 1861, p. 125.
"Hon. Salmon P. Chase, of Ohio, Secretary of the Treasury," Mar. 23, 1861, p. 189.
"General Sam Houston, Governor of Texas," Mar. 30, 1861, p. 204.
"Hon. William H. Seward, Secretary of State," April 6, 1861, p. 209.
"Mrs. General Gaines," April 13, 1861, p. 225.
"Hon. Charles F. Adams," April 20, 1861, p. 241.
"President Lincoln," April 27, 1861, p. 268.
"Col. Wilson, of Wilson's briggade (sic)," May 11, 1861, p. 289.
"The Late Colonel Ellsworth," June 8, 1861, p. 357.
"Stephen A. Douglas," June 15, 1861, p. 381.
"Winfield Scott, Commander-in-Chief of the United States Army," July 13, 1861, p. 440.
"Speaker Grow," July 20, 1861, p. 461.
"General McDowell," Aug. 17, 1861, p. 516.
"General Mansfield," Aug. 17, 1861, p. 516.

"Colonel Blair," Aug. 17, 1861, p. 516.
"General McClellan and Staff," Aug. 24, 1861, p. 532.
"Brigadier-General Burnside," Aug. 24, 1861, p. 541.
"The Rebel General Lee," Aug. 24, 1861, p. 541.
"Flag-officer Stringham," Sept. 14, 1861, p. 577.
"Major-General McClellan, U. S. A.," Sept. 21, 1861, pp. 600–601.
"The Late General F. D. Baker, Killed October 21, 1861," Nov. 2, 1861, p. 693.
"Captain S. F. Dupont, Commanding the Great Naval Expedition," Nov. 9, 1861, p. 705.
"General Hunter, Commanding Our Army in Missouri," Nov. 23, 1861, p. 705.
"Thurlow Weed, Esq.," Nov. 23, 1861, p. 749.
"Captain S. F. Dupont, U. S. N.," Nov. 30, 1861, p. 764.
"Commodore Wilkes, U. S. N.," Nov. 30, 1861, p. 765.
"The Captured Rebel Commissioner Mason," Nov. 30, 1861, p. 765.
"The Captured Rebel Commissioner Slidell," Nov. 30, 1861, p. 765.
"Hon. George Opdyke, Mayor Elect of New York," Dec. 21, 1861, p. 805.

HARPER'S WEEKLY, 1862

"General Burnside, Commanding the Burnside Expedition," Jan. 18, 1862, p. 36.
"Lord Lyons, British Minister to Washington," Feb. 22, 1862, p. 116.
"M. Mercier, French Minister to Washington," Feb. 22, 1862, p. 116.
"Baron Stoeckel, Russian Minister to Washington," Feb. 22, 1862, p. 116.
"Brigadier-General Burnside," Mar. 1, 1862, p. 136.
"The Late General F. W. Lander," Mar. 15, 1862, p. 136.
"Hon. Andrew Johnson, Military Governor of Tennessee," April 5, 1862, p. 221.
"Lieutenant Morris, U. S. N., Commander of the *Cumberland*," April 5, 1862, p. 221.
"Major-General Buell," April 12, 1862, p. 225.
"Brigadier-General Shields," April 12, 1862, p. 225.
"Major-General Pope," April 26, 1862, p. 268.
"Commander Foote," April 26, 1862, p. 268.
"The Late Martin Van Buren, ex-President of the United States," Aug. 9, 1862, p. 497.
"Brigadier-General Keyes, U. S. A.," Aug. 9, 1862, p. 508.
"The Rebel General Stonewall Jackson," Aug. 30, 1862, p. 556.
"The Late General Isaac I. Stevens," Sept. 20, 1862, p. 604.
"The Late General Phil Kearney," Sept. 20, 1862, p. 604.
"Major-General Hooker," Oct. 4, 1862, p. 629.
"Major-General Franklin," Oct. 4, 1862, p. 629.
"The Late General Mansfield," Oct. 4, 1862, p. 629.
"The Late General Reno," Oct. 4, 1862, p. 629.
"Scenes on the Battlefield of Antietam," Oct. 18, 1862, pp. 664–665.
"Brigadier-General Wadsworth, Union Candidate for Governor of New York," Oct. 25, 1862, p. 685.
"Major-General William S. Rosecrans, Commander of the Army of the Ohio," Nov. 8, 1862, p. 705.
"Mrs. Lincoln, Wife of the President," Nov. 8, 1862, p. 709.
"Hon. Horatio Seymour, Governor-Elect of the State of New York," Nov. 22, 1862, p. 737.
"Brigadier-General Thomas of the Army of the Ohio," Nov. 22, 1862, p. 749.
"Major-General A. E. Burnside, Commander of the Army of the Potomac," Dec. 13, 1862, p. 785.

"Major-General Nathaniel P. Banks, United States Army," Dec. 6, 1862, p. 769.

"Major-General Burnside and the Division Commanders of the Army of the Potomac," Dec. 13, 1862, p. 785.

"Rev. Morgan L. Dix, Rector of the Trinity Church, New York," Dec. 13, 1862, p. 797.

HARPER'S WEEKLY, 1863

"Brigadier-General J. G. Foster," Jan. 10, 1863, p. 21.

"Major-General John A. McClernand," Feb. 7, 1863, p. 81.

"Major-General Joseph Hooker, The New Commander of the Army of the Potomac," Feb. 7, 1863, p. 93.

"Major-General Daniel Butterfield, Chief of Staff to General Hooker," Feb. 14, p. 109.

"Mr. and Mrs. Charles S. Stratton (Gen. Tom Thumb and Wife)," Feb. 21, 1863, p. 113.

"Major-General Hooker, Commanding the Army of the Potomac," Feb. 28, 1863, p. 129.

"Major-General David Hunter, U. S. A.," Mar. 14, 1863, p. 165.

"Hon. John Van Buren," Mar. 21, 1863, p. 177.

"James F. Brady, Esq.," Mar. 21, 1863, p. 177.

"Major-General Ulysses S. Grant, U. S. A.," June 6, 1863, p. 365.

"Clement L. Vallandigham," June 6, 1863, p. 365.

"Major-General George G. Meade, the New Commander of the Army of the Potomac," July 11, 1863, p. 432.

"The Late Rear-Admiral Foote," July 11, 1863, p. 445.

"Major Kiernan," July 11, 1863, p. 445.

"The Late Brigadier-General George C. Strong," Aug. 15, 1863, p. 525.

"Residence of John Burns, at Gettysburg, Pa.," Aug. 22, 1863, p. 529.

"Major-General Stoneman," Aug. 22, 1863, p. 541.

"Rear-Admiral David G. Farragut, U. S. N., Aug. 20, 1863, p. 545.

"General Quincy A. Gilmore," Sept. 12, 1863, p. 584.

"Major-General George H. Thomas, U. S. A., The Hero of Chickamauga," Oct. 10, 1863, p. 641.

"Our Russian Visitors," Nov. 7, 1863, p. 708.

"Rev. Henry Ward Beecher," Nov. 14, 1863, p. 733.

"Major-General C. C. Washburne," Nov. 28, 1863, p. 764.

"Charles G. Gunther, The Mayor Elect," Dec. 19, 1863, p. 813.

"Hon. Schuyler Colfax, The New Speaker of the House," Dec. 26, 1863, p. 817.

HARPER'S WEEKLY, 1864

"General Wm. A. Averill," Jan. 16, 1864, p. 36.

"The Late Most Reverend John Hughes, D. D. Archbishop of New York," Jan. 16, 1864, p. 44.

"Major-General Francis J. Herron," Feb. 6, 1864, p. 85.

"Brigadier-General George A. Custer," Mar. 19, 1864, p. 177.

"Brigadier-General Judson Kilpatrick," Mar. 19, 1864, p. 180.

"The Late Colonel Ulric Dahlgren," Mar. 26, 1864, p. 193.

"Brigadier-General Henry E. Davies," April 2, 1864, p. 209.

"General W. F. Smith," April 2, 1864, p. 209.

"Major-General John A. Dix, President of the Metropolitan Fair," April 9, 1864, p. 228.

"Rev. Henry W. Bellows, D.D., President, United States Sanitary Commission," April 9, 1864, p. 228.

"Major-General David M. Gregg, May 7, 1864, p. 300.

"General Thomas E. Greenfield Ransom," May 14, 1864, p. 309.

"The Late Major-General John Sedgwick," May 28, 1864, p. 349.

"General Gouverneur K. Warren," June 11, 1864, p. 369.

"Governor Andrew Johnson of Tennessee," June 25, 1864, p. 401.

"Lt.-General Grant at His Headquarters," July 16, 1864, p. 449.

"General Meade and His Staff," July 23, 1864, p. 469.

"General Burnside and His Staff," July 23, 1864, p. 409.

"Army of the Potomac, General Warren and His Staff," Aug. 13, 1864, p. 517.

"Army of Potomac, General Hancock and His Staff," Aug. 13, 1864, p. 517.

"Hon. Fernando Wood," Sept. 3, 1864, p. 573.

"Clement L. Vallandigham," Sept. 3, 1864, p. 573.

"The Most Reverend John M'Closkey, D.D., Archbishop of New York," Sept. 10, 1864, p. 577.

"Major-General Wright and Staff," Sept. 10, 1864, p. 589.

"Rear-Admiral David G. Farragut, U. S. N.," Sept. 17, 1864, p. 597.

"General Jefferson C. Davis," Sept. 17, 1864, p. 605.

"Hon. George H. Pendleton," Sept. 17, 1864, p. 605.

"Private Miles O'Reilly," Sept. 24, 1864, p. 621.

"Hon. Reuben E. Fenton, Union Candidate for Governor of N. Y.," Sept. 24, 1864, p. 620.

"Major-General Philip H. Sheridan," Oct. 8, 1864, p. 641.

"Major-General David B. Birney," Oct. 15, 1864, p. 661.

"The Late Chief Justice Roger B. Taney," Oct. 29, 1864, p. 693.

"Captain Napoleon Collins," Nov. 26, 1864, p. 753.

"Major-General Gershom Mott," Nov. 26, 1864, p. 764.

"W. W. Wood, Chief Engineer, U. S. N.," Nov. 26, 1864, p. 764.

"Major-General George H. Thomas," Dec. 17, 1864, p. 801.

"Major-General William Tecumseh Sherman," Dec. 17, 1864, pp. 808–809.

HARPER'S WEEKLY, 1865

"The Late Hon. William L. Dayton," Jan. 14, 1865, p. 29.

"Hon. William Dennison, Postmaster General," Jan. 28, 1865, p. 49.

"General H. W. Slocum," Jan. 28, 1865, p. 49.

"The Late Lieutenant Samuel W. Preston," Feb. 4, 1865, p. 69.

"The Late Lieutenant Benjamin H. Porter," Feb. 4, 1865, p. 69.

"Brigadier-General Adelbert Ames," Feb. 4, 1865, p. 76.

"Hon. Daniel S. Dickinson," Mar. 4, 1865, p. 141.

"Hon James Harlan, Secretary of the Interior," Mar. 25, 1865, p. 181.

"President Lincoln at Home," May 6, 1865, p. 273.

"Sergeant Boston Corbett," May 13, 1865, p. 292.

"President Lincoln's Funeral Procession in New York City," May 13, 1865, pp. 296–297.

"Sherman and his Generals," July 1, 1865, p. 405.

"The Prince Napoleon," July 1, 1865, p. 412.

"Major-General Charles Griffin," Aug. 5, 1865, p. 493.

"Brevet Major-General Nathaniel A. Miles," Aug. 19, 1865, p. 513.

"Rear-Admiral Henry H. Bell," Aug. 26, 1865, p. 540.

"William Cullen Bryant," Sept. 2, 1865, p. 549.

"Hon. Preston King," Sept. 2, 1865, p. 556.

"Rear-Admiral Francis H. Gregory," Sept. 2, 1865, p. 556.

"Major-General John G. Parke," Sept. 16, 1865, p. 589.

"General H. W. Slocum," Oct. 7, 1865, p. 628.

"Bishop Quintard of Tennessee," Oct. 7, 1865, p. 628.

"The Embassy from Tunis," Oct. 21, 1865, p. 660.

"Major-General Francis Barlow," Oct. 21, 1865, p. 669.

"Hon. Charles F. Adams," Nov. 11, 1865, p. 705.

"The Balloon Bridal Party Starting on Its Aerial Tour from Professor Lowe's Amphitheater, Central Park," Nov. 25, 1865, p. 745.

"The Late Hon. Preston King," Dec. 2, 1865, p. 757.

"Hon. John T. Hoffman, Mayor-elect of New York City," Dec. 23, 1865, p. 801.

FRANK LESLIE'S ILLUSTRATED NEWSPAPER, 1860

"Hon. Robert Toombs, Ga."; Hon. James Chesnut, S. C.";
"Hon. Alexander Stephens, ex-Sen. of Ga." Dec. 1, 1860, p. 24.

FRANK LESLIE'S ILLUSTRATED NEWSPAPER, 1861

"M. B. Brady's New Photographic Gallery," Jan. 5, 1861, p. 108.

"Adolphus H. Davenport, Esq., Comedian," Jan. 26, 1861, p. 157.

"Miss Isabella Henkle, Prima Donna at the Academy of Music, N. Y.," Feb. 2, 1861, p. 165.

"Lt. Hall, U. S. A., Bearer of Dispatches from Major Henderson to Gov. Pickens," Feb. 2, 1861, p. 168.

"Gallery of Illustrious Americans, Ladies, No. 3. Mrs. John Crittenden," Feb. 9, 1861, p. 185.

"Col. Isaac W. Hayne, Bearer of Dispatches, of the Ultimatum from South Carolina to the Government at Washington," Feb. 16, 1861, p. 197.

"Hon. John Tyler, ex-President of the U. S. and President of the Peace Convention Sitting in Washington," Feb. 16, 1861, p. 204.

"Jefferson Davis, First President of the Confederacy," Mar. 9, 1861, p. 241.

"The Late John Francis of New York," Mar. 9, 1861, p. 252.

"Lincoln's Cabinet: Hon. Gideon Welles, Secretary of Navy; W. H. Seward, Secretary of State; Montgomery Blair, Secretary of War; Caleb B. Smith, Secretary of Interior; Edward Bates, Attorney General," April 16, 1861, p. 311.

"A. B. Roman of Louisiana, John Forsyth of Alabama, Martin Crawford of Georgia, Commission at Washington from the Confederacy," April 13, 1861, p. 321.

"Brigadier-General Wm. S. Harney, U. S. A.," June 8, 1861, p. 54.

"Capt. Roger Jones, U. S. A., Promoted for Destroying Arms and Government Buildings at Harper's Ferry, April 18, 1861," June 22, 1861, p. 90.

"The Late Col. Noah L. Farnham of the First Regiment, New York City Fire Zouaves," Aug. 31, 1861, p. 245.

"Mayor Derrett of Washington, Now a State Prisoner in Fort Lafayette," Sept. 7, 1861, p. 272.

"The Late Col. E. D. Baker, U. S. Senator from Oregon, Killed at Ball's Heights, Va.," Nov. 9, 1861, p. 389.

"General William Hardee of Georgia, Commander of Troops in Missouri," Nov. 9, 1861, p. 395.

"Brig. Gen. Louis Blenker, Commanding a Division of the National Forces in Va.," Nov. 16, 1861, p. 410.

"Brigadier-General Samuel P. Heintzelman, Commanding the Occoquan Division of the U. S. Army on the Potomac," Nov. 23, 1861, p. 6.

"Brigadier-General John Buchanan Floyd, Late Secretary of U. S., Now Commanding the Rebel Forces in Western Virginia," Nov. 23, 1861, p. 11.

"Commodore Samuel F. Dupont, Commanding the U. S. Naval Expedition to Port Royal," Dec. 7, 1861, p. 37.

"Commodore Charles Wilkes, U. S. Navy," Dec. 7, 1861, p. 44.

"William McGwin, Late U. S. Senator from California, Now under Arrest on a Charge of Treason," Dec. 21, 1861, p. 70.

FRANK LESLIE'S ILLUSTRATED NEWSPAPER, 1862

"Brigadier-General Daniel E. Sickles, Excelsior Brigade," Jan. 11, 1862, p. 128.

"Brigadier-General James Shields of California," April 12, 1862, p. 356.

"Major W. F. Arny, U. S. Agent for the Territories, Successor to the Famous Kit Carson," July 5, 1862, p. 213.

"Hon. Edward Stanley, U. S. Provisional Governor of North Carolina," July 5, 1862, p. 225.

"Lieutenant-Colonel William Carey Massett, of the 61st N. Y., Killed at the Battle of Fair Oaks, June 1," July 12, 1862, p. 241.

"Brigadier-General Joseph Hooker, now Commanding the Advance of the Union Army before Richmond," July 12, 1862, p. 252.

"Brigadier-General Henry W. Benham, Commander of the Federal Forces at the Battle of Secessionville, James Island, S. C.," July 19, 1862, p. 257.

"Colonel James M. Quade, 14th Regiment New York Volunteers," July 19, 1862, p. 268.

"General Edwin V. Sumner," July 26, 1862, p. 284.

"The Rebel General Thomas J. Jackson, Commonly Called Stonewall Jackson," August 9, 1862, p. 305.

"General Henry Wager Halleck, Commander-in-chief of the Federal Armies," August 9, 1862, p. 309.

"Brigadier-General John M. Schofield," Aug. 23, 1862, p. 348.

"Brigadier-General Samuel D. Sturgis," Aug. 23, 1862, p. 348.

"Brigadier-General King," Aug. 30, 1862, p. 356.

"Brigadier-General Tyler," Aug. 30, 1862, p. 356.

"Brigadier-General Michael Corcoran, Late Colonel 69th N. Y. S. M.," Sept. 6, 1862, p. 381.

"Major-General John Pope, Commanding the Army of Virginia," Sept. 13, 1862, p. 385.

"Gen. Robert Edmund Lee, Commander-in-chief of the Rebel Army," Oct. 4, 1862, p. 29.

"Brigadier-General Wm. Benjamin Franklin, Commanding a Division at the Battle of Antietam," Oct. 11, 1862, p. 37.

"General Fitzjohn Porter," Oct. 25, 1862, p. 68.

"Brigadier-General George W. Cullum," Nov. 1, 1862, p. 83.

"Mrs. Jefferson Davis, Wife of the President of the So-Called Southern Confederacy," Nov. 1, 1862, p. 88.

"Brigadier-General Quincy Adams Gillmore," Nov. 15, 1862, p. 125.

"The Late Major-General Israel B. Richardson," Nov. 15, 1862, p. 125.

"Hon. Horatio Seymour, Governor Elect of the State of New York," Nov. 22, 1862, p. 129.

"M. P. T. Mason, the Celebrated Lecturer," Nov. 29, 1862, p. 156.

"Madame Genevieve Guerrabella, the American Prima Donna," Dec. 6, 1862, p. 169.

"Artemus Ward (Charles F. Browne)," Dec. 13, 1862, p. 188.

"Rev. Morgan Dix, Rector of Trinity Church, N. Y.," Dec. 20, 1862, p. 197.

"Gen. George L. Hartsuff," Dec. 20, 1862, p. 197.

FRANK LESLIE'S ILLUSTRATED NEWSPAPER, 1863

"Rear-Admiral Lisovski, of the Russian Navy," Nov. 7, 1863, p. 1.

FRANK LESLIE'S ILLUSTRATED NEWSPAPER, 1864

"John N. Pattison, The Young American Pianist," Mar. 26, 1864, p. 5.
"Col. Ulric Dahlgren, U. S. A.," Mar. 26, 1864, p. 13.
"Gen. George A. Custer, U. S. A.," Mar. 26, 1864, p. 13.
"Rev. Henry W. Bellows of New York, President of the U. S. Sanitary Commission," April 16, 1864, p. 53.

FRANK LESLIE'S ILLUSTRATED NEWSPAPER, 1865

"The Late James William Wallack, as Benedict, in Shakespeare's Comedy of 'Much Ado About Nothing,'" Jan. 14, 1865, p. 268.
"Reuben Fenton, Governor of the State of New York," Jan. 14, 1865, p. 268.
"Hon. Daniel S. Dickinson," Feb. 25, 1865, p. 365.
"Andersonville," Sept. 23, 1865.
"G. F. N. Hashem, Ambassador from Tunis," Oct. 28, 1865, p. 84.
"Sergeant Boston Corbett, the Man Who Shot Booth," May 13, 1865.

PICTURE INDEX

INDEX